The Catholic Family: Image and Likeness of God

VOLUME 1

Family Life

D1004724

The Catholic Family:
Image and Likeness of God

VOLUME 1
Family Life

Deacon Dr. Bob McDonald

PUBLISHING COMPANY
P.O. Box 220 • Goleta, CA 93116
(800) 647-9882 • (805) 692-0043 • Fax: (805) 967-5843

Library of Congress Number #, Pending

Published by:
 Queenship Publishing
 P.O. Box 220
 Goleta, CA 93116
 (800) 647-9882 • (805) 692-0043 • Fax: (805) 957-5843

Printed in the United States of America

ISBN: 1-57918-118-X

Dedication

*"Now a great sign appeared in
the sky, a woman clothed with
the sun, standing on the moon
and on her head a crown of
twelve stars."*

(Rev. 12:1)

This book is dedicated to the Queen of Heaven, on whose feast
day I was ordained a Permanent Deacon.

For my ordination gift I asked her that I would always preach
and teach the truth with love. *"Veritatem facientes in caritate"*
(Eph. 4:15). May this work give her the honour she is due as the
Mother of Jesus and may it give glory to God in the hearts of
Catholic couples everywhere.

Acknowledgements

A book such as this can never be the work of one person alone. I am so grateful for the love, the work, the countless hours, the support and the dedication of my wife, Rita, without whose wisdom and patience this book could never have been completed. She typed and retyped, read and reread the manuscript, always suggesting modifications with wisdom and tact. She never lost faith in the importance of the task and she never lost faith in me. Above all, she never lost faith in God and continued to believe in his holy will for this work.

My very special gratitude to Mark Sebanc, author of the wonderful novel *Flight to Hollow Mountain,* for his fearless editing and the expertise which he generously shared with regard to grammar and my poor literary style. It is not easy to make a silk purse out of a sow's ear.

My heartfelt thanks to my equally talented friend and mentor Michael O'Brien, artist and author of *Father Elijah* and numerous other works of literature, for his reading of the manuscript, pointing out errors and the need for clarification of many points which might otherwise have been misunderstood.

I am deeply grateful for the expert editing by Chris Zakrzewski, former editor of *Nazareth Magazine.* His input was given with such gentleness, yet at the same time he was firm in his conviction that the book should be brought to completion.

A special mention must be made to my fellow Secular Franciscan, Eric MacDonald, who was the expert "glitch-remover" for my computer. He made himself constantly available at all hours to assist, to advise, and to correct. I am sure that St. Francis is delighted with his spiritual son.

Above all, I humbly give *all* the glory to the Holy Spirit, Spouse of Mary, to whom I have prayed throughout the entire task of writing, and I also pray that this work reflects his guidance and inspiration.

Feast of Pentecost and the Visitation
May 1998.

CONTENTS

CHAPTER 1

The Story of Becky and John:
The Anatomy of a Catholic Marriage

"You hate those who pay regard
to worthless idols but I trust
in the Lord. I will exult and
rejoice in your steadfast love,
because you have seen my
affliction; you have taken heed
of my adversities."

(Ps. 31:6-7)

Becky and John were both baptised as infants into the Catholic Church. This would have been a wonderful thing except that they were raised with the lukewarm idea that one only needs to do the minimum for one's own salvation. True, they had to go to Mass on Sundays, but apart from that, there was no real sense of loving God or growing in holiness. These things were for saints only! In all honesty, they found Church to be boring and they were always glad when Mass was over, because then they could play with their friends. Becky's parents were modern liberal thinkers, who saw no problem with rejecting some of the teachings of the Church, especially if these were inconvenient or difficult. As a result, once Becky reached fifteen years of age, they decided to have her take the birth-control pill "as a precaution." They believed that this was a rational and intelligent thing to do, given the growing temptations out there in the world. After all, what could be worse than getting pregnant? That would bring shame to their good family name in the community. Becky meanwhile, quickly came to believe that if it was alright to be on the pill, then pre-marital sex must be no big deal. She assumed her parents could hardly disapprove.

John's parents were middle-class, educated people, who considered comfort and status to be more important than loving. They were determined that John should have a good education but this was so important to them that they tied their love to John's academic performance. If his grades were good, they showed him their love by buying him a coveted toy. If his grades were poor, they punished him. There were rarely any hugs or kisses for John. He soon learned that his value as a person depended upon his achievements and so he set about excelling in his studies. Deep within, he craved his parent's love, but he knew he had to earn it. As a result, he eventually entered university to study economics and with sheer hard work was turning out straight A's. In spite of his academic excellence, he never really experienced any profound sense of peace or joy, but he simply put this down to his personality. It never entered his head that this emptiness was connected to the way he had been raised. Somewhere deep within, there lurked a sinister feeling that he could never be good enough.

Unlike John, Becky never had any excessive demands made on her by her parents. They were too busy with themselves, enjoying trips, friends and pleasures. Becky had to fend for herself and enjoyed all kinds of freedom to do as she pleased with her peers, especially now that she was "protected" by the pill. She lost her virginity at age sixteen and from then on, sex was not so much a joy as just something a girl had to do in order to keep a boyfriend. Her school grades were never good, and by age seventeen she had dropped out and was drifting from job to job. By the age of twenty-one she was working in a café as a waitress and life was going nowhere. She did not seem to have any firm direction or purpose, but simply clung to a vague notion that somehow things would get better.

John dated a few girls while at university and even lived with one for a few months, but that ended in a very bitter break-up. He continued to go to Mass on Sunday, but only if he did not have something more important to do. He thought nothing of receiving Jesus in communion even though he had not confessed his sexual sins. No one had ever told him what a sacrilege was, and worse still, he had no notion of the state of his own soul. For him, religion was simply a habit, not a vital source of love and life. He would have scoffed at the suggestion that true religion could have anything to do with peace and joy, the very things he yearned for in his heart.

After graduation with full honours, he landed a job with a marketing firm and the prospects were excellent. He soon impressed his superiors with his competence and his personable nature, with the result that he began to climb the corporate ladder at a rapid rate. He was now twenty-six years old.

It was a bright spring morning when John wandered into the café where Becky was working, and as soon as he laid eyes on her, he was smitten. He could hardly drink his coffee, he was so intent on drinking in Becky. Her smile, her eyes and everything about her made him feel weak at the knees. He desperately wanted to speak with her, but all he could manage was a useless stammer. After that, he ate lunch there every day for two weeks before he plucked up enough courage to ask her for a date. Meanwhile, Becky was wondering if he would ever ask her out. She had been dreaming about him ever since he first walked in.

The romance blossomed at such an exciting pace that within three months, John had proposed to Becky and she joyfully accepted. They were deeply in love and they decided on a short engagement. John's parents did not really approve of Becky, but then no girl would really have been good enough for their son. Becky's parents seemed pleased enough, but really they were just relieved that she might settle down at last. Now they were both plunged into a flurry of arrangements. It was a given, that they would be married in a Catholic Church, but they had very little idea of marriage as a sacrament. They were more interested in the glitter of the ceremony than in its substance, and they spent all their energies planning the wedding reception, the cake, the limousine, the speeches and of course, the honeymoon in the Caribbean. By the time they had planned the perfect wedding, it was going to cost close to twenty thousand dollars and that did not include the absolute necessity, by their way of thinking, of a brand-new fully furnished bungalow. They were going to start married life at the top and they did not worry that such a start meant a huge debt load.

The wedding day was a dream. The sun was shining brightly, the wedding guests were beautifully turned-out, and while John was handsome in his tuxedo, Becky was stunning in her designer wedding dress. In all their careful planning, they never thought to include the Sacrament of Reconciliation prior to the great day, so they both received Jesus in a state of serious sin. In actual fact, neither of them had ever confessed their previous sexual adventures. Why should they, when they had always been told that God loved them so much that he would always understand? But that was not going to spoil their day. The priest delivered a beautiful homily on the solemn nature of marriage as a sacrament and as a covenant. He talked about true love as a willingness to sacrifice oneself for the other. Sadly, Becky and John never heard it. They were both too caught up with anticipating the reception, the honeymoon and their future life together.

Not long after settling into their perfect little bungalow, it began to lose its attraction for them and so they talked about buying a bigger, more opulent house in the suburbs, preferably with a swimming pool. Naturally, this meant that Becky would have to work, in order to save for the down-payment and meet the higher mortgage payments. It seemed logical then, to postpone having children, and so Becky continued to take the birth control pill.

They both still went to Sunday Mass, but occasionally they would skip it if they felt too tired or if they had planned an outing. They never thought to ask themselves why they should go to Mass at all; that was just something that Catholics did. Naturally, it never entered their heads to pray together.

After a couple of years, they had saved enough for the down-payment on their dream-home and they triumphantly moved in, believing that now they would be really happy. Sure enough, they were, for about four months, and then Becky pointed out that she needed to have her own vehicle. John readily agreed. They wanted children eventually, but that could wait until they became a two-car family. Before long, they were able to boast of having two shiny brand-new vehicles in the driveway and, to themselves at least, these were a sure sign of their success in life. Now they expected to be content.

John was by now rising very fast in the company and had to be away from home a lot, at seminars, sales meetings and picking up contracts. He was more and more wrapped up in his work, with the result that when he was ever home, he was withdrawn and uncommunicative, and spent more time in front of the computer screen than with Becky. Not surprisingly, Becky began to realize that the romance was losing its former lustre and she felt increasingly lonely and frustrated. They hardly ever made love these days since John seemed to be so tired all the time. He had decided that they needed to acquire a boat and in spite of her misgivings, he assured Becky that it would be the perfect answer. They could cruise on the lakes, sleep on the boat under the stars, and really get closer to one another. It would give them both a break from work and from the house, which by now had become more of a dormitory than a home. Becky wanted so much to believe in John's promise and so she continued to work and to put off having a baby. Maybe the boat really would be the answer to the emptiness she felt inside.

Eventually, they purchased a twin-engine cruiser, which meant taking out a loan from the bank, but it also meant purchasing a contract for docking facilities, and the boat was eating up gasoline at a phenomenal rate. John seemed to brighten up for a while, enjoying his new toy for three whole weekends that summer. But his work was becoming more pressing and soon he did not have the time or the energy for the boat anymore. It ended up being a major frustration to get the thing out of the water and into dry dock for the winter. From a plaything and a source of pleasure, the boat had become another drudge.

In the next few months, Becky experienced two episodes of unexpected heavy bleeding, and her doctor was convinced that these had been miscarriages in spite of her being on the pill. She was deeply wounded by this revelation. All of a sudden, she realised how empty her life had become and she knew she desperately wanted a baby. It was with a growing feeling of alarm that she also knew John had other priorities in his life. Gradually, she became more and more discouraged, more and more unfulfilled, and to make matters worse, John did not seem to notice. He was too busy saving money for his latest solution to all their problems. He was now fixed on buying a luxurious motor home. They were going to have a lot of fun with that.

They were fighting a lot these days and it slowly dawned on John that Becky never seemed to be content. She was complaining most of the time and exploded into anger or burst into tears at the slightest provocation. This really hurt him a lot. After all, he was working day and night to give her everything she could ever want. He told himself he was doing his very best to make her happy, and from time to time, he even wondered why he had ever married her. Becky began to drink too much.

One awful day, they had a huge fight. It was over a very trivial matter, but the years of pent-up frustration soon erupted into rage and all the resentment came pouring out. Becky accused him of not loving her anymore, while John completely lost his temper, threatened her, and almost struck her. They were both stunned at the power of their own feelings and they knew that something was terribly wrong. How had this ever happened? Where had they lost their way? Here they were, successful, with a beautiful house, a swimming pool, two cars, a luxury cruiser and the prospect of a top-of-the-line motor home, and yet they had become strangers to one another. John thought that Becky was no longer the wonderful girl he had met in the café fifteen years ago, while Becky could not understand how John had changed so much. All their striving and all their hard work seemed to be for nothing. What had happened to the wonderful dreams they had once dreamed together?

It took a couple of days for the anger and hurt feelings to settle down, and during that time, they did not speak a word to each other. Then Becky, realising her marriage was in serious trouble, decided it was time to have a heart-to-heart talk with John. Anxiously, she asked him to sit down and listen to what she had to say. He felt very uncomfortable and he was not sure that he really wanted to hear this. Becky, her voice trembling, then said, "John, we have everything, yet we have nothing. We are losing our love for each other and that scares me. Surely our love is the most important thing in our lives." Then, not being able to keep it in any longer, she blurted out in a pleading sob, "I want a baby!" John snapped back, "Oh sure! A baby will solve everything. If the two of us can't get along, how will three of us make things any better?" It was as though Becky had been stabbed with a knife. All of her dreams were shattered. Her hope of happiness had slipped through her fingers, and she had no idea how to recapture it. In desperation, she had a crazy thought, and like a drowning man clutching at a straw, she gave voice to it. "John, I love you and I don't want us to split up. We have tried to make it on our own and it isn't working. How about we ask God for some help? Maybe it wouldn't hurt to pray." By now, John was too defeated to argue. He just nodded his head.

Becky rummaged in a drawer and found a white mother-of-pearl rosary which one of her aunts had given her on her wedding day. It had never been used, but better late than never. They quietly recited the beads, each praying from the heart that their marriage could be saved. It was awkward at first, but as they progressed, they began to feel an unfamiliar sense of peace. The gentle rhythm of the prayers seemed to give them some hope that God really did want to be included in their troubles. Afterwards, Becky put her arms around John and they hugged one another for a long time. Then they just sat out the evening in silence, not really knowing where to go from there.

Two days later, there was an unexpected knock at the door. The new parish priest had decided to do the rounds and was calling on his parishioners in order to introduce himself to his flock. He was quite young and when Becky answered the door, she noted that he was wearing his Roman collar. They had never had a priest in their home before, so they felt a little embarrassed, nor had it even entered their heads to have their home blessed, and they both were feeling a little guilty for not having attended Mass the previous Sunday. They wondered if he had noticed. But before long, they knew they really liked Fr. Bill. He seemed so relaxed and genuinely interested in them, and it was soon clear that he had not called to take them to task.

After the usual formalities and good-mannered preliminaries, Fr. Bill looked around and asked, "Do you two have any children?" Becky and John felt immediately uncomfortable, but after a moment of embarrassed silence, Becky glanced at John. He nodded and she opened up. She told Fr. Bill about their problems, how they had been slowly drifting apart and how they had avoided having children for the sake of a better standard of living. She was surprised that she found it so easy to bare her soul to this man who seemed to genuinely care about their happiness. Fr. Bill listened intently to every word and it was clear to the unhappy couple that he was silently praying through it all. When Becky had finished, Fr. Bill thought for a while and then he said, "Becky and John, you are two beautiful people. You have so much to offer to the world, but you have gotten lost along the way. It seems to me that your priorities in life have been disordered and therefore you inevitably became more and more unhappy. Disorder always ends up in misery. Would you allow me to help you re-arrange those priorities so that you can have a second chance at the happiness you both long for?"

He had thrown down the gauntlet, and Becky and John eagerly accepted the challenge. John, with a resigned shrug, said, "Fire away, father. At this stage in our marriage I'm ready for anything."

Fr. Bill then settled down more comfortably in the plush chesterfield and he began to speak. "You two, whether you remember it or not, entered into a solemn covenant with each other and with God to be a holy people for his kingdom. This may come as a surprise to you, but your primary calling was not to pursue happiness in earthly wealth, but to find it in God and God alone. Your second calling was to have children and raise them to be children of God since they would be his as well as yours."

Becky and John sat up more attentively at that. They had never heard this before and they were eager to hear more. What they did not realize was that they *had* heard it before. They had been told the same thing in the homily given on their wedding day, but they were not listening then. They were definitely listening now.

Fr. Bill talked some more about what true love is, and how love demands self-sacrifice, rather than mere self-gratification. He gently pointed out, "Falling in love does not mean that you will satisfy all my needs. That is of little importance. What it means is that I desire to give myself completely to you with no strings attached. Even if you do not meet my needs, I still love you and will always place your well-being above my own. Meanwhile, both partners always place God first in all things."

For Becky and John, this was like a completely new revelation, and yet deep in their hearts, it had the ring of pure truth. It was as though the very thing they needed most had been right there all along, but they had been too blind to see it. How could they have missed something so obvious? In the ensuing silence, they could hear the monotonous tick-tock of the big grandfather clock out in the hall.

Fr. Bill sensed their eagerness and excitement, and knowing this was the moment of truth, he took a deep breath and said, "There is something more which you need to understand, but you may not like it. Please, at least accept that I value your immortal souls so much that I have to be honest with you." They both signalled for him to continue. What had they to lose? They were miserable enough as things stood. "Well," Fr. Bill ventured, "you really have been walking down the broad, easy road away from God. How could Almighty God help you two, when you had cut him out of your lives?" Becky, feeling the need to defend herself, jumped in and said, "But we go to Mass on Sundays, father." Father nodded. "Yes, but was that ever enough? When did you last clean house and go to Confession?" The resultant silence said it all.

"Now, listen carefully. It is clear, in the short time I've known you, that you are as ready as you will ever be to hear this, so here goes. The first serious disorder in your lives has been that you made success and things your first priority. You allowed them to displace God in your hearts and so they became false gods — empty idols. Such things can never bring true peace and you have both discovered that. Does that make sense to you?" Becky and John already realised this deep within, but this was the first time anyone had had the courage to tell them. They felt they could trust this Fr. Bill and they could sense the love he nurtured in his priestly heart for them and for the pain of their predicament.

John then spoke up, "Father, what you say is absolutely true. I take the burden of blame for that. Becky wanted to have children, but I always wanted to put it off in order to acquire more toys. I have denied her, and so I suppose I have been a rotten husband." Becky reached out, touched his hand and threw him a smile which radiated forgiveness, understanding, love, and above all, the light of a dawning hope. As he saw the look in her lovely eyes, the very look for which he had longed all these years, his heart seemed to crack open and he began to sob. Fr. Bill sat quietly, allowing them to minister to each other as only a wife and husband can.

After a few moments, John managed to choke out, "Fr. Bill, you said that was our first serious disorder. Is there a second?" And he replied, "Yes, John. There is. You have been using artificial contraception in order to promote your selfish life-style. Forgive me for being blunt, but you have both cut God out of your Covenant. It is God's right to bless you with children and his alone, but when you began to contracept, you usurped God's holy prerogative and reserved it for yourselves. That saddens God very much. I know it all looked very logical and reasonable at the time, but I can see that you are both bereft of the greatest blessing God could give to you. That gift is a child. Ask yourselves this. What has been the fruit of your love for one another? It looks to me that the answer is a big house and some expensive toys. Surely, the most sublime fruit of love between a husband and wife is a new life, a precious little soul to be raised for God's Kingdom." Now, it was Becky's turn to sob and the tears ran down her cheeks and splashed onto the hardwood floor.

John wanted to defend Becky and so he blurted out, "We were never told about this stuff. How were we to know this? Why were we not told?" Fr. Bill looked sad and said, "You're probably right John. But there is little to be gained by pointing the finger at anyone. What matters is that you are hearing it now and God willing, if you both have a child, you can ensure that he or she is not deprived of the truth. You can see to it that your little one is raised in the fullness of the Faith. Surely that is a marvellous thought."

By this time John had his head in his hands and he quietly said, "There is more isn't there?" The priest looked intently at him and nodded. "This is the worst part. You have both been receiving Jesus, the very Son of God, in Holy Communion, with mortal sin on your soul. You have been bringing great sadness to Jesus, inviting him into an unclean place. Think about it. If you knew Jesus was coming here tonight, you would rush around cleaning and tidying up the house to make it fit to receive the King of kings. Well, what about the house of your soul? It needs cleaning up even more than this mere building."

Now both Becky and John were in tears. The good priest allowed them to sob it out, knowing that it was not the moment for more words. He just prayed quietly inside, asking the Holy Spirit to fill their hearts and enlighten them with the love of God. The grandfather clock kept up its steady tick-tock out in the hall, marking out the relentless passing of these precious seconds. Becky was the first to compose herself. "You know Father, John and I were so desperate the other night, we actually said a Rosary together. We had never done that before and as we prayed, I knew that we had somehow lost God's blessing, but I did not know how to put it into words. Worse, I didn't know how to get it back. I am beginning to think that your visit was God's answer to our prayers. What would you advise us to do?"

The worst was over. Father Bill let out a deep sigh and with a sparkle in his eye, he said, "Now, that is the easy part. The first thing is to make a good general confession, and if you'd like to take a few minutes to examine your conscience, I can hear your confessions individually right now. Why put it off? The next step is to get to Mass as soon as possible and experience the joy of receiving Jesus into a soul that is free of sin, a soul as pure as it was on the day of your Baptism. The third step is to commit yourselves to a life of daily prayer together, asking God to take his rightful place once more in your marriage. One more thing. Stop the pill!" Becky was stunned. She hadn't told Fr. Bill that she was actually on the Pill. "How did you know that, Father?" He smiled knowingly. "It wasn't too difficult to figure out. You'd be surprised how many Catholic couples think it is OK to be on the pill."

That evening, Becky and John made a heart-felt confession. They were astounded at their overwhelming feelings of relief, cleansing, peace and joy. It was as though fifteen years of baggage had been lifted from their shoulders and their hearts. They profusely thanked Fr. Bill and it was obvious to all three of them that they were going to become fast friends.

After that, Becky and John grew rapidly in a whole new understanding of what it means to be Catholic. They became faithful to prayer, and to the Sacraments. They began to go to Mass on weekdays, whenever possible, in addition to Sundays. To their great delight, Mass was no longer an obligation, but the sheerest joy. They received the Sacrament of Reconciliation faithfully once a month, and became involved in lay ministry to young married couples in the parish. Fr. Bill came round for dinner every week and their wonderful conversations centred on God and their new-found faith. After dinner, they always said a Rosary together.

John sold his boat and never did buy that motor home. Six months later, Becky announced that she was expecting a baby. She and John both knew that this child was the most precious of all possible blessings from God and at last, after all these years, they experienced the joy they had been searching for in all the wrong places.

CHAPTER 2

Husband and Father:
Real Men Do Cry

*"That men may appreciate
wisdom and discipline, may
understand words of
intelligence."*

(Prov.1:2)

There is a great and growing distortion in our society today. The battle of the sexes has now become open and total warfare, thanks, of course, to the unrelenting efforts of Satan to destroy the sanctity of the family. As a result, our world is peopled by the walking wounded, broken men who do not know how to be real men, and broken women who have rejected everything that is feminine. A powerful spirit of misogyny (that is to say, a hatred of the female) has taken a hold of our souls, so that men believe that the only way they can survive is to dominate and abuse women, while women, who also would like to survive, are denying the best of what it means to be female, in order to embrace the worst of what it means to be male. Misogyny has become so prevalent, that men hate and suppress their own femininity, while women try to escape from their femininity by becoming competitive, aggressive and power hungry.

This distortion between the sexes was prophesied by God after the sin of Adam and Eve in the garden. God said to the woman, "Your yearning will be for your husband, and he will dominate you" (Gen. 3:16). The power struggle between men and women, the so-called battle of the sexes, is a direct consequence of original sin. Satan is cashing in on this perversion, and is successfully setting men against women and women against men, thereby destroying family peace. Even more alarming is the fact that he is leading us to raise children who no longer know what true love is all about.

The great majority of men today do not have a clue what it means to be a real man. They have been raised by broken fathers, and so their masculine image is distorted by their own inadequate fathering experience. Dad was never really present to them. He was away at work all the time, or he was drunk most of the time, or he was caught up in his own selfish pursuits. Whatever the problem, he was emotionally a thousand miles away from his son. And even when he was physically close, he likely indulged in anger, physical beatings, or relentless put-downs of his children. With such a role model, what sort of image of manhood is a boy likely to internalise? Because he desperately wants his father's love and admiration, he either imitates dad and becomes another bully or he seeks his father's love in other men and commits himself to a homosexual life style, trapped in the prison of gender confusion. Others are so destroyed by dad's put-downs, they really believe that they will never amount to anything. They develop a crushing sense of worthlessness and go through life in constant fear, often totally controlled by their wives, their bosses at work, and even by their own children. They never knew a real man, a man whom they could have as a hero and who, in turn, could love them, encourage them, teach them and spend time with them. When dad is not a hero, men turn to other men to be their heroes. If they are fortunate, it will be a good model, a man of goodness and honour. If not, they will fashion themselves in the image and likeness of an anti-hero, whose example leads them farther and farther away from Jesus. So often they choose another dysfunctional man, such as Rambo the killer, or James Bond the womaniser, or Joe Big Bucks, the ruthless business man. If we do not have a father, we will invent one. Our need for fathering is that great. It is a built-in drive.

Nowadays, many men think that being a man means never to show emotions, other than anger, of course. Real men never ever cry. Real men get drunk on weekends. They hunt and fish, play endless golf, and neglect their families. They never indulge in tender hugs for their wives or children. They leave child-rearing to their wives. A real man never does housework. He must never be romantic, unless he is sexually aroused. Also, he must pretend to be a gold medal Olympic sexual athlete and brag about it to his male friends. His religion is sports, and his gods are hockey and football stars. He must succeed in the workplace, dominate his wife, and conquer the world. Naturally, real men must always indulge in some form of prejudice, because it makes them feel superior. Accordingly, a Hispanic becomes a Spic and a Caucasian becomes a Honky. A Catholic might be derogatorily referred to as a Papist, while a Protestant is labelled a Heretic. The ugly mind of a prejudiced man has to reduce a person to a single epithet, in order to cope with those who are "different." Prejudice makes no room for the love of Jesus Christ, which embraces all men and women regardless of race or creed. On top of this, of course, a real man never prays with his family. Prayer is only for women!

The tragedy is that such men are truly miserable and unhappy creatures. They become more and more neurotic, unable to understand why their wives become unhappy too. They fail to make the connection between their own behaviour and the disobedience of their children. When their kids become powerful teenagers, into drugs, alcohol, sexual pleasure and maybe even crime, they blame everything and everyone else but themselves. And if they ever suspected for a moment that they were actually dysfunctional, they would never come to a therapist for help, because that would be a sign of weakness, and real men can never admit to a weakness.

No wonder there is feminism in today's world. No wonder women are lashing out at men who are abusing them. No wonder more and more women are turning to each other for love and opting for lesbian relationships, given the risks they run in seeking true love from men. Something is seriously wrong. There is a major sickness in our world. In a word, it is the breakdown of God's order. God's design for men is being mutilated, which means that they must rediscover what God intended them to be. In fact, I would hazard a prediction right now. If men will turn around and become obedient to God's vision of who they are, not only will men become real men, but feminism will disappear from the face of the earth. It will simply become obsolete.

When men live out their true vocation of manhood, women will once again become secure, loved, respected, protected and provided for, and they, in turn, will rediscover their God-given role as receivers and nurturers of life and love. They will once again become man's helpmate, as God intended. The family will be restored to its holy order, and God will reign in our families as he should.

For men to reclaim their manhood, they would do well to take a good look at three heroes, three role models vastly different from the kinds of heroes they are exposed to by movies and television. Forget Archie Bunker and our over-paid sports stars. We need to open our hearts and look at God the Father, Jesus Christ the Redeemer, and St. Joseph the Foster-Father. Each of them is a treasure house of wisdom for men.

God the Father

"This then is what I pray, kneeling before the Father, from whom every fatherhood in heaven or on earth takes its name. In the abundance of his glory, may he, through his spirit, enable you to grow firm in power with regard to your inner self, so that Christ may live in your hearts through faith" (Eph. 3:14-17). From this we learn that, first and foremost, our fatherhood derives from the fatherhood of God. Our paternity is a gift from the paternity of God. A man is indeed the head of his household, but he is not given human power. He is given *divine* power, which he must exercise in accordance with the Father of fathers in Heaven.

"Whoever does not love does not know God, for God is love" (1 John 4:8). Love is the key to the Fatherhood of God. Love, therefore, must also become the key to our human fatherhood. If a man does not know how to love, he has not yet discovered what real manhood is all about. But what is love? St. Paul tells us, "Love is patient, love is kind, love is not envious or boastful or arrogant or rude. It does not insist on its own way. It is not irritable or resentful. It does not rejoice in wrong doing but rejoices in the truth. It bears all things, believes all things, hopes all things, endures all things" (1 Cor. 13:4-7). That does not seem to fit with today's ideas about manhood. This kind of manly loving is a far, far cry from the angry, fury-driven, hard drinking, wife abuser of today. The man who follows St. Paul has, as his model, God himself. The angry, fury-driven man models himself on Satan. That is the difference, and it makes all the difference.

"My son, do not disdain the discipline of the Lord or lose heart when reproved by him, for whom the Lord loves, he disciplines" (Heb. 12:5-6). As fathers, men stand in for the Lord and so they have the duty to discipline their children. This duty is not to be dumped onto their wives. It is true that wives must also discipline the children, but they derive that authority from their husbands. Husbands derive their authority from God the Father himself. It is a man's job, and he shirks it at his peril. God the Father disciplines and he expects earthly fathers to do the same. It goes with the job. If fathers do not take this task seriously, then their own immortal souls will be in grave danger. Read the Old Testament and see what happened to Eli the Priest, when he failed to discipline his sons. God said, "I condemn his family for ever, since he is aware that his sons have been cursing God and yet has not corrected them" (1 Sam. 3:13). Eli failed in his duty towards his sons and so deserved to be cursed by God. All fathers, therefore, are duty-bound to give godly discipline to their children.

A wise man once said, "Fathers are pals nowadays, because they don't have the guts to be fathers." Faithful Catholic men must decide to become true fathers and bring discipline to their homes. They begin this task by disciplining themselves. If they demonstrate obedience to God the Father in Heaven, then they have a right to demand obedience from their children. God the Father has rights over earthly fathers and they, in turn, have rights over their families. That is God's order. But just as God exercises his rights with love and mercy, so fathers must show love and mercy to their wives and to their children. "And parents, never drive your children to resentment but bring them up with correction and advice inspired by the Lord" (Eph. 6:4).

A real man knows his Father-God in heaven, and in turn, becomes a godly father in his own home.

Jesus, The Christ

Jesus, to be sure, was the perfect model of manhood, and he modelled his Father in Heaven perfectly. Indeed, Scripture tells us that we are to put on the mind of Christ. He said, "Learn from me for I am gentle and humble of heart" (Matt. 11:29). Jesus did not say, "Learn from me for I am powerful and arrogant of heart." If we are to be like him and become real men, we are to give up all notions of power or violence, and become gentle-men, humble in our relationships with our wives, our children and our neighbours. Rambo will waste you. Jesus will bless you. Violence is Rambo's way. Meekness is Jesus' way. We must not think that being meek or gentle is only for weaklings. On the contrary, meekness is for very brave and courageous men. Which is easier, to shoot a man or to allow him to shoot you? Jesus allowed violent men to nail him to a cross. Was that the action of a coward or a real man? When evil men come to kill my wife and my children, perfect conformity to the example and lessons of Jesus, as found in the Gospel, would require me not to kill them. This would be the heroic, Christ-like course of action. The consistent teaching of the Church, however, allows us to take life in extreme situations of self-defence. I am not sure what I would do in such an instance, but I do know this: they would have to climb over my dead body to get to my family. My manhood would demand this sacrifice for my wife and children. As a husband and father, I must be prepared to lay down my life for my family. That means dying to self every day, and it may one day mean a sacrificial death in reality. This is not just a lofty theory. This is the very life blood of my vocation as husband and father.

"You have heard how it was said, eye for eye and tooth for tooth, but I say this to you. Offer no resistance to the wicked. On the contrary, if anyone hits you on the right cheek, offer him the other as well" (Matt. 5:38-39). This, of course, goes against all of our natural, animal instincts and all of our training as males. Yet Jesus demands that we rise above any immediate urge to violence or retaliation against others. He teaches us that the most effective response to evil is goodness. If we punch the man who punches us, we only add to the evil in the world and we give Satan more power, because he feeds on evil. But if we give back goodness for evil, we neutralize it, there is rejoicing in heaven and Satan retreats in frustration.

Jesus also told us he came to save the world, not to condemn it. He never condemned sinners. He always encouraged them, built them up, and called them to a higher good. We too must never condemn others. We must also imitate Jesus and build others up, calling them always to bring out the best in themselves. This is especially pertinent in the case of our wives and our children.

"Love one another as I have loved you" (John 15:12). Once again it all comes back to love. God *is* love, and Jesus commands us to love. Love, then, is the foundation of true manhood. Men must become lovers, real lovers, which might even mean laying down their lives for their families, just as Jesus laid down his life for all of us. They are to sacrifice their own selfish desires and needs for the sake of their loved ones. They are to die to self if they are to truly find the happiness they desire as men.

In Michael O'Brien's novel, **Plague Journal,** one of his characters declares with great insight: "I didn't know it then, but the cost of a happy family is the death of selfishness. The father must die if he's to give life to his spouse and his children. Not a pleasant thought, but a true one. An entire life-time can be spent avoiding it. It's simply not enough to provide and protect. In themselves, of course, providing and protecting are good and necessary things. That's our responsibility. But a father can provide a mountain of material goods for his family and defend it against all kinds of inconveniences, thinking he can rest easy, having done his part, and still have missed the essential thing: he is called to be an image of love and truth."

Jesus tells us how to be happy as men, how to have a happiness which endures, not fleeting earthly pleasure. In the Sermon on the Mount, he preached on the richness of the Beatitudes, and there he said, "How *happy* are the poor in spirit ... happy the gentle ... happy those who mourn ... happy those who hunger and thirst for what is right ... happy the merciful ... the pure in heart ... the peacemakers." If men read this passage over and over again and truly welcomed these wonderful words into their hearts, they would be guaranteed a deep, abiding happiness within. Jesus promised it and he, as we all know, is the Prince of promise-keepers. The world tells us that we can only be happy if we strive to amass money and power, or if we frantically seek pleasure, if we accumulate things, get a bigger house, a bigger boat, and drink the right beer. Jesus had very different ideas.

Happiness is not to be found in the world and its trinkets, but in following his way, which is the way of the heart. And if we follow his way, we will also become the beneficiaries of the fruits of the Spirit, which St. Paul tells us are: "Love, joy, peace, patience, kindness, goodness, trustfulness, gentleness and self-control" (Gal. 5:22-23). Is there any man who does not want these treasures? If we do not follow Jesus, we are doomed to reap the opposite of these wondrous fruits. Once again, as St. Paul says, "When self-indulgence is at work, the results are obvious: sexual vice, impurity, and sensuality, the worship of false gods and sorcery, antagonisms and rivalry, jealousy, bad temper and quarrels, disagreements, factions and malice, drunkenness, orgies and all such things" (Gal. 5:19-21). The man who opts for these is indeed an unhappy man.

Is this the life a real man wants? Is this the life any man wants? Sin and misery come out of self-indulgence. Peace and happiness come out of being the husbands that God calls men to be. "Happy the man who trusts in the Lord" (Ps. 84:12). This is a profound truth. If men really trusted that God will take care of them, even in the little things, they would give up their neurotic, masculine need to control their own little world. They would relax and stop worrying, believing that all things are being worked towards their good by a wise and loving God. It is not by conquering the world that men will find peace. It is only by becoming like little children and placing all their trust in their Abba, their Papa-God, that they will find peace. Man cannot control the world, but our Father God can and it was Jesus who showed us how.

St. Joseph

St. Joseph was the step-father of Jesus. He was well aware that Mary, his wife, was the special gift of God to him. He knew he had been chosen by God to care for Mary and her Son, and he joyfully took on the task.

The Gospel of Matthew tells us that Joseph was a just man. Scripture is full of references which explain what it means to be a just man. "Wisdom comes from the lips of the just and his tongue speaks what is right. The law of God is in his heart, his foot will never slip" (Ps. 37:30-31). "The just always lend generously, and their children become a blessing" (Ps. 37:26). "He speaks truth from his heart. He keeps his tongue under control" (Ps.15:2-3). "The path of the just is like the light of dawn, its brightness growing to the fullness of day" (Prov. 4:18).

Good St. Joseph was all of these things. He loved Mary, his betrothed, and refused to hand her over to the law, even when it looked like she had become pregnant by another man, which must have struck him as the only natural explanation. His actions were informed by the law of love engraved deep within his heart and not by the human demand for vengeance. In spite of his hurt, he returned mercy for hurt. He decided to legally divorce Mary rather than openly condemn her, which he had every right to do under Jewish law. That is the mark of a just man. A real man knows how to be merciful.

St. Joseph exhibited eight singular qualities, which constitute a shining example to all who would become real men: loving man, chaste spouse, protector, provider, worker, teacher, faithful husband and servant. St. Joseph knew how to love. He sacrificed his own natural desires for fatherhood in order to do the Will of God. He loved God first and after that he also loved Mary and Jesus. He was chaste, but chastity is not to be confused with celibacy. Husbands are not all called to be celibate although some couples may generously choose this holy sacrifice later in life after having raised their family. They are free to enjoy a loving sexual life, but at the same time all men are called to chastity in their sexual lives. St. Joseph protected his little family, especially when he had to flee to Egypt to save them from Herod's murdering soldiers. He provided food, clothing, and shelter for Mary and Jesus by doing good, honest, hard work every day, excepting the Sabbath, which he insisted on keeping holy in accordance with the commandment of Yahweh. He taught Jesus carpentry, and he also taught him the Scriptures. St. Joseph was utterly faithful to Mary, his wife. There was no room for any other woman in his heart and, of course, he placed himself totally at the service of Mary and Jesus for their well being and happiness. How many of today's husbands know how to serve their wives and children? How many husbands today dedicate themselves to making their wives happy and content? How many husbands today spend time with their children? A real man understands his priorities in life. He puts God first, his wife second and himself third. That is God's order. It is God's design for husbands. Of course, for a wife it is God first, husband second, and herself third.

St. Paul calls on married couples to serve each other. My job as a husband is to put my wife ahead of myself, to love her as I love myself. I am called to do everything in my power to make her feel secure and loved. Then and only then do I have the right to expect her to serve me, building a home for me and my children. This sounds like a tall order, especially if I do not acknowledge one thing as certain: I am never going to succeed in doing this under my own power. I am going to need the power of God, which is God's grace, to accomplish this. That is why I am called by God to be holy and to pray every day, calling down upon me and my wife all the graces of our marriage sacrament. Prayer is not primarily for women. Prayer is in fact the fundamental obligation of the man of the house. I must be the prayer leader of my family, summoning my family to regular prayer time in the home. I am the *intercessor* before God for my wife and my little ones. God looks to me to guide my family in the ways of truth and holiness. If I fail in this task, I must answer for it before the Lord just as Eli the Old Testament priest had to do. My eternal happiness depends on my being the holiest husband and father possible. Marriage demands no less.

The family Rosary is a powerful prayer for unity, love and protection, and it is the man who should lead it. The man must constantly ask God the Father to give him the grace he needs to be a godly husband and father. He must see to it that his children are brought up in the faith and that they attend Mass, always on Sundays, and during the week if possible, and that they go to regular confession and communion. Such a man will be able to stand one day before Jesus, confident that he has lived out his Christian duty in the eyes of the Lord. But such a man is also promised great blessings by God even in his earthly life. "Your own labours will yield you a living. Happy and prosperous will you be. Your wife a fruitful vine in the inner places of your house. Your children round your table like shoots of an olive tree" (Ps. 128:2-3). God is promising that the faithful and holy husband will be blessed and that this will be manifested in fruitful work, in happiness, prosperity, in a contented wife and in godly children. This is an offer too good to refuse.

In chapter 10, it is pointed out that a father models an image of God to his young child. But the role of father becomes even more powerful when the child becomes older. He will model an image of *manhood* to his children, and this has major implications for their sexual development. From the age of ten to sixteen years, the most indispensable person in the child's life is father. It is especially during these years that a child desperately needs dad to model ideal manhood. If a child is deprived of fathering during these years, either by dad being physically absent, emotionally withdrawn or consistently drunk (which is the same thing), then dire consequences can ensue.

A male child needs dad to be his hero. He craves dad's love, and if he does not get it, he is devastated. This need is so great that he will search elsewhere for it. Indeed, the need may express itself in a homosexual preference whereby he may invite another man to give him the love he never received from his dad. His need for his father's love is that powerful.

Daughters who feel unloved by their fathers will come to hate dad for not loving them. From this they may come to hate all men in as much as they represent dad to them, turning to lesbian relationships as the only reliable source of love in their unhappy world.

The "gay" subculture refuses to accept the psychodynamics of its own disorder. Indeed, most of them try to prove that homosexuality is genetic. But even if that could be proven, which I seriously doubt, it is still a disorder. A genetic mutation cannot be used to justify an immoral lifestyle. The fact is, I have treated many homosexual patients, and in all cases I have found absentee or dysfunctional fathering in their critical years. Many also found healing when they came to experience the perfect fatherly love of God, the Father of all fathers.

When it comes to family relationships, a man needs to understand the "feminine" within himself. To accomplish this, he so often needs to overcome his own conditioning. Our parents meant well, but so often they raised us in their own image of what a man should be. Add to that the Hollywood brainwashing of boys and men to be a one-man army, and it is easy to see how the inborn feminine nature of the male can be crushed. We may believe that the macho image is the only valid way to be a real man, but that is absurd. It is interesting to look at Rambo after he has brutally killed scores of other men. He stands with the smoking gun in his hand surveying the mayhem he has created. Does he look happy? On the contrary, he looks alone, isolated, and unfulfilled. His vengeance did not bring him peace of mind. That is just as true for all of us men. When we follow the paths of the world, in violence and in denial of our own tenderness, we too will find ourselves alone. We will cut ourselves off from the life-giving love of our wives, our children will grow to despise us, and we will end up killing our own capacity for love.

The real man is the one who has discovered the God-given balance within and is not ashamed of it. He recognises that all men are really scared little boys inside. Men are expected to go to war, but they do not want to die. We are afraid. The real man has come face to face with his true inner self, the self that is loving, tender, gentle, self-giving, forgiving, understanding, and filled with compassion for lesser men. He faces the truth about himself and, like any other little boy, he is eager to rush into the protecting arms of his mother when he is frightened. The Blessed and Great Mother of God is ready to throw her arms around him, if only he will come to her. She of all people understands the heart of a man, from whom so much is expected and needed by his wife and children. She also understands the demands made on him by a perverse and sinful society. After all, Mary understood her Son and his Sacred Heart in all its beauty, its weariness, its deprivations, and even its fears. Jesus asked his Father to take the chalice away from him, but immediately submitted to his Father by asking that his will be done. This is the perfect model of how men, as husbands and fathers, should pray. Like Jesus we should admit that we are often "sorrowful unto death" (Matt. 26:38). We should kneel before the Father and tell him so.

Then, like Jesus, we can ask for what we want. "Father, if it be possible, let this cup pass me by" (Matt. 26:39). A real man then goes all the way in generosity and prays, "Not my will but thine be done" (Matt. 26:39).

A true husband knows how to be gentle with his wife. He offers her the words, "I love you" more than he needs to, but not just the empty words. He proves what he says by his loving actions. He knows when she is tired, or discouraged or sad and willingly gives her the strength of his arms. Nothing speaks more eloquently to a woman than a manly hug. He listens to her concerns. He never scorns her apparent lack of logic. To his delight, when he does listen, he usually finds that what he thought was illogical was actually wisdom. He knows how to sacrifice his own needs for her, and he learns that best from seeing the way she constantly sacrifices her needs for him. He indulges her little demands of him, as best he can, and thinks of her before he thinks of himself. He never criticises her or judges her, and absolutely never allows anyone else to do so.

On a certain occasion, when he was eleven years old, a holy priest whom I know defied his mother in angry and petulant rebellion. He and his mother were standing at the foot of the stairs in their house at the time. This good priest says that his father was upstairs, but came from out of nowhere, as if he had been shot out of a cannon, and planted himself in front of the boy. He took him by the lapels and said, "Don't you ever speak to your mother like that again. But never mind that, nobody speaks to *my wife* like that. Nobody." That young boy never ever forgot this lesson, even after he had grown up to become a priest. His father was a real man and he rushed to defend his wife as all real men should. He was teaching his son that the relationship with his wife was paramount and took precedence over all other relationships, even his relationship with his son. A man's wife is God's precious gift to him and him alone. God expects him to defend her against all-comers, including and perhaps especially, the children.

A real man is not ashamed of his tender heart. He is able to feel the pain of those he loves and to weep with them. So many men refuse to do this and see themselves as fixers. When his wife comes to him with her pain, he dispassionately offers her five solutions to "fix" her feelings. This is not what she is asking for. She merely longs for him to understand her, to accept her feelings without judging them, and to give her that magic manly hug. Again, the real man knows this and does it.

At the same time, a Christian man shares all of his income and his goods with his family. He does not hold back money for his own selfish pursuits at the expense of his wife and children, and especially not at the expense of their necessities. He does not hide money in a separate bank account and he never insists on "mine and yours." He rejoices that all of the family assets are "ours." Such a man recognizes his wife as his true partner in life in all things, and that she has equal right and access to the family goods and property.

As a father, the real man is willing to have his need for leisure and rest challenged. Children are spontaneous and in great need of affirmation. A good father is willing to submerge his own needs, to sit down, listen to their ideas and dreams and give them the wisdom of his gentle direction. His words have power in their little hearts, because they see him live out those words. He is a living example of his own wisdom. He knows how to play with them, to have fun, to let them jump all over him, even if he is tired. He sets aside time to take them to a ball game or to ballet or to a concert. He does not discriminate between one child or another, nor does he show a preference for boys over girls. I remember once organising a fishing trip for my son. This was to be the big father-son bonding experience. My daughter Kirstie was listening to our plans and with a kind of pleading look on her face, quietly said, "Dad, I like fishing too." It was like a bombshell to me. My lovely daughter also wanted to be a part of this special time with me. She was paying me the ultimate compliment of a daughter to a father and showing me the yearning in her heart for her father's love. So I happily took her along on the fishing trip, and it turned out she caught the biggest bass of the day, my son caught a couple of keepers and I caught the one that measured all of two inches from nose to tail. I have a snapshot to prove it. I know that a powerful and beautiful bonding was given expression on that memorable day. My daughter still loves to talk about it and we all chuckle at my mighty tiddler. It is one of those memories which will never lose its flavour. A good father knows how to give his children memories to be stored forever as priceless treasures.

A real man never backs down from his duty to discipline the children he loves. Indeed, it is because he loves his children that he takes the time to discipline. He knows his own strength, and so he always disciplines with love, never with anger. He appreciates that anger is by its very nature violent and can lead to abuse. He corrects, admonishes and instructs his child with the authority of God himself. Therefore, he knows that he is not imposing his own will on his children, but rather calling them to be obedient to the will of God, the Father. At all times, he supports his wife in the discipline of the children. He never contradicts her in front of them, although he may in private, later on, gently ask her to reconsider a harsh punishment.

Real men do cry. A manly man knows when to let the tears flow. He is not ashamed to show his wife and his children that the true heart of a man is capable of such tenderness. His tears are the silent sign of a compassionate heart. "Happy are those who mourn" (Matt. 5:4). Such a man is not stingy in offering comfort to those who need it, nor is he too proud to ask for it when he is the one in need.

My daughter Fiona once composed a little poem for me when she was a small child. She wrote,

> Pops are tops.
> My dad is too.
> He plays with me
> and takes me places.
> But best of all he loves me.

For me, that was a wonderful testimony to my own fatherhood and I will treasure it for ever. Could any father ask for more?

So now it is easier to appreciate the awesome responsibility that goes with being a husband and a father. Life does not come with an instruction manual. That's why we have fathers to instruct their families. A wife needs love and security. A child needs love, security and training. A man needs to provide all of these things to fulfil himself and to draw his family closer to God.

So what is a real man?

A real man is a lover, a great and wonderful lover, who follows God's way of love and not the world's way.

He is God-centred and never self-centred.
He is gentle and never violent.
He is peaceful and never angry.
He is kind and never mean-hearted.
He is firm and never controlling.
He is just and never unfair.
He is available and never absent.
He is humble and never proud.
He is faithful and never adulterous.
He is a promise-keeper and not a renegade.
If married, he is a husband and never a bachelor.
And he is a father in accordance with God the Father.
Above all he is a living model of Jesus Christ.

CHAPTER 3

Wife and Mother: Real Women are Mystery and Masterpiece

"A gracious woman does
honour to her husband."
(Prov. 12:4)

The Church is very often accused these days of having oppressed women down through the centuries. She is perceived as a male-dominated hierarchy, deliberately structured so as to keep women from realising their full potential and dignity. This is simply a lie, but then if a lie is repeated often enough, most people soon come to believe it. Satan understands this very well and so he keeps on telling and re-telling the lie. But it is a lie for the simple reason that the Bible from its beginning to its end honours the role of women in salvation history. It not only places woman firmly in a position of equal dignity with men, but it also highlights her very special feminine charisms. These are gifts from our loving God who, on the one hand, emphasises her equality with men, but at the same time rejoices in that which makes her irreplaceable and unique. The Catholic Church is the Bride of Christ and, as such, is obedient to Jesus who is the Word of God and the Bible is the Word of God. The Church therefore in that spirit of obedience has always elevated woman to her proper God-given dignity. She could do no less. Countless holy women have been recognised and canonised by the Church. Numerous seminaries for young men aspiring to the priesthood were run and taught by holy, highly educated women. It could not have been otherwise, since the Church models herself on Mary the Mother of Jesus and he founded the Church in the first place. Certainly there are countless examples of women being oppressed and dominated by men, even by priests who ought to have known better, but this was always contrary to the teachings of the Magisterium of the Church. Domination was never preached by the Church. Pope Paul VI, who conferred the title of Doctor of the Church upon St. Teresa of Jesus and St. Catherine of Siena, thus recognising their powerful contribution to the clarification of the truths of the Catholic Church, said, "Within Christianity, more than in any other religion, and since its very beginning, women have had a special dignity of which the New Testament shows us many important aspects … it is evident that women are meant to form part of the living and working structure of Christianity in so prominent a manner that perhaps not all their potentialities have yet been made clear." In other words, the mystery of what it means to be female has not yet been fully revealed, and this is precisely because being female is indeed a profound and wondrous mystery. We can never fully understand a mystery. Both men and women need to explore this hidden reality in ever greater depth, because the more we learn about woman as God intended her to be, the more we learn about God himself. Men should be overawed at the beauty and the truth of women. The more they discover, the more they will revere their wives and all women and the less likely they will be to dominate, abuse and use women for their own selfish purposes.

The Second Vatican Council states: "The hour is coming, in fact has come, when the vocation of women is being acknowledged in its fullness, the hour in which women acquire in the world an influence, an effect and a power never hitherto achieved. That is why, at this moment when the human race is undergoing a deep transformation, women imbued with a spirit of the Gospel can do so much to aid humanity in not falling."

Are these the words of a Church which oppresses women? On the contrary, the Church is suggesting that much of the salvation of the human race is in the hands of godly women who choose to live out the Gospel of Jesus. The Church recognises that it is the quiet strength, courage, fidelity, wisdom and above all the love of women which will call men to be true disciples of Christ and, together with men, to change the world.

The Bible is a treasure house of insights into the mystery of woman and femininity. Right at the beginning in the book of Genesis we are told, "God created man in his own image, in the image of God he created him: male and female he created them" (Gen. 1:27). Therefore both male and female are human beings to an equal degree. Both are created in God's image. But while male and female are equal in dignity, they are not identical. God created real differences, not only to distinguish the sexes, but also that together we might be better equipped for our unique and special roles in the formation of family and community life. These differences are not simply in our physical bodies, but rather are more profoundly spiritual, psychological and emotional. There is therefore a God-given complementarity between men and women. "This is why a man leaves his father and mother and becomes attached to his wife and they become one flesh" (Gen. 2:24). Man is not complete without woman and she is not complete without man. But together they become one flesh, united in giving glory to God. God understood this emptiness within Adam and said, "It is not right that the man should be alone. I shall make him a helper fit for him" (Gen. 2:18). "Then Yahweh God made the man fall into a deep sleep. And while he was asleep, he took one of his ribs and closed the flesh up again forthwith. Yahweh God fashioned the rib he had taken from the man into a woman and brought her to the Man. And the man said, 'This one at last is bone of my bones and flesh of my flesh. She is to be called woman because she was taken from man'" (Gen. 2:21-24). We can therefore conclude that man and woman are made *for each other.* Each needs the other. Eve is a vital part of Adam, being made out of his rib and she is there to be his helper and to be one with him. It is important to note that God made her to be a helper "fit for him," which means she was the perfect mate for the man in every possible way. She was to be a helper, not in the sense of a slave jumping to his every command, but in the sense of sharing with him in "subduing the earth" (Gen. 1:28). She is his life's companion and Adam's highest calling on earth is to exist in relationship, first with God and then with the woman. Yet at the same time, it is in his relationship with woman that he finds his true relationship with God. Before the Fall, this union of Adam and Eve was so perfect that "Both of them were naked, the man and his wife, but they felt no shame before each other" (Gen. 2:25). Therefore, even their sexuality was totally pure and free from the darkness of lust. They both lived as truly equal persons, giving of themselves totally one to the other, and that is still the secret of any happy and successful man-woman relationship today. It was and still is God's intention for us and it is the only way in which we will find peace and happiness with one another.

Unfortunately, the tragedy of the apple spoiled the perfection which before had come so easily to them. Now they were both distorted by the Original Sin and all of us, to this day, share in that distortion. God himself pronounced the sentence upon them both. "To the woman he said, 'I shall give you intense pain in child-bearing, you will give birth to our children in pain. Your yearning will be for your husband and he will dominate you.' To the man he said, 'Because you listened to the voice of your wife and ate from the tree of which I had forbidden you to eat, accursed shall be the soil because of you. Painfully will you get your food from it as long as you live'" (Gen. 3:16-17).

Therefore the unity of the two was now disrupted. A woman would be the victim of her own emotions, *yearning* for her husband, that is to say, needing more from him than he could ever give, knowing that he could never fully satisfy her deepest self. As a result, she is often tempted to become a seductress just like Eve in order to get what she yearns for, thereby denying her own holy femininity. She may use her beauty to get what she thinks she wants or become demanding or complaining. She may begin to value trinkets because she cannot have what she truly values, namely a deep and abiding intimacy with her husband. As a result, she destroys her true self in order to satisfy her false self. A man on the other hand tends to dominate his wife and stifle her womanhood. The very thing he needs in order to be complete and happy is the very thing he destroys by his drive to dominate. This terrible consequence is in full swing today, dividing male and female, destroying marriages and families. The original God-given equality of man and woman is now violated and while it is clearly to the disadvantage of the woman, it also diminishes the true dignity of the man. The more he lords it over his wife, the more he violates himself. The battle of the sexes becomes total war. It is interesting to note that in this all-out battle, men do not try to win it by becoming like women. Instead it is women who take on the men on their own ground by trying to become like men. Pope John Paul II in his letter *Dignity and Vocation of Women* said, "Consequently, even the rightful opposition of women to what is expressed in the biblical words 'He shall rule over you' must not under any condition lead to the masculinization of women. In the name of liberation from male domination, women must not appropriate to themselves male characteristics contrary to their own feminine originality. There is a well-founded fear that if they take this path, women will not reach fulfilment but instead will deform and lose what constitutes their essential richness. It is indeed an enormous richness." The one and only hope for the human race is not militant feminism (although a woman's cry for equal dignity is a perfectly valid Christian principle) but to rediscover what God originally intended, to honestly face our post-original sin distortions, to repent of them and to strive to become true children of God, fully male and fully female.

It is true that St. Paul says, "Wives be submissive to your husbands as to the Lord" (Eph. 5:22), and Peter, the first pope, echoes this when he says, "You wives should be obedient to your husbands" (1 Pet. 3:1). Taken out of context, it looks like God is demanding a master-slave relationship. That is why it is vital to take the *whole* passage of Scripture and not a quotation in isolation, because therein lies the serious risk of misinterpreting the holy Word of God. First of all, as soon as St. Paul asks for wives to submit to their husbands, he immediately commands that "Husbands love your wives as Christ loved the Church" (Eph. 5:25). This passage demands our fullest understanding. We must ask ourselves, "How did Christ love the Church?" He *submitted* himself to it. He *obeyed* it. Did he not say, "Whatever you bind on earth will be bound in Heaven? Whatever you loose on earth will be loosed in heaven" (Matt. 16:19)? Therefore Jesus deliberately chose to be *obedient* to his own Church. Not only that, but he washed the feet of his disciples, powerfully demonstrating his desire to *serve* the Church. Husbands therefore are also called to submit to their wives and to serve them, to obey them and to be at their disposal. Likewise, when St. Peter asked wives to submit to their husbands, the whole passage reads, "You wives should be obedient to your husbands. Then if there are some husbands who do not believe the Word, they may find themselves won over, without a word spoken, by the way their wives behave, when they see the reverence and purity of your way of life" (1 Pet. 3:1-2). In other words, wives are indeed called to be submissive just as husbands are called to be submissive, but in a wife's silent submission and good example, she can draw her husband closer to God and truth. In fact, St. Paul makes this interpretation very clear when he says, "Be subject to one another out of reverence for Christ" (Eph. 5:21). Pope John Paul II re-emphasises this truth in the *Dignity and Vocation of Women,* when he writes, "In the relationship between husband and wife the subjection is not one-sided but mutual." Therefore, a husband governs and his wife rules. He is the king and she is the queen. He is the head and she is the heart. *He is the moral authority. She is the love authority.* This is equality in diversity. Catholics must reorganise their thinking. Jesus calls men and women to be equal before God and one another. The age of male domination must come to an end if humanity is ever to be restored to its original harmony and blessing.

Am I obedient to my wife? Yes I am. I recognize that she has wisdom in so many things and I listen to that wisdom. Her wisdom and intuition have saved me from many a rash and ill-considered decision. At a more mundane level, she has wonderful managerial skills with money and finances. I do not. I therefore am totally obedient to her in all matters to do with spending or saving money. In fact I often blissfully walk around with no money in my pocket, knowing that all such things are being prudently and wisely cared for by my life's partner. She runs my medical office and without her, my work would be a shambles and so I obey her in everything that has to do with organization. In turn she obeys me in all things medical because those are my skills. Likewise, she defers to my ministry as Permanent Deacon and does everything in her power to support that ministry. We have discovered each other's gifts and deficiencies and we have learned how to bring them together in a beautiful complementarity. Together we have found oneness and wholeness.

When we are of one mind and heart on an issue, we know that the Holy Spirit is present in and approves of our decision. But what does a Christian couple do when there is a stalemate? If man and wife cannot agree on an issue, how should they handle it? First of all they should set aside useless feelings of hurt, pride or anger. Bad feelings only cloud our reason and block our access to wisdom and truth. Then the couple should kneel down together and ask the Holy Spirit for guidance. If the Lord answers them, the next step is simple. Obey the Lord. If there is no obvious answer then God wants to test our love commitment to one another. At such an impasse one of the two must *defer* to the other. This is a test of humility, to submerge one's own opinion out of love. Because the woman is love, it is in fact easier and more likely that she will defer to her husband. Her having done so, the husband, as head of the household and deriving his authority from God the Father, has the right to lovingly override her act of submission and to submit to his wife, but if he chooses not to, then his decision stands. In submitting, the wife is fulfilling her role as helper or helpmate to her husband and in submitting, the husband is fulfilling his role as loving husband. If the wife defers to her husband, then he and he alone has to take full responsibility before God for the consequences of his decision. Such situations are a powerful test of love between man and woman and that is God's order for marriage. Love, for it to be true, has to be constantly tested.

Yet, as was stated earlier, this equality does not eliminate the essential differences between male and female. God ordained these differences and they must be better understood if we are to live more fully in the brilliant light of God. Woman is a mystery created out of *love,* by love and for love, and she is God's masterpiece of love. The sublime perfection of womanhood in the mind of God was, of course, the Blessed Virgin Mary, who attained the awesome perfection of both *virgin* and *mother*. She was *entrusted* by God with carrying and giving birth to the Son of God. After Adam, no man has ever been born without original sin, apart from Jesus, who was both God and man. Only a woman has been given that privilege and this is rooted in the very nature of Mary's womanhood and femaleness. If we are to come anywhere close to an appreciation of the mystery of woman, we must understand these four great feminine characteristics of love, virginity, motherhood and trustworthiness.

While it is true that both men and women are called by Jesus to love, there is a huge difference in the way that they do. Men have to learn how to love. They stumble over it because it goes against their sin-nature, which is to dominate, and love and domination cannot co-exist. Therefore man constantly has to strive to defeat his sin-nature if he is ever to become a true lover. Women, on the other hand, instinctively embrace love. Love pulsates deep within their very essence so powerfully that one could say, "A real woman is love." Love is what drives a woman. Love is what she lives for. Love is what she is created for. Love is her very breath and without it she withers and dies inside.

Men are capable of survival without love by sinking all their energy into work, power, domination and success. They are capable of *feeding* on these sad substitutes for love. A woman simply cannot do this without destroying herself as a woman. To do so, she has to renounce her femininity and become a sad imitation of a man. A woman feeds on love, not power. There is an old proverb which says, "What a woman wants, God wants." This saying recognizes that when a woman is fully female, she intuitively wants the things of God because God is love and the woman wants love above all things. When she is not loved, she becomes unhappy and it is her unhappiness which leads her to become self-absorbed, demanding, complaining, taking refuge in meaningless things like clothes or jewellery or expensive trips. These become poor substitutes for what she really wants, mere soothers to replace her real food, which is love itself.

A man who withholds love from his wife is slowly killing her and will answer to God for destroying that which is most beautiful and precious in her, namely her likeness to God, who is love. She is the very heart of the home, and for a man to abuse that heart, which was personally given to him in marriage by God, is to abuse himself. He needs a heart for him to be complete and his wife is that heart. A man should treat his wife as his most precious jewel because that is what she is. He should make her feel cherished and special. He should delight in her femaleness, loving to adorn her, taking a holy pride in what he is able to provide for her.

When I was in Ethiopia during the great famine of 1985, an Afar tribesman, when faced with the prospect of starvation, would first sell his weapons. For him these guns, swords and daggers represented his masculine pride because that is how he earned respect from other men. Among Afars, a real man had to be able to defend his family and his tribe, yet his weapons were the first to go in order to obtain food for his family. The very last thing to be sold was his wife's jewellery and this was the ultimate tragedy and defeat for that man. The wife knew this and she would humbly and sadly hand over her poor trinkets to her husband, knowing it was tearing him apart and that it was his last resort for survival. She, as a woman of love, set about comforting her crushed husband, building up his defeated ego and continuing to trust in his manliness. She was willing to stand by his side even to death itself. Is that not something which can only be done out of love? A woman, because she is loved, becomes a fountain of love which she shares generously with others, especially her husband. He is a creature of *action* and so he instinctively provides and protects. She has to *nurture* to be a woman and so she can quietly accept her husband's flaws and failings, never destroying his need to feel like a man and always encouraging and building him up.

The woman's highest calling of love is to love God above all. It is she who intuitively understands what it means to love God and so she draws her husband closer to that same calling. She fills her heart and her home with God. Prayer comes easily to her or at least, more easily than it does to a man. For a woman, prayer is like breathing, while for a man, prayer has to be a project. As a result of his wife's quiet blessing, the husband finds himself freed to become the spiritual leader of his family as he should. It is his duty to be that spiritual leader, but he needs his wife to sanction it, otherwise he is likely to falter and lose courage. If a wife blesses her husband's holiness and quietly calls him higher, he will respond in a manly way, but if she showers him with scorn, he will be tempted to give up. If she mocks him when he takes out his rosary, he is likely to put it down.

Recent research has shown that when a baby is being formed in the mother's womb, numerous rich connections develop between the right brain and the left. This is true of both male and female babies. At thirteen weeks, when the baby's sexual characteristics are being formed, the females retain these rich connections between right and left brain while in the male, many of them cease to function and they atrophy. In other words, men are mostly left brain creatures. They can still access the right brain, but it is not easy for them. This is not too difficult to understand, since they need to operate from the left side of the brain for most of their time. Out in the world, they need uncluttered logic, mathematical skills, and mechanical skills in order to solve problems and to survive. They cannot afford to be trammelled by emotions. Women, on the other hand, are in a way more complete. They are in equal touch with both sides of their brain. The right hemisphere is responsible for such wonderful qualities as intuition, wisdom, poetry, creativity and music. The result is that men focus more on problem-solving while women, like the Blessed Mother, ponder things in their hearts. Of course men can be great poets and musicians and artists but to accomplish this they must learn to quieten the left brain and listen to the right.

God built these differences into our very brains with the result that women find it much easier to tap into wisdom and intuition and to be creative. To do this well, they need their husbands to be out there doing left brain things because this frees her up to build that which we call a home. A man can build a house but only a woman can build a home. She should not have to build the house because that will drain her energy for making the home. That is why it is such a tragedy that there are so many single mothers and working mothers these days, who have to go out to work in order to build the house. They have little or no energy left to build a home for their children. The husband also pays a high price for insisting that his wife contribute to building the house by going out to work. He desperately needs a home too. He needs a sanctuary to which he can escape after his day's work, where he can take delight in his wife and his children, where he can take off his false mask of invincibility and admit to his weakness, where his flaws are accepted, where his wife encourages and compliments him and where he can be a true king hidden from the world. This is not intended to imply that a woman cannot assist her husband with regard to income and the promotion of a better standard of living for her family. This is a legitimate pursuit but it must never take precedence over her primary duties as wife, mother and heart of the home.

Needless to say, if a mother of young children has to enter the work force, then her children are also robbed of their birthright, which is to be loved and taught the faith by their very own mother. This is what fulfils a wife who is loved. It is she who creates the loving space. She chooses the colours, she chooses the furniture, she puts her mark and her love in all the corners of the home with pictures, mementoes, and signs of her Christian faith. Her smile decorates that space and her arms are always ready to receive her troubled husband and to scoop up her frightened children. Where else can man tap into the mystery of love but in the arms of his wife? Where else, apart from prayer, can he find solace and renewed energy?

Men like to think that a woman is more emotional than a man. This is not true. Certainly she is more in touch with her emotions than a man and is therefore more comfortable with emotional language. It is also true that when a woman allows herself to be dominated by her feelings instead of her wisdom, then things go seriously wrong. But that is just as true of men. If a man allows his angry feelings to rule his head, then he too can do a lot of damage. For both men and women, the will must dominate our feelings. Feelings are fickle and inconstant and should never be allowed to override the higher faculty of the will.

It is a fact that a woman quivers less than a man to a sudden explosion. In regard to pain and suffering she is much less cowardly than many a soldier. She can bear suffering without complaining. She is not disturbed by sickness. She does not give in to her own sickness as easily as a man does, nor does she flinch at the sickness of others. Rather, she rolls up her sleeves and gets on with the job of nursing, no matter how disgusting or exhausting it may be. It is as though her capacity for the pain of childbirth gives her the strength to face other forms of pain. It is a well known fact that a real woman tends to be serene, sure and deep-rooted.

This mystery of the feminine applies equally to the priest and the nun who have entered a different kind of marriage. The priest is married to the Church and it is only in the arms of his bride that he will find his true manhood. He needs the love of his flock, which is the Church, as much as a man needs his wife. I therefore appeal to all Catholics to love their priest. They should treat him as they would their very own husband or father. He should be invited to our homes and given the encouragement and love which help him to persevere, so that he can be for us the "other Christ," the *alter Christus,* the dispenser of the sacraments, which we all so desperately need. Never criticise a priest. That is the same thing as a wife criticising her husband and a man is easily crushed by a woman's scorn. The priest needs his parish to build him up and appreciate his efforts, otherwise he becomes defeated and discouraged. He needs the love of his bride. The religious sister on the other hand is married to Jesus, not to the Church. She is his bride and he looks to her for the love that he craves for, just as he does to the entire Church which is also his bride. She is most fulfilled by her divine husband, who never stops treating her as his most precious jewel. She is the apple of his eye, and so she can be a true lover also, totally loved and able to love the whole world in return.

This leads into the role of virginity for all women. Virginity is badly misunderstood if it is envisioned as something merely physical. The virginity of our Blessed Mother was much more than simply a body which did not know a man. It was for her a mental, emotional and above all a spiritual reality. She was literally married to the Holy Spirit and therefore her entire being was focussed on and dedicated to God. She was a perpetual virgin. She had to be, because of her spiritual marriage. She could never have had relations with St. Joseph because that would have been infidelity to her Divine Spouse. Likewise, all women are called to a spiritual virginity. This is of course, a physical thing in the unmarried, but that physical virginity becomes transformed by marriage. This spiritual virginity of woman should not be abandoned just because she is now united in one flesh with her husband. In fact she must nurture her spiritual purity all the more. She must be totally faithful to her husband and must be totally faithful to God. She must preserve, not only her body for her husband, but must preserve her soul for God, in purity and in chastity.

A man must see this reality in his wife if he is to delight in her and be constantly amazed at her mystery. Many women today refuse to see Mary as their ideal. They reasonably say that there is no way they can be both virgin and mother, and so they put Mary aside as irrelevant to their practical lives. But this is a serious mistake. It is true that God elevated the Mother of Jesus to the fullest perfection of virginity and motherhood, but in doing so, he wanted her to be the shining example of perfection to all women. In a deeply spiritual sense, all women are called to preserve within their deepest essence, that spiritual virginity for their husbands and for the Lord, just as they are called to motherhood, whether that be physical or spiritual motherhood. A real woman intuitively knows this, and when her husband sees the secret smile of knowing on her face, he can only gaze in wonderment at the secrets stored in her heart.

Scripture tells us that Mary "pondered these things in her heart" (Luke 2:51). That means she treasured the mysteries of God deep within her being and marvelled at them. All women are able to do this. They may not often be able to put the mystery into words because it is so profound, but they are able to let that mystery fill them with life. A man can only stare at the mystery, as something outside of himself. A woman lives it in her very heart. This is spiritual virginity and it truly reveals a woman as God's secret. She is his mystery given to him for his delight, to wonder at, and to explore.

The highest of all vocations for a woman, which at the same time is what makes her fully female, is motherhood. This does not necessarily mean having a child of her own, although that is the usual meaning. It also includes the motherhood of all women to all humanity. That is why Mary was not only the physical mother of Jesus in the fullest sense, but she was also given as mother to the entire world when she stood at the foot of the cross.

While Eve was given to Adam as a helper, woman is not merely a helper to her husband alone but is also a helper to God in the mystery of motherhood. God creates. Woman procreates. The distortion that occurred in the Garden of Eden took place because Eve wanted to become like God and to do her own creating. She wanted to devise her own rules of good and evil. The ultimate tragedy of that disorder is seen in those women of today who not only want to be like God and to create, but who also want to un-create by killing their own babies in the womb. Naturally, fathers who aid and abet in the crime of abortion are equally guilty. A real woman relishes her privilege to procreate, which means to cooperate with God in carrying and giving birth to new souls for God. In welcoming new life within her she says, "Fiat" to God. "Let it be done unto me according to thy word" (Luke 1:38) and to rejoice in it.

It is very important to understand that pregnancy is almost entirely a womanly experience. The father has planted his seed and certainly must now create a safe place for his wife so that she can give herself over completely to the new life growing in her, but he can never be plunged into the experience of pregnancy in the same way as his wife. Once more, he can only stand and stare at the mystery of what she is "pondering in her heart." He can never truly know. She is experiencing a profound change in her body, which is now directing all of its energies to the welfare of the baby. More importantly, she undergoes a transformation in her spirit and in her soul as she touches on the mystery of new life. Her entire being becomes expanded and it pulsates with its God-given purpose, which is to become love itself. Only a woman truly knows this. I can talk about it, but I have to eventually run out of words, because as a man, I do not know and I can never know. As a father, a man can rejoice in his paternity but try as he might, he still stands outside of his wife's profound and total transmutation.

The woman will, like Mary, give birth and she will hold the world in her arms, a living breathing miracle which she and God have given to the human race. Of course it was her husband who lovingly planted the life-giving seed, but there is an emptiness within him as he feels he is on the outside looking in. This is the critical time when he must conquer an urge to be jealous. He may be a proud father but he has to recognize that a bond has been forged between his wife and this child, into which he can never be fully absorbed. For the wife, this is also a critical time. While she rightfully rejoices in this deep bonding with her infant, she must remember that her husband may feel out in the cold. She has to have a heart big enough to reach out to him, to love him, to express her gratitude to him, to include him and to nurture his right to feel like a proud father. After all, he is the father of the miracle in whom she now delights.

Both mother and father must now set about the most important and valuable career in the world, which is to raise their child to be a godly child and ultimately a godly man or woman. Mothering cannot be compared to being a doctor, or a president of a corporation. It is laughable to even try. The future of the world and the future of the Church depends on mothering and fathering. No doubt, doctors and business people are important, but their fruits can never be compared to the fruits of godly parenting.

Even the woman who cannot have children of her own body, either by infertility or because of consecrated virginity in the religious life, must learn to become a mother if she is to be fulfilled. She too is created with the power for love, and so the childless woman can mother children by adoption. Likewise the religious sister can mother countless children by her love, her smile, her womanly understanding, her work, her prayer and the hospitality of her heart. Hospitality of the heart is the mystery of motherhood and motherhood is the supreme sign of what it means to be a woman. We as men should stand in awe and in wonder as we gaze upon the miracle of motherhood in our wives and in other women. It is his wife's motherhood which calls a man to be a real man. Motherhood is the life-blood of the human race and this priceless role has only been given to women. Women are indeed God's masterpiece.

The last, but not the least, of the quartet of womanly mysteries is the quality of trustworthiness. At the Annunciation, God entrusted the Virgin Mary with the care of his only son, Jesus the Messiah. God trusted the woman, who was still a mere human creature, even though she was immaculately conceived, to nurture him in her womb, to be a living monstrance of Jesus-incarnate for nine months. He trusted her to raise that divine and human child in holiness and in wisdom so that she might release him one day to the cross of Calvary. God's trust in her was well placed, as all mankind knows. "From this day, all generations will call me blessed" (Luke 1:48). At the same time he entrusts all of his human children to his human mothers. Each one of us had to trust the mother to whom God entrusted us. As Karl Stern, a great psychiatrist and convert to the Catholic faith observed, "The paradox of being human resides in the fact that, while we are the summit of God's creation, each one of us must, in order to enter this life, pass through a period of utter helplessness and dependence." We must trust our mothers because we are given no alternative. That is why abortion is so horrible a crime, because it utterly destroys the trust that the unborn child must invest in its mother to care for him, to welcome him and to protect him. In killing her child, a woman murders not only her child but murders all that is good in herself. She cannot be entrusted. But a real woman is trustworthy. Her children are entrusted to her in order that she can enable them to entrust themselves to others, initially their father and then ultimately, their eternal Father, God. Because the mother is trustworthy, she can also protect her children from all that is not trustworthy, namely malicious people or bad friends, unsuitable television programs, unholy music, false teaching and occasions of sin.

Satan understood this realm of trust and knew, that if he could distort it in Eve, then Adam would be no problem. So he sowed suspicion in Eve's heart. He directed her trust away from God and towards himself and his own lies. Eve then believed that the serpent was to be more trusted than God and so she ate the apple. Mary, the second Eve, entrusted herself fully to the truth of God and therefore was herself trustworthy. Likewise, if any woman wants to be fully woman, and to rejoice in her total femininity, she too must trust completely in God. In so doing, she also lures her children and her husband into a deeper and deeper trust in God. The entire family then, becomes more and more like the image and likeness of God in which it was made. It becomes akin to Adam and Eve before the fall, ever more pure, and ever more resistant to sin.

The book of Proverbs has a great deal to say about who a real woman is and how she behaves. "The truly capable woman, who can find her? She is far beyond the price of pearls. Her husband's heart has confidence in her, from her he will derive no little profit. Advantage and not hurt she brings him all the days of her life. She selects wool and flax. She does her work with eager hands. She is like those merchant vessels bringing her food from far away. She gets up while it is still dark giving her household their food, giving orders to her serving girls. She sets her mind on a field, then she buys it. With what her hands have earned, she plants a vineyard. She puts her back into her work and shows how strong her arms can be. She knows that her affairs are going well. Her lamp does not go out at night. She sets her hands to the distaff, her fingers grasp the spindle. She holds out her hands to the poor, she opens her arms to the needy. Snow may come, she has no fear for her household, with all her servants warmly clothed. She makes her own quilts, she is dressed in fine linen and purple. Her husband is respected at the city gates, taking his seat among the elders of the land. She weaves materials and sells them, she supplies the merchant with sashes. She is clothed in strength and dignity, she can laugh at the day to come. When she opens her mouth, she does so wisely; on her tongue is kindly instruction. She keeps good watch on the conduct of her household. No bread of idleness for her. Her children stand up and proclaim her blessed, her husband too sings her praises. 'Many women have done admirable things, but you surpass them all.' Charm is deceitful and beauty empty; the woman who fears Yahweh is the one to praise. Give her a share in what her hands have worked for and let her works tell her praises at the city gates" (Prov. 31:10-31).

This is a hymn to womanhood and to what a real woman is all about. It is not too difficult to translate this Old Testament passage into the realities of the modern woman. A woman is capable and priceless to her husband. He has the utmost confidence in her and because of her prudence with the family income, he will find that she can always make ends meet. The good woman works for her husband's advantage because his good name is her good name. She works hard and does it eagerly. She rises early to take care of her loved ones before they go off to work and to school. She decides what would be good for the family and what the family needs. She saves her money out of the budget and then joyfully goes out to purchase it. She is strong in her work, as strong as a man and never shirks it. She takes a deep personal pleasure for herself when things are going well for the family, because she knows that she has played her part in their good fortune. She is generous to those worse off than herself. She always gives to the poor and those in need and does it out of her means, and always with love. She sees to the material needs of her husband and children, making sure she buys the proper clothing for them, the best affordable nutritional food, and the items they need for their work and school. She is creative. She dresses modestly and within her budget. Because of her goodness, her husband is respected in the community. She has strength, dignity and a light heart in the face of the day's worries and challenges. She has control of her tongue. She speaks with wisdom and is always ready to instruct her children with kindness. She is not a gossip or a slanderer. She watches over her loved ones constantly with the concern of a wife and mother. Because of her love, her children cannot help but love her in turn, and they bless her and bless God for her. Her husband is proud of her and is eager to sing her praises to others. Above all she fears God, and since the fear of God is the beginning of wisdom, she is wise in all she does.

Is this too tall an order? Not according to God. It is an ideal, and surely we all fall short of the ideal, but if we do not know what is perfect then we will never know what to strive for. I recommend that both men and women should read Proverbs 31 over and over again. It will lead a woman to understand her own nature more clearly, and it will lead a man to see the beauty in his wife, never take her for granted, and to appreciate the wonderful gift that she is in his life.

So what is a real woman?

A real woman is love.
She loves God, her husband, her children and the whole world.
She is wisdom and she is intuition.
She is a receiver of life and not a contraceptor.
She is a nurturer of life and not an abortionist.
She is trustworthy and not fickle.
She is the heart of the home and not its head.
She is a queen and not a king.
She is a forgiver and not a grudge-bearer.
She loves and never rejects.
She is obedient and deserves obedience.
She is content and not a complainer.
She is gentle and not a tyrant.
She is courageous but never rash.
She is strong but never masculine.
She is sacrificial but never a victim.
She is humble but never a doormat.
Above all she is the mystery and masterpiece of God.

CHAPTER 4

Relationships:
Woman Wounded; Man Maimed

"Then the eyes of both of
them were opened and they
realized that they were
naked."

(Gen. 3:7)

As soon as Eve believed the lie of Satan and as soon as Adam believed the lie of Eve, the terrible original sin was committed. From that moment on, Adam and Eve and the entire human race were condemned to a ***sin-nature.*** It is very important to understand what it means to have a sin-nature. It means to fall from innocence, and to become twisted and deformed. Before the fruit of the Tree of Life was violated, Adam and Eve were not conscious of any darkness in their relationship with one another. "Now both of them were naked, the man and his wife, but they felt no shame before each other" (Gen. 2:25). When Adam looked at Eve, he felt only delight and wonder at the miracle of her as God's gift. There was no lust in his heart but the great and first sin changed all of that. "Then the eyes of both of them were opened and they realized that they were naked" (Gen. 3:7). This terrible realization of their nakedness not only made them prey to shame and lust, but it also revealed to them their spiritual and psychological nakedness.

Humanity would, from then on, be prone to dark deeds, driven by lust for sex, money, power and things, while all of these excesses would fill the human soul with shame. What a shame that we must suffer shame! Shame is the sword which repeatedly stabs our human hearts and it leads to woman-wounded and man-maimed. Shame is the legacy of the Original Sin.

All men and women are damaged. We are damaged by our very genetic structure, which we inherited from our equally damaged parents who ultimately inherited their characteristics from Adam and Eve. Starting with our genetic distortions, we are then further damaged by life's experiences. We can have negative and frightening experiences in the womb. We are then further damaged by our parents (even by parents who love us and do their very best), our teachers, our relatives and friends and by strangers. And so we adults all have a storehouse of memories of being unloved or put down or used or discounted or scared. Our own sin-nature becomes further distorted by the sins of others and this is the human tragedy.

Give thanks to our loving God who never gave up on us. Praise him for his redemptive action which restores us to our inheritance as sons and daughters and which makes it possible for us to grasp heaven. But, while the Sacrament of Baptism washes us and makes us new creatures in Christ, we are still victims of our sin-nature and it is this which makes our marital relationships so difficult to perfect. It is because we act out of our own hurt, self-centeredness, anger, jealousy, greed, lust and pride that we experience relationship breakdown. We are so blind to this truth that we usually blame our partner for what we ourselves have done.

I remember as a little boy asking my mother how I came to be born and she delighted in telling me that one day she was lying in a hospital bed. Suddenly the window opened and a beautiful little angel flew in to the room. It was a boy angel and he flew up and down the ward till he finally recognized my mother and came and nestled into her arms. She told me how happy she was that the angel had chosen her. The angel was of course me! I loved that story and would ask her to repeat it to me over and over again. Often I would wonder what had happened to my wings and I know I grieved a little over their loss and longed to have them back again so that I could fly.

When I discovered how babies were really born, I was hurt. I "knew" that my mother had lied to me and I felt foolish in being so naive as to believe such a story. How could I ever have believed that I was once an angel? For many years after that, if ever I thought of the angel story, I felt a deep and strange mixture of delight and embarrassment. As a more mature Christian, I am able to re-evaluate my mother's little story, and I realize that she was trying to teach me a truth which she instinctively knew in her soul. She had a simple faith and was much closer to wisdom than I have ever reached with all my book learning. She intended to instill within me the important truth that we all come from God. God creates our immortal soul and human parents cooperate with him in creating the physical body of their child.

There is one fundamental truth upon which we should agree; all of us are born into post-Adam-and-Eve *dysfunctional* families. There is no escape from the perpetuated consequences of original sin, which are sickness, sadness, death and an attraction to sin. Nevertheless, it is still possible for parents to provide a reasonably healthy environment for their children. This should consist of being welcomed into the family and of being loved. It should include cherishing, touching, relationships, warmth, food, protection from harm, permission to explore the environment and to return to safety when it hurts or bites, encouragement in learning and praise for achievements.

Unfortunately for the majority of us, the child is soon disillusioned. We are all too quickly robbed of our birthright. We are neither freely loved, nor perfectly nurtured. We are abandoned, rejected and often increasingly abused by physical violence, emotional violence and sexual violation. Fifty percent of girls and twenty-five percent of boys are sexually abused. We are distorted by broken parents who were raised by broken parents. We find ourselves less and less focussed on our legitimate needs because we must focus on the most fundamental need of all, which is survival at all costs. We all learn different ways to survive and they all usually work for a while. Most of us survive to adulthood, but sooner or later, these same survival techniques will come back to haunt us. Somewhere in our adult lives our grieving, angry, brutalised child will at last break through. What was once Innocence-personified has now become sadly distorted.

There are many different survival techniques which children adopt. Because they know they are being cheated of their birthright, they may become hard of heart, overly timid and compliant, afraid to speak up, over-demanding, chronically depressed, angry, disobedient to authority or chronic complainers. In their teenage years they may also become sinfully involved in sex, drugs, alcohol or crime. Whichever of these dysfunctional survival techniques they embrace, the result will be unhappiness deep within. This is why so many adults, sooner or later, wind up in a therapist's consulting room. Ultimately, the only healing is to recognize that the survival technique is itself a disorder, to take it to the cross of Jesus Christ, renounce it and follow his way of love, forgiveness and peace.

In the light of all this, let us consider woman-wounded and look at how things were meant to be and how they became disfigured. *The Poem of the Man-God* by Maria Valtorta is a novel about the life of Jesus. She puts words into the mouth of the Lord and while these are not to be read as authentic private revelation, nevertheless they provide a penetrating insight into woman's reality. At one point, the women disciples are growing in numbers and Jesus is compelled to give them a teaching on their particular ministry. In the interest of clarity I have paraphrased a little, and so Jesus says: "In the closed religion of Israel, all the shame fell upon women, the origin of sin. In the universal religion of Christ, all that is changed. All the grace was assembled in one woman and she delivered it to the world that it might be redeemed. Woman therefore is no longer the anger of God but the help of God. How great is the necessity of woman near the altar of Christ. The infinite miseries of the world can be cured much more and much better by a woman than by a man ... woman must receive the broken as if they were dear children led astray, who are coming back to their father's house and dare not face their parent. You are the ones who will comfort the sinner and placate the judge.

"Many will come to you seeking God. You will welcome them as if they were tired pilgrims saying, 'This is the house of the Lord, he will be here at once and in the meantime you will envelop them with your love. A woman knows how to love. She was made to love. She might degrade love into sensual lust, but true love, the gem of her soul, is still imprisoned in the depths of her heart, a love made of angel wings, of pure flame and remembrances of God, of its origin from God and its creation by God. Woman is the *masterpiece of goodness* near the *masterpiece of creation* which is man, 'And now I will make Adam a help-mate that he may not feel alone.' Woman must take the faculty of loving and make use of it in the love of Christ and for Christ among her neighbours. She must be charitable to repentant sinners. She should tell them not to be afraid of God. How often a mother's little ones or a sister's young brothers were ill and needed a doctor and they were afraid. But with caresses and loving words, they relieved them of their fear and so, no longer terrified, with their little hands held by the women, they let the doctor cure them. Sinners are your sick brothers and children who are afraid of the Divine Doctor's hand and of his sentence. Since women know how good God is let them tell sinners that God is good and no one must be afraid of him.

"Be sisters and mothers to holy people. They too need love. They will become tired and worn out in evangelising. They will not be able to do all that is to be done. Help them, discreetly and diligently. Women know how to work at home and in everything that is needed for everyday life. The future of the church will be a continuous flow of pilgrims to the places of God. Be their kind hotel-keepers, taking upon yourselves all the most humble work so that the ministers of God may be free to continue the work of the Master. When cruel times come, man is never very strong in suffering. Women instead, as compared to men, enjoy the true kingliness of being able to suffer. Teach men, supporting them in the hours of fear, discouragement, tears, tiredness and bloodshed. Women are heroines of sorrow, the solace of martyrs and martyrs themselves, who can be silent priestesses who will preach God by their way of living and who with no other consecration but the one they received from the God-Love, will be consecrated and worthy of it."

A whole book could be written on these words and the exalted role of women in the eyes of God. However I want to emphasize the very first statement made by Jesus. "In the closed religion of Israel, all the shame fell upon women, the origin of sin. In the universal religion of Christ, all that is changed. All the grace was assembled in one woman and she delivered it to the world that it might be redeemed. Woman therefore is no longer the *anger* of God, but the *help* of God."

This is crucial to a fully Christian understanding of woman. The Old Testament religion viewed woman as the originator of man's downfall and so women were disdained and regarded with fear as though they were constantly primed to lead innocent man into sin. Thus man's control over woman was self-righteously justified. But Mary, the second Eve, has changed all of that. All of the grace, that is to say, Jesus, was assembled in one woman, who was Mary, and she delivered it to the world. Woman was therefore fully redeemed along with man, and ought to have been restored to her rightful place and role in the New Testament religion and indeed the Catholic Church has consistently taught this truth. Unfortunately to this day it is as though woman had never been redeemed, at least in the hearts of many men. Deep down in the male psyche, woman is still looked upon as the first Eve, still preferring the apple to innocence, still the temptress. Man blindly distorts the Genesis story. He continues to believe that he was basically a victim, artfully seduced by scheming woman. He believes that if it had not been for Eve there would have been no Fall. But Scripture makes it abundantly clear that Adam was a full cooperator in Eve's sin. If he had exercised his rightful authority as husband and said, "no" then none of us would be under the curse. Adam was even cowardly enough to blame Eve when he was challenged by God and to this day he continues to blame woman for his woes, and even for his sins. By the same token, Eve could only say, "The devil made me do it" and since in modern times, she has been duped by militant feminism into believing that man is the devil, she continues to say, "The devil made me do it." The stage is therefore set for a deep life-draining wound between the sexes. Man believes he is a victim of the seductive woman. Woman believes she is a victim of the devil-man.

Woman is the gifted mystery of God's loving creation. She does not need to become a priest. She is already the "silent" priestess of new life, just as Mary was the "silent" priestess who brought Jesus to us. She is made for love. She is our love teacher, the human archetype of love, the indispensable repository of the love memories of the race. Destroy her and we destroy love on the face of the earth. We fail her when we do not treasure her for herself, protect her in birth-giving, or provide for her mothering. Only she can teach our children how to love. Do we prostrate ourselves at the altar of God in gratitude and thanksgiving for the gift of such a jewel? Only a man who perceives the truth of the mystery can do so, and he is as rare today as he was yesterday.

Many women today are deeply damaged. If they escape being aborted, they face being rejected, not just because they are human, which is bad enough, but often because they are female. Un-nurtured and un-cherished, they are puzzled and devastated by their parents' broken-ness. Violence is perpetrated upon them. They are sometimes sexually invaded as little children, deeply damaged by the self-hatred of their raging fathers or brothers and undefended by their own mothers, who are so often conspirators of silence. Thus abandoned and violated, they grow into caricatures of womanhood. They become sleepwalkers in a nightmare, smouldering volcanoes of anger, hosts to the devouring worm of self-loathing and worst of all, death-dealing deniers of new life. Abortion is a lot easier for a woman when her precious femininity has been violated as a child. Violence begets violence. The damaged become damagers and so become impervious to love, both in giving it and in receiving it. As a child she craves her father's love, but perceives that somehow she is flawed and not worthy of it. So she goes through life searching endlessly trying to fulfil this deepest of needs. She either punishes herself for her own unworthiness or punishes her father in an endless rejection of all men. She may even embrace the counterfeit love of other women since a pretend love is much better than the terror of emptiness.

Likewise many men, equally flawed, respond by despising the shrew. They are terrorised by the new woman castrator and so they defend themselves by retaliation. They abuse their natural strength by rejecting, despising, using, beating and raping. They dominate and thereby confirm that they are right. They are no longer certain of women. They no longer perceive their male role with clarity.

Instead of offering men one apple, women are shaking the tree and hundreds of apples are falling down about their heads. Men are becoming scared out of their minds, but think it would be unmanly to admit it. We are discovering a new reality today or perhaps resurrecting a very old one, that if we add woman's fear to man's fear, we incarnate Satan's hatred.

Men try to explain away the woman wound with fatuous cliches such as, "It's her hormones." This is a terrible rejection of the female experience. If it is indeed her hormones, then as a doctor, I can tell you there is something very wrong with her hormones. She is ill. Men have no right to opt out of their duty to heal the woman-wound by naively explaining away her pain as merely hormonal. That is a lie to women and an insult to God.

Worse still, when woman is broken, impaled by violence, robbed of her birthright of love, men have no idea how to heal because the onus of loving them back to life falls on them and they are poor lovers. It is much easier to reject her, to dominate her, to call her names like shrew or nag and to abandon her to the coldness and loneliness she feels. But in so doing, men banish themselves into their own painful world of domination, which they use to hide their own terror. Men need to know that if women are wounded then the whole race is wounded.

If woman today is wounded, then man is maimed. He is also a victim. He has been tempted by Eve and found to be willing. Deprived of his birthright, he has also been distorted by his parents and by a society which idolises egoism, pride, impurity, money and power. Trained by playing with war toys, he has learned that might is right. Battle is the only valid arena in which disputes can be settled. Whoever is left standing must have been in the right, regardless of the issue. He has been robbed of his God-given sonship which calls him to grow in peace, strength, courage, gentleness, fortitude, perseverance and work. Instead he has become a grotesque caricature forced to wear a macho mask to conceal his terrifying inner darkness. "I am a man. I must at least pretend to be brave. I must not weep. I must take what I want even if that means taking a woman. I must bludgeon my enemies into submission and that includes any woman who challenges my assumptions. I am angry but it is justified." But how can that be when anger is a sin against justice? "Keep this in mind dear brothers. Let every man be quick to hear, slow to speak and slow to anger. For a man's anger does not fulfil God's justice. Strip away all that is filthy, every vicious excess. Humbly welcome the word that has taken root in you, with its power to save you. Act on this word" (James 1:19-22).

Some men are so threatened by the new aggressive female that they run and run and seek their solace in the arms of other threatened men. Mother damaged and unfathered, they confuse their gender identity and cannibalise other men in a frantic search for their true maleness, which is never to be found. They miss the mystery of Christian life which is to seek their wholeness in the very pain which terrifies them. Sooner or later, they must turn their face to woman, confront their fear and trust in Jesus if they are ever to find lasting peace.

Since secular psychology teaches that all of us must *self-actualise* and realize our full potential without God, then society concludes that it must be morally right to be self-centred. My greatest good, therefore, is to survive, not to love. A man can now justify beating his complaining wife and a woman feels no guilt in crushing her wimpish husband. Today many men despise women for not being women and women despise men for not being men and this is called society. What we call community or civilisation is nothing more than a thin veneer, easily rubbed off. It is predator and prey in an endless after-the-Fall survival of the fittest. Now we must contracept, because new life is too burdensome. We must abort, brutalise and euthanise if we are to survive. We in effect join forces with Satan, to de-create with him, to de-value life, to destroy the good within us. We cry out in our pain, proclaiming our tragedy but we cannot hear the pain of the other over our own din. I have a right to be hurt but you do not. We have forgotten how to father and mother each other. We have lost our compassion for our wounded partner in life because we have not learned how to be other-centred and so we persist in being self-centred.

If healing of this depressing wound is ever to occur, we must all turn to Jesus Christ. He was immersed in this wound when he lived among his fellow humans and he understood it very well. He also offered us the medicine for it and *he is that medicine.* We must stop devouring each other. Men must renounce their brutality and risk the healing of women. Women must give up being victims and stop avenging themselves on men.

The truth will set us free and the truth is that there is no difference in our wounds. They have the same sick root and Satan would like us to believe that it is not so. He cries in triumph, "You can never be reconciled" but God whispers to us, "You are both wounded by lack of love, but I can heal you." This lack of love is a sin and we sin when we blame each other. Man blames woman and becomes a woman-beater, while woman blames man and becomes a man-eater.

The fact is that no man and no woman causes our anger or deserves our disdain. We cause our own anger, we dance with our own disdain and both are sins. We may be distressed, distorted and twisted out of shape, but we are redeemed none-the-less. We lost our paradise by our sin but Jesus proved we can regain it. Since he did all the work, can we not then reclaim our former beauty?

The healing can and must begin. We can restore God's love in our marriage relationships. We must rediscover what it means to be fully woman and what it means to be fully man. Woman-love plus man-love equals God-love. It is in communion that we reflect more brightly the perfection of God's love. We are made in God's image and likeness but if the sexes remain divided, it is only half an image. We both need the complementarity of the other in order to be whole. We may therefore delight in our differences but recognize our fundamental equality as children of God. We modern Christians must affirm that what Jesus promised to the brothers, he also promised to the sisters. We are all entitled to love, respect and education in the fullest sense of these words. If we deny women's right to equal dignity, then we still regard woman as the post-fall seductress, the unredeemed first Eve. Our healing as husband and wife begins when we open our eyes and see woman as the post-resurrection mediatrix of love called forth by Jesus himself and perfectly incarnated in his Blessed Mother. Shall we act as if Jesus was mistaken?

This is not meant to imply that healing is for one or the other of the protagonists. Both sexes need healing. This is not a war, or at least there is no need for it. As long as we see only the enemy in each other we will never heal. If instead, we see the victim, then we can rescue one another from the battlefield. Healing must begin with **both** of us. Feminism is not wrong when it asks for healing, but it becomes terribly disordered when all it does is point the finger at men and remains blind to woman's own need for healing. "Why do you observe the splinter in your brother's eye and never notice the log in your own?" (Matt. 7:3). Healing begins when we all, men and women alike, cry out without shame to each other, "I am broken. I am a distortion of what the good God created. I need you. Could you not also need me? Let us hold each other in the dark and call upon the Lord." Man must rush into the arms of the broken woman and beg for comfort. Woman must lovingly melt her heart and joyfully receive the broken man. You comfort me and I will treasure you. God's life can then be re-kindled as it becomes re-incarnated in the re-union of male and female.

The real soul-healing takes place when we rival each other in the service of each other. Serve and you will be served. Serve and marriage will be restored no matter how distorted it may have become.

There are seven basic steps to the healing of marriage relationships.

1. Open your eyes to the miracle of yourself. You are totally and passionately loved by God. Love what God loves. If you do not, you reject his gift.
2. Open your eyes and see in your spouse a miracle of creation. The one with whom you fight so much is totally and passionately loved by God. Love what God loves. He or she is not an enemy but a fellow victim of original sin. Compassion is called for, not criticism.
3. Pray out your anger and self-loathing. Own it. Do not justify it by blaming the skeletons in your mental cupboard; mother, father, all men or all women. This is a cop-out. Reclaim your gift of free will. You are free to choose to refuse to be angry with your spouse. You are free to choose to refuse to abuse your spouse. This is the message of Jesus. He affirms our free will. My spouse does not make me angry. I choose it. Rediscover and rejoice in your freedom to do otherwise.

4. Have some one pray over you and over you and over you. We all desperately need prayer and it is good and powerful to have other Christians lay on hands and beg God to heal our marriage wounds.

5. Listen to the pain of others. Set your own pain aside for a time and enter into the heart of your neighbour. His or her pain is just as real. This activity brings you out of your own suffering and helps you to appreciate the suffering of the other. It stimulates compassion, empathy and identification. If the other's pain only causes impatience or scorn within you, then you are not listening. You do not have to offer fatuous advice. In a sense you only have to hold the other and soothe him or her by your attentive presence. Let what little strength you possess flow out and strengthen the one who is weak. Remember, it will be the other way around when it is your turn to feel weak. Strangely enough, when we do forget self by loving our brother or sister, our own pain becomes easier to bear.

6. Fearlessly proclaim your needs but without self-pity. If you are healing the other with love, the other will heal you. So take the risk and tell of your needs, give the other an opportunity to hear your pain and to perhaps meet those needs. Pain is pain. Hurt is hurt. You have every right to grieve, so comfort each other, hold each other, rock and cradle each other. You are all treasures of God, so treasure each other. Tell woman it is holy to be feminine, tell man it is holy to be masculine, but let us return to God's truth about what feminine and masculine are supposed to be.

7. Finally, there is no wholeness without holiness. Jesus knew that. But holiness is a lonely climb if we try it alone. Man, take woman by the hand and together climb the mountain. If you climb separately, then when you fall, no one can hold on to you. But, roped together, you can stop the fall and regain your foothold. Paradise awaits you but you need not suffer hell on earth. The good news is that for us Catholics, we are not cast adrift without help. Jesus is in the boat with us, waiting to rush to our aid in the storm. If we call out to him, he will rise up and command the wind and the waves to be still. We

have the Sacraments and the Sacrifice of the Mass by which we can confidently ask Jesus to enrich us with his grace. As St. Paul tells us, it is in our own flawed human weakness that we find the very strength of God. By grace and with Jesus we can defeat our failings and rise ever higher towards that perfection which God the Father intended for us. Surely we are deformed by sin, but Jesus can unravel that deformity for us if only we say, 'Fiat' to his will.

This chapter has focussed on the wound of our nature as male and female beings. The next chapter will look at those mental and emotional characteristics which mark out the differences between men and women. It will also help, not only to know what the differences are, but also to understand one another in joy instead of frustration. We *can* live in happiness with each other because we are followers of Jesus Christ who conquered sin and death. In restoring us to our inheritance as sons and daughters of God, he is able and eager to give us all the help we need to be revived as an image and likeness of God.

CHAPTER 5

Relationships: The Difference Makes all the Difference

> *"The husband must give to his wife what she has a right to expect, and so too the wife to her husband."*
>
> (1 Cor. 7:3)

It is self-evident that men and women are different. They are different physically, which is obvious, but they are also different psychologically, emotionally, socially and spiritually. This is simply a scientific fact verifiable by observation. Numerous psychologists have grappled with the problem of describing these differences in an orderly way but while they may often disagree with one another about the nature of these, they have always agreed that indeed men and women are very different. This may seem like flogging a dead horse since most of us know deep down that male and female are not identical, but there is a distorted faction in our time which is trying to eliminate gender altogether by moving towards an *androgynous* society, that is to say, a willful and distorted attempt to eliminate our unique sexual nature in order to create one sex out of the two. This usurps and denies God's holy intention when he created both male and female. Such people deliberately dress in such a way as to make it difficult to distinguish men from women and of course the end-point of their disorder is that they come to condone bisexual acts. But our escape from the battle of the sexes will never be found by eliminating our gender differences. It can only be regained by accepting our God-given sexual nature as male and female and rejoicing in it.

Let it be abundantly made clear that God decreed the differences and these are life-giving and good. As pointed out in chapter 3, God laid down our male and female characteristics in our very brains. Men find it easier to follow the left brain, given that it is neurologically difficult for them to access the right half of the brain. Women are comfortable using both sides of the brain and this simple anatomical fact helps us to understand one another's unique approach to life. The separate characteristics of male and female are therefore *genetic* in nature.

This genetic diversity between the sexes is then further entrenched by parents and by society. Boys and girls are socialised differently, with the result that they tend to think, feel, act and interact, play and pray differently. Unfortunately, men and women who fail to appreciate or understand these natural features react to one another, thereby provoking unnecessary fights and arguments. Those who do understand make allowances for their spouse, eliminate their adversarial attitudes and are less likely to fall into fighting. As any couple will admit, fighting resolves nothing and always leads to hurt feelings whereby love is eroded. Christians should do everything to avoid bitter wrangling, because both husband and wife adopt a stance of self-righteousness, a self-centred belief that their opinion is right, a determination to prove that the other is wrong and therefore stupid. It always includes criticism and judgement of the other, which is directly opposed to the commandments of Jesus Christ. "Love your enemies, do good to those who hate you, bless those who curse you, pray for those who treat you badly" (Luke 6:27). "Do not judge and you will not be judged because the judgements you give are the judgements you will get and the standard you use will be the standard used for you" (Matt. 7:1-2). How many Catholic couples believe in their faith and yet make a mockery of it by fighting with one another and telling themselves that it is not sinful? If I have a vicious, no-holds-barred fight with my wife, I am violating the woman who is a temple of the Holy Spirit and who has been given to me by God as pure gift. That is a sin for which I should rush to Confession.

There are many ways to help couples give up this disordered behaviour and not all of these can be covered in this book. Perhaps the most helpful strategy is to bring the reader to an understanding of why a spouse thinks and speaks in the way that he or she does. Montaigne, a French philosopher, once wrote, "To understand all is to forgive all." Understanding then, is the key to marital peace and harmony. Once we understand, it becomes easier to forgive. To achieve this new vision of each other, I have borrowed heavily from the work of Deborah Tannen, *You Just Don't Understand Me,* and the classic work of John Gray, *Men are from Mars, Women are from Venus,* Both of these books are straightforward, easy to read, very informative and for the most part are "easily baptised" into a Christian view of who we are.

This is not to imply that this is the only valid way to describe male/female differences. It is also important to understand that such attempts can only be generalisations at best. Every human being is unique and so the following observations can never be true of every man or every woman. Nevertheless, they can help us towards a better understanding and appreciation of ourselves as male and female.

The fundamental cause of strife between a husband and a wife is the fact that a man assumes his wife should think like him while she believes that he should think like her. Since both do not think alike, this illogical belief makes discord inevitable. The fact is, as Dr. Gray asserts, men and women might as well come from different planets. Each has his or her own reality, and each sees the world in a different way. More importantly, each has a different objective in relating to others. The world is not the same for men as it is for women. But just because they see reality differently, this does not mean that one is right and the other is wrong. Both are in their own way right. It is in accepting each other's separate realities that harmony is to be found. It is arrogant to assume that my reality is the only valid reality.

First of all, a man tends to be concerned about his *status* when he is interacting with others. He is constantly evaluating the pecking order and will do almost anything to avoid feeling inferior to someone else, especially a woman. He will always try to have the upper hand, not because he desires to crush another person, but simply because he hates to feel or to be perceived as inadequate. That is why he is driven to competition, power and success. He may not understand that, he may not even want to understand that, but it is true nonetheless.

A woman has very little interest in status. She desires *intimacy.* For her, connectedness and closeness bring inner feelings of warmth and security. The psychologists who have verified these truths are merely confirming the prophecy of Yahweh who said, "You will *yearn* for your husband and he will *dominate* you" (Gen. 3:16). Man therefore is driven by the need for independence while woman is driven by the need for intimacy.

This was perfectly demonstrated by my own experience. Some years ago, my wife and I were driving for the first time through the city of Barcelona in Spain. Neither of us spoke Spanish and so we could not understand many of the road signs. I was driving. I got lost, of course, and we found ourselves back in the city centre. I tried again and once more we were back in the centre. My wife pleasantly suggested we stop and ask for directions. I boorishly ignored that suggestion and kept on driving. Eventually, I was heading deeper and deeper into the suburbs of Barcelona, thoroughly lost, but the last thing I was going to do was stop and ask. My wife was by now very upset that I would not do the thing which was logical to her and ask a passerby for help. I became more upset with her, and before long we were into the inevitable shouting match. By now we were getting low on gasoline, but I was determined to find the airport under my own steam and at all costs. No pleading from my wife would make me pull over and ask a passerby. I did manage to find the airport in the end, but the next morning while apologising to my wife for my behaviour, I was really struggling with how I could have been so stupid and stubborn. I did not understand at the time the dynamics of that experience, but I do now, and my wife and I chuckle at it to this day.

As a man, I found it repugnant to ask for directions from anyone because that would have automatically placed me in an inferior position. I would have been the ignorant one needing help from someone who knew what I did not. Therefore, rather than accept the simple truth, I was unconsciously and irrationally willing to drive all night rather than lose status. For my wife, it was an entirely different situation. Since status is not important to her, she would have cheerfully stopped to ask the way and would have enjoyed it, because she could thereby connect with a stranger and feel warm feelings of gratitude for his or her help. Now that I understand this, I have learned not to feel so threatened by asking for advice. But I did have to work at it and I still get a vague feeling of discomfort when I do. I am certain that if my wife had been driving, we would have reached the airport a lot sooner. Needless to say, my wife loves to tell that story around the dinner table.

Since a man is driven by a need to be independent, he will often make arrangements without consulting his wife. He believes he is being generous when he announces the big surprise that he has purchased tickets for a show. He wants to delight her and to feel strong in his decision. She however is hurt and this deeply puzzles him. She would never dream of doing such a thing, not because she needs her husband's permission, but because she wants to feel united and close to him as they make plans together. She wants him to share in her excitement. Because of his independent decision, she feels left out.

A man likes to make his own decisions while a woman prefers consensus. Since a man is a being of action and needs to *act,* he feels trapped by lengthy discussions, especially on what he considers trivial matters. When his wife says "What do you think?" he assumes he is being asked to decide. He fails to understand that what she wants is a cosy intimate interaction. He prefers to believe "We are separate and different." She wants to believe "We are close and the same." He prefers to act. She prefers to interact.

Women generally want to do what is asked of them. Men will reflexively resist when they feel they are being told what to do. That is why army officers feel they must train soldiers by physical exhaustion and by humiliation in order to break their independent spirit, so they will automatically obey an order in battle. If a man offers to help a woman, she will gratefully accept. If a woman offers to help a man, his first impulse is to refuse because it makes him feel inferior. For her, she is saying "I want to be close to you and in helping you I feel connected." He does not hear that at all.

When she tries to help him he hears "You need my help because I am more competent than you."

A woman who displays a need for intimacy is easily misunderstood by the man who is only seeing the world through the eye-glasses of status. He sees her as insecure and incompetent, while she sees him as unfeeling and distant. This is not to say that men only want self-determination and women only want interdependence, but it is a matter of degree.

It is very informative to watch children at play. Boys tend to play in large groups which are structured according to status. They constantly brag about their skills and bravery. They usually have a leader and their games have winners and losers. In my own group, I was the leader. I was Robin Hood and the others were Little John, Will Scarlet, Friar Tuck and Allan-a-dale, and we always thoroughly defeated the evil sheriff of Nottingham. But while I was flattered to be the leader, I was secretly uneasy inside because I had to give orders and the orders always had to be right. A woman would do well to understand, that in spite of her husband's need to appear strong, independent and resourceful, he is probably very scared deep down. He lives in fear of being exposed as incompetent or cowardly. She should never let him suspect that she knows the awful truth behind his mask.

Girls play very differently. They tend to play in small groups or in pairs. The key to their activities is intimacy. Everybody gets a turn and there are no winners or losers. Girls do not boast of their talents. They do not give orders but prefer to make suggestions and to listen to the suggestions of others.

As might be expected, boys are more competitive in play while girls are more cooperative.

There is a funny story, told by men of course, which relates that if a dinner guest asks a man "Where did you get the beef?" the man will say "at the supermarket." If he asks the woman, she may say "Why? Don't you like it?" The story is meant to be a humorous put down to women. But there is a beautiful truth hidden in it. For the man, he felt superior in being asked a question and so he was able to give a straight forward answer. The woman however was motivated by her desire to please her guest, and so she asked a perfectly reasonable question in return. She needed to know if the beef was to his satisfaction because it was important to her that he enjoy his meal.

The difference between men and women is poignantly illustrated by the following interactions, first between two women, and then between one of the women and her husband.

1. **Woman:** "I feel violated by my breast surgery."
   Woman friend: "I know just how you feel. I would feel less of a woman if that happened to me. In fact that is just how I felt when I had my hysterectomy."

2. **Wife:** "I feel violated by my breast surgery."
   Husband: "Its no problem honey. You can have a surgical implant and no one will know the difference."
   Wife: "So you don't like the way I look anymore."

In the first encounter, the two women were exercising their need for connection. When the woman expressed her devastation, the friend immediately accepted her feelings and tried to connect by sharing a similar experience. In the second encounter, the man equally felt his wife's devastation but he blew it by trying to fix it. His wife interpreted that as a rejection of her post-surgical appearance. She was hurt and he was puzzled.

This desire to be a fixer gets men into a lot of trouble with their wives. If a woman says "I feel depressed" her husband will jump to the wrong conclusion and assume that he is being asked to fix her depression. He will then reel off five solutions. This is the last thing she wants. In fact she feels rejected by his response. What she is asking for is that he understand and accept her feelings and perhaps give her a reassuring hug. She just wants to connect. A woman appreciates a man who can fix mechanical things but she resents him trying to fix her feelings.

This works two ways. If a man says to his wife, "I feel depressed" she will in her desire to show solidarity with him, say something like, "Oh, I know just how you feel. I was depressed last week." Now he is the one who feels hurt. He thinks she is trivialising his real feelings by comparing his experience with hers. What he really wants from her is encouragement, to be assured that he is still a man and not a weakling. He may even want a little mothering but he does not want what he perceives to be condescension. Strangely enough, he is hoping she might be able to *fix him.* It is an interesting thing that men give to women what they themselves would like to receive and vice-versa.

There was a marriage counsellor who was helping an elderly couple who, after many years of happy marriage, were now fighting constantly. After a few sessions, he was still puzzled by their bickering. In desperation, he asked Joe if there was anything which Sarah did which really annoyed him. He said, "Oh yes. Whenever I am sick in bed she insists on bringing me hot sweet tea. I hate hot sweet tea." Sarah then jumped in and said, "Well, while we are on that subject, whenever I am sick, he always gives me hot lemon and I hate hot lemon." The counsellor was stumped for a while and then in a moment of inspiration, he said, "Joe, when you were a little boy, what did your mother give you anytime you were sick?" Joe instantly replied, "Oh she always brought me hot lemon. It made me feel loved." Needless to say, when Sarah was asked the same question she reported that her mother always gave her hot sweet tea. The problem was solved. Joe loved Sarah and so gave her what made *him* feel good. Sarah loved Joe and gave him what made *her* feel good. But that never works. Joe and Sarah wanted to express care and concern for one another but they did it by giving what the giver would like, not what the receiver would like. Once this was pointed out to them by the counsellor, they were delighted with this new insight and put it into practice. The answer is always to find out what your spouse would like and give it generously, even if you yourself would hate it.

Many men object that women want to talk endlessly about their problems. Men prefer to deal with issues quickly, forget them and move on. A woman cannot quite do that. She needs to "ponder these things in her heart," to talk them out before bringing them to closure. For example, a man could insult his wife vehemently in the evening, then get up in the morning, give her a big kiss and cheerfully go out to work. She is stunned. "How could he just walk out of here as though nothing had happened last night?" He has put it out of his mind and for him it is over. For her it is not nearly over and she needs to talk about it. If she tries to do this, he reacts by accusing her of refusing to forgive and forget.

A woman, on the other hand, will often be heard complaining that her husband does not talk enough. She cannot understand why she has to do all the talking at home, yet when they are somewhere else, he is the life and soul of the party. The truth is that men and women both do plenty of talking but talking serves a different purpose for them. Men talk more at meetings, in groups or in classrooms. At a meeting is it not always a man who asks the first question? He enjoys relaying factual information in order to preserve his status and to show off his knowledge and skill. She talks to achieve rapport with others and so she prefers to talk in an intimate setting. He, on the other hand, prefers pontificating in large groups. He is a public speaker. She is a private speaker. As a result, men are uncomfortable with intimate talk at home and they find "small talk" unworthy of their attention. Men often do not know what women want and women often cannot understand why men find it so difficult to know what women want.

The classic scenario is the breakfast table where the husband is hidden behind a newspaper while the wife, who would like to talk, share and feel close, is staring at her non-present spouse. She may indeed talk, but all she gets is a disembodied "Humph" now and then. She feels he is not there at all and worse still she feels discounted. In fact, she feels the need to talk even more than usual when he is deep in his newspaper, precisely because of this sense of being invisible. She does not understand his need to withdraw while he does not understand her need to relate. I remember a very funny cartoon where a couple are at the breakfast table. He is holding up a newspaper so his wife cannot even see his face. She is clutching a set of bag-pipes and she says, "Bob, marriage is about communication and I am about to communicate!" This poor woman is going to try anything to get his attention.

Dr. Gray touches very well on this theme when he writes about how men and women deal with problems. When troubled, the man will go off "into his cave." He will disengage and withdraw to think out the problem alone. Not until he has decided on a solution or a course of action will he re-emerge from the cave and rejoin his wife.

She is often hurt by this, but if she understood that this behaviour is not an insult but a male strategy which he needs to indulge in, then she would be more likely to give him his space, knowing he will eventually come back. It is his way of solving his problem.

A woman rarely goes into her cave. Instead, she handles a problem by talking about it and so she needs someone to talk to, usually her husband. It is by talking around the problem and coming at it from a variety of directions that she brings it to resolution. If the husband does not understand this, then he will think it is stupid to go on and on about an issue (because it is not his way and therefore must be wrong). If he learns that this is a woman's problem-solving technique, then he will more likely be prepared to sit down with his wife, listen to her and allow her to give voice to her thoughts and her feelings. It is not that she needs any response from him, other than acceptance. She really only needs to hear her own thoughts out loud. Verbalising for her is a way of organising the problem. The solution is really not very difficult. A wife needs to respect her husband's need to go into his cave. He needs to respect his wife's need to be heard. Couples who take this advice to heart find that they greatly reduce the number of their arguments and have a lot more time left over to enjoy one another.

Men often complain that their wives rake up the past. As soon as they get into a disagreement, she will then bring up incidents from out of the dim and distant past, incidents long forgotten by him. He feels this is unfair and he is hurt that she has clearly not forgotten or let go of his past sins. But he is again misinterpreting what is going on in her mind. She is simply taking the opportunity of a particular offense, occurring in the present, to point out a wider pattern of his general behaviour by relating it to past examples. She deeply desires him to see the pattern clearly so that he can begin to work against it. It is not that she has not forgiven. For her it is a way of asking him to change an undesirable habit. Meanwhile, he can see no point in digging up a corpse to see if it is still dead. Again, if he can understand this strategy, he will be less likely to react, and by listening, may hear what he needs to hear about his way of behaving.

Women accuse men of not looking at them when they talk. This is not really an avoidance strategy on his part. It makes good sense to him. He avoids eye-contact because with another man, it could look like an aggressive challenge. He avoids it with a woman because it could be interpreted as flirting. In avoiding eye contact, he is expressing a desire for friendship.

When a woman sees her husband performing a task, it is the most natural thing in the world for her to offer to help. She is again expressing a desire to cooperate with him, to feel close and to make things easier for him. She may in her eagerness even jump in and take over, because she thinks her's is a better way of doing the task. Her intentions are admirable, but he is more likely to react by feeling utterly incompetent and inadequate. He wants to feel strong and independent and sees her offer of help as a put down.

Much of the misfiring of communication between spouses boils down to the use of language. A man is very literal in his interpretation of what is said to him. He hears the words being used and takes them at their face value. After all, that is how he thinks he speaks. A woman however, uses language in a very different way. There is meaning behind her words that is never immediately obvious to a man, although it always is to another woman. Therefore men and women need to learn how to interpret "man-ese" and "woman-ese" if they are ever to understand one another. They must learn each other's "gender-speak." After all, they do come from different planets!

The mistake we all make is in thinking that there is only one way to think (my way), one way to talk (my way), or one way to listen (my way). Nothing hurts more than to be told your intentions were bad when you know they were good, or being told you are doing something wrong when you are just doing it your way.

Dr. Gray's book covers this language problem very well, but I will give a few examples by way of illustration, together with some of my own.

Women like to use the words "never" or "always" and "should." Men take it literally and so they get it all wrong.

Mistranslation

Wife: "We never go out."
Husband: "That's not true. We went out last Wednesday. How can you lie like that?"

Wife:	"No one ever listens to me."
Husband:	"That's stupid. I listen."
Wife:	"I always feel tired these days."
Husband:	"You were full of beans at the Joneses on Sunday. I just don't understand how you can exaggerate like that."
Wife:	"You never give me flowers."
Husband:	"I bought you a new coat a month ago. Would you rather have flowers than a coat?"
Wife:	"You should do it this way."
Husband:	"You're saying I am incompetent."

If he had studied gender-speak, he would have heard something very different:

Translation

Wife:	"We never go out."
Translation:	"I'm feeling overwhelmed. I wish we could go out together and just be relaxed and close."
Wife:	"No one ever listens to me."
Translation:	"I feel un-cherished and discounted. Please be there for me right now."
Wife:	"I always feel tired these days."
Translation:	"I am emotionally drained. Just accept my feelings and do not judge me. Give me your strength."
Wife:	"You never give me flowers."
Translation:	"I feel unloved and lonely. I need a big warm hug."
Wife:	"You should do it this way."
Translation:	"I want to help. If you let me, I'll feel nice and close to you."

When a man learns "woman-ese" he finds it much easier to respond by understanding her needs and meeting those needs. He really does enjoy giving his wife what she wants because it makes him feel needed. The problem arises when he does not know what she wants. That scares him to death. It works the other way around too.

Mistranslation

Husband:	"I hate my job."
Wife:	"Oh no! If he quits, how will we survive?"
Husband:	"That makes me angry."
Wife:	"It's not my fault you are angry."
Husband:	"I'm too tired right now."
Wife:	"I know just how you feel. I get tired too."
Husband:	"It's nothing."
Wife:	"Yes, it is. Something is bothering you. Tell me what it is."

What did he really intend to convey?

Translation

Husband:	"I hate my job."
Translation:	"Sometimes I feel inadequate as a man. I need you to build me up."
Husband:	"That makes me angry."
Translation:	"I'm scared of my anger. Please don't provoke me."
Husband:	"I'm too tired right now."
Translation:	"I have things on my mind. Could you let me be alone for a while till I figure them out?"
Husband:	"It's nothing."
Translation:	"I'm in my cave. Don't follow me in there. I can handle it by myself."

A man is not as intimately aware of his emotional life as a woman is, except when it comes to anger or fear and so he is uncomfortable when his wife wants him to talk about his inner being. So when she asks, "What are you thinking?" he usually says, "I don't know." This may well be the truth for him. He feels that his passing thoughts are not worthy of mention. She, on the other hand, values all of her thoughts and likes to share them in closeness with her husband. She verbalises thoughts. He filters his. If she has negative thoughts about her husband she will tell him, assuming that he will not be hurt and that it will help him to change. He rarely tells her his negative thoughts about her (unless he is angry) because he does not want to be a bully and hurt her. Paradoxically his silence hurts her more.

The aforementioned differences do not reflect a *communication problem,* which these days has become the big excuse for couples to separate and give up on each other. They are merely signs of a different *communication style.* It is easily resolved once each spouse learns to translate the language. Why should I assume that my spouse is out to destroy me or to score points at my expense? It is far more logical to believe that he or she wants to be happy and that my spouse wants me to be happy also. My spouse may fumble it from time to time but he or she usually means well. I fumble it too and I *know* that I mean well.

The Bible book of *Jesu ben Sirach* (or *Ecclesiasticus*) instructs married couples how to interpret the Word of God in regard to relationships. "A man with no understanding has vain and false hopes" (Sir. 34:1). Such a man not only does not understand the things of God but he will also not understand his wife. He has "vain and false hopes," which means he will foolishly have expectations of her which she cannot meet, and because he does not understand her language, he will be hurt by her words.

"Blessed the soul of the man who fears the Lord.... He lifts up the soul and gives light to the eyes; he grants healing, life and blessing" (Sir. 34:15 and 17). A man who fears the Lord has the right disposition and so is inspired by grace to bring healing to his wife's hurts, to give her life (which is love) and to bless her in all she does. "He who acquires a wife gets his best possession, a helper fit for him and a pillar of support" (Sir. 36:24). A man's wife is his supreme boast. God gives him a "helper" fit for him, and so he must see her as a specially chosen gift from God himself. If he treats her as a treasured gift, then she will always lovingly support him and he deeply needs her support to boost his sense of manhood. "If kindness and humility mark her speech, her husband is not like other men" (Sir. 36:23). This speaks to the amazing power of a good wife to bring out the very best in her husband. By her kindness, her womanly humility and her way of speaking, she helps him to feel like a man, to feel strong and to interact with confidence in the workplace and elsewhere outside of the home.

Once we open our eyes and our ears to the separate reality of our spouse, once we realize that he or she does not think, feel, speak or act in the way we do, then the light bulb can go on. We quickly begin to come to a new understanding of one another and to a new appreciation of one another. This is a whole new level of loving. It is a deepening of the love we felt in courtship. It is a post-honeymoon awakening of the soul which now becomes the major player in our love interaction. When the soul is now in love with the soul of our spouse, we enjoy a love that cannot die. The roots of love now run deep and in turn nourish us as a covenant couple free from competition, free from the need to manoeuvre or to outsmart or play games. We are free to grow in spirit because we are immersed in a confident love. We can joyfully accept the differences between us, because the difference makes *all* the difference.

CHAPTER 6

Troubled Marriages:
From Conflict to Communion

"Where do these wars and
battles between yourselves
first start? Is it not
precisely in the desires
fighting in your own selves?"

(Jas. 4:1)

In the Scripture passage quoted above, the apostle James goes right to the heart of the matter. Conflicts and battles in a marriage really begin in our own hearts. As victims of a sin-nature we tend to be blind to our own sins and at the same time we are driven to blame our spouse or anyone else for our own bad behaviour. Therefore if I am yelling in a rage, it is only because my spouse "made me angry." If I seek illicit sexual gratification in the arms of another person, it is because my spouse "does not love me." If I am cold and withdrawn, it is because my spouse "does not understand me." On the other hand, if my spouse is angry with me then he or she is at fault for giving in to sinful anger against innocent me. If my spouse is unfaithful, how could I ever forgive such a betrayal? If my spouse is cold and withdrawn, there must be something wrong with him or her since I have done nothing wrong. Therefore if I am behaving badly, it is my spouse's fault. If my spouse is behaving badly it is also my spouse's fault.

This flawed mind-set is a prescription for conflict. It is founded upon a self-centred and disordered ego which is blind to its own defects and only too willing to allot blame to others (chapter 4). The Christian life calls us to renounce this unholy attitude, to examine and root out our own personal flaws and to respond to our spouse with understanding and compassion. A real Christian acknowledges and faces up to his sinful tendencies and repents of them. If anger is a problem, he works against it. If he has to struggle with lust or disordered sexuality he prays about it and engages his free will in the fight to overcome it. If he is cold and withdrawn, he can choose to become warm and loving.

So many of us justify bad behaviour by telling ourselves, "I can't help it." This is a lie which denies our free will, the very gift given to us by God, by which we either choose heaven or choose hell. To convince ourselves that we do not have free will does not make free will disappear. Even if we distort our intelligence to the point of being convinced that we can't help it, God will not be convinced. A fool can fool himself but never God.

Conflicts in marriage are therefore a serious risk if only by the fact that we are sinful by nature. But they also occur for several other powerful reasons. Men and women think and act differently. These differences lead to misinterpretations and misunderstandings which so often propel us into conflict. Another reason for arguments is that we too easily give in to our negative feelings. Thus, when our spouse is behaving in a non-loving way, we find ourselves experiencing hurt, rejection, failure, sadness or anger. If we allow these feelings to dominate our thinking, then we will act out of these feelings and in turn justify our own non-loving behaviour. Again, Jesus calls us to rise above our feelings, not to allow them to dominate our will and to continue loving no matter what. Surely Jesus was the perfect example of how to do that. If he had acted upon his feelings in the Garden of Gethsemane, he would have abandoned the painful work of redemption. If we act on our negative feelings then we will abandon the work of loving our spouse. True love stands on its own. It is not dependent on whether my spouse loves me back. Even if my spouse does not love me, I will still love. Anything less than that is conditional, and sends the message that "I will love you only so long as you love me."

A major cause of marital conflict is that somewhere after the bliss of the honeymoon, the partners come face to face with each other's flaws. The flaws were always there of course, but infatuation had blinded them. Now they are coming to the forefront and have to be dealt with. This is a very precarious time in a marriage and can lead to the destructive habit of "weather proofing" the relationship. The truth is that Christian love overlooks the flaws in my spouse rather than focussing on them. Weather-proofing is an arrogant attempt to change my spouse into the perfect fantasy in my mind of what a spouse should be, and that is a dangerous illusion. Love on the other hand accepts the other as he or she is, "warts and all!" Love is grateful to God for the priceless gift of the other and rejoices in the gift. Certainly I can lovingly provide the encouragement and the environment by which my spouse can grow, even to overcoming his or her weaknesses and defects, but I must not judge or demand. "Judge not that you may not be judged" (Matt. 7:1). Judging and criticising are not my God-given rights. In fact, it is sinful because only God has the right to judge. When I judge I am telling my spouse that I am a superior being and that he or she is not good enough for me. Husband and wife are equal partners, equal in dignity and equal before God.

A major stumbling block to peace in a marriage is the sudden, awful realization that my spouse cannot meet all of my needs all of the time. If, on my wedding day, I laboured under that naive illusion then I am in for a rude awakening.

My spouse is not my perfect fantasy and I have to undergo a reality check sooner or later. No human being can meet all of my needs, ever. We spouses are all finite beings struggling with our own baggage and now we are challenged to struggle with the baggage of our spouse as well. Not only are we male and female and therefore conditioned differently, but we come from two totally different family backgrounds and experiences. Now we expect to come together and create a harmonious and peaceful new family as though that should be automatic and effortless. It is more like trying to mix oil and water. Marriage is a sacrament, which means that it needs sanctifying grace in abundance for it to succeed in uniting two strangers in harmony. Human effort alone will never be sufficient.

It is bad enough that I must come to the realization that my spouse cannot meet all of my needs, but it is even more alarming to realize that perhaps my spouse also expects *me* to meet all of his or her needs. Broken marriages are littered with unrealistic expectations. So many immature persons get married and expect impossible perfection from the other. When the spouse turns out to be a poor flawed human creature just like them, they react with disproportionate anger or hurt or resentment. *Our spouse is not God.* Only God is God. We therefore do well to put our expectations of perfection onto God, who alone is perfect, and accept our spouse as merely human.

It is true that the badge of real love is self-denial and self-sacrifice for the other. Without this willingness to die for the other, it can hardly be called love at all. "Love one another as I have loved you" (John 15:12). But that does not mean that one can ever hope to meet all of another's needs. It simply means that one gives oneself completely and hopes that it will be enough. What more can a human lover do? This gift of self should be accepted graciously by the other and cherished as any other priceless treasure. I cannot give one ounce more than my complete self.

Many of us foster conflict by presuming malice in whatever our spouse does. In other words, if my spouse is critical, complaining, cold, demanding or childish, then it must be because he or she is out to get me. He or she cannot wish me well and so is deliberately trying to wound me. This is almost always not true. If my spouse is behaving in this way then he or she is feeling insecure and maybe even unloved. Insecurity leads to low moods and a low mood causes us to lose our warm feelings. It makes us lose our bearings and so we likely fall into habitual behaviour which, at first glance, is ugly and destructive. But it is really a cry for love. It is an appeal for us to respond, not with rejection, scorn or criticism, for that only engages us in battle, but with compassion for and understanding of our spouse's insecurity.

If we claim to love then we should be sensitive to our spouse's low moods and be eager to help him or her recover. Recovery will never take place if we try to talk the other out of the low mood or if we try to cheer him or her up. Humour in this situation only trivialises the other's low mood. Perfectly good logic appears to be totally illogical to the victim of the low mood. If I am in a low mood and my spouse tries to reason with me it will not work. In a low mood, I am no longer in touch with logic or reason. I am the victim of my own distorted thoughts and I cannot see reality for what it is. The only effective response is compassion. Compassion does not judge the other, it accepts the other's temporary low mood and it wraps the other in serenity, thereby promoting security. As one's spouse begins to feel more secure, his or her mood begins to rise and will once more break out into the sunlight where thoughts and feelings are once more logical, objective and warm.

Meanwhile how should we react to our spouse when he or she is in a low mood? Believe it or not, it is surprisingly simple. If the reader will take the following strategy to heart and put it into practice then I guarantee that arguments and conflicts will practically disappear.

Some years ago, I realised that I was often caught up in mind-games with my wife. I always had to guess whether she was in a low mood or not, just as she had to somehow read my mind and decide if I was in a low mood or not. Sooner or later our low moods would become obvious, because we were indulging in destructive behaviour, but even then I had no idea as to how to react, nor did my wife. I could also see that once we were expressing our low moods in a negative way, the damage was done and more difficult to recover from. There had to be a way to catch the problem and contain it *before* it became a source of argument. So one day, I shared my thoughts with my wife. Naturally, I chose to do this when we were both in a high mood. This was important because it is always easy to know when your spouse is in a high mood and it is only in a high mood that we are objective, logical, gracious to each other and willing to make things even better. It is only when we are in a high mood that we can have an intelligent and productive conversation. I asked her if she would be willing to tell me that she was in a low mood as soon as she was aware of it. She agreed and of course I also undertook to tell her when I was in a low mood. Now we would no longer have to guess at what was going on in the other's mind. At least we would now know that the other was in a low mood before it led to a fight. But it was not going to solve our conflicts to simply be aware that the other was feeling insecure. There had to be a way of helping the other *feel* more secure. So I asked my wife, "Whenever you are in a low mood, how would you want me to respond?" She thought about it and said, "Give me a hug. Then if you maybe could do some little thing that shows you love me, I would like that. Maybe you could make me a cup of coffee or sit down and listen to my thoughts." When she shared that with me, it all seemed too simple and yet it was like a gift from her to me. Now I knew what to do to help her at those times and I really wanted to help her. Then she asked me what I would like her to do when I am in a low mood. I replied, "leave me alone!" She instantly understood that this was how I cope with my own low moods. I need to "go into my cave." She agreed to give me that gift.

The result is, that whenever my wife informs me that she is in a low mood, I launch myself into hug-mode and help her feel more secure. She in turn allows me the space to deal with my own low mood knowing that my mood will eventually come back up, as it always does. Meanwhile, we never discuss serious subjects when one of us is in a low mood. The problem will keep till we are both in a high mood and it will then be an exciting challenge rather than a problem.

The rules then, are quite simple:

1. Agree to inform your spouse when you are in a low mood before it explodes. Your spouse is not a mind reader.
2. Tell your spouse how you would like him or her to respond when you admit to a low mood.
3. Be eager to find out how your spouse wants you to respond to his or her low moods.
4. Just do it.

You will be amazed and delighted at how arguments simply become unthinkable. Like every change in behaviour, it will take a commitment, but unlike other changes in life, this is much easier than you think, since the rewards are immediate and gratifying. If, as you try to put this into practice, you find yourselves in a major, hurtful yelling match, do not treat it as a huge tragedy or failure. Once you are both in a high mood again, you can think clearly once more, discuss what happened and then get on with practising your new strategy. Both spouses really want the same things. They want peace, love and harmony in the home and in their relationship, and when they begin to see it actually happen as they live out this new strategy, they will never give it up. It is too rewarding.

The above recommendations work when only one of the spouses is in a low mood and the other is in a secure high mood. But what should we do when both of us are in a low mood at the same time? This is a recipe for disaster if we both try to interact in such a state since neither of us is in a healthy frame of mind. We will be embroiled in a terrible fracas in no time. "If you go snapping at one another and tearing one another to pieces, take care; you will be eaten up by one another" (Gal. 5:15). There is only one answer and it is to *disengage.* Both spouses should agree beforehand, that if ever this happens, they will leave each other alone, deal with their own low mood by themselves and reconnect when they feel better. This is the only way to avoid unnecessary damage.

That is the "McDonald Technique," pure and simple, and I can attest that it works for my own marriage and I have recommended it to numerous couples who report on its effectiveness for them. It is a lot better than fighting.

When it comes to really troubled marriages, naturally one has to consider professional marriage counselling. There is nothing wrong with seeking the help of an objective and skilled counsellor. But before entering into a client-therapist relationship, it would be essential to know if the counsellor is really committed to saving your marriage. It is a sad fact that many counsellors give up all too easily and recommend separation and divorce. They often may pontificate and declare that the spouses are not compatible and therefore would be happier living apart. This is not therapy. It is certainly not Christian therapy. If you are fortunate enough to have a Christian therapist, then he or she will usually believe in the sacredness of marriage and will counsel accordingly.

Another very important aspect of marriage counselling is that often the couple comes in with a hidden agenda. The husband or the wife may enter therapy earnestly desiring that the marriage get back on track. However, one of the partners may simply be there because he or she feels dragged into it and wants to pretend to be open to healing, when in fact this is not the case. Such a spouse is dishonest and merely engineers the failure of therapy so he can then say, "Well I tried and it did not work so I am justified in calling it quits." Another difficult problem in therapy is where one partner is convinced that there is nothing the matter with him or her and that the therapist's job is to "fix" the other. This never works because it is a lie. Both partners in a troubled marriage need to learn how to change if love is to be rekindled. Marriage counselling works best if both partners desire help and if both are willing to honestly look at their own responsibility in the relationship. Nevertheless, this is not an absolute rule. I have seen marriages recover simply because one partner decided to change. The other unwilling spouse then felt more secure and also began to change. The new loving behaviour in one spouse brought out the best in the other. Nonetheless, counselling is a lot easier when both partners are open. Christian counselling calls forth this necessary sense of responsibility and encourages the partners to reach for the goodness within.

It is very important to eliminate a misunderstanding about how marriage counselling works. The process is not a mere matter of problem-solving. In fact, this is usually bad therapy, although there is sometimes a place for it. Most couples, by the time they are desperate enough to seek counselling, are caught up in the pain of their own damaged feelings and they are focussed on their major areas of disagreement. They expect the therapist to come up with a magic solution to their problems and that is very wrong. Some therapists do get drawn into these problems, but it is a lost cause. A marriage will never be without problems, so if I as a therapist am merely a problem-solver, then I should move in with the married couple. I could be their live-in guru to be consulted every time a problem arises. This of course, would be laughable, but it is no more laughable than the therapist who restricts his role to mere problem-solving. It does not work in the long haul. The real skill of therapy is to help couples solve their own problems. If they do this with love, then their solutions will be far more ingenious than anything I could come up with. In the end, my solutions are only good for *my* marriage, not yours. If, as so often happens, the therapy focuses only on individual problems, it soon gets bogged down in recriminations, low mood feelings and in the futile search for solutions. The couple leaves the office in a lower mood and more discouraged than when they came in, only to return next time with a new set of problems for the therapist to solve.

There has to be a better way and there is. It is called "high mood therapy." The basic principle of high mood therapy is to offer hope to the distressed couple. Focussing on problems is low mood therapy and drags down the couple's spirits, thereby creating a deeper and deeper despondency which defeats the very purpose of therapy. A high mood therapist takes the "high-road," is optimistic about the couple's potential and calls them to greater confidence in their recovery. As a result, couples should leave the office with a deeper sense of closeness, a greater sense of hope and a willingness to come even closer together. They leave the office believing that it might be worth the risk to try again. If a couple were to go sight-seeing in a city, would they go and visit the town dump? Not likely! They would visit the gardens and the beautiful art galleries. So it is with therapy. Low mood therapy visits the dump. High mood therapy prefers the gardens.

There are a variety of schools of therapy. Some use Cognitive techniques, some use Gestalt, some use Behaviour Modification Principles, but whichever modality your therapist employs, success will still depend on the high-mood approach.

Good therapy therefore helps a couple to recall the heady days of what it was like to be in love with each other and to assure them that their love has not died. It has merely become paved over by the cares of life. This will mean re-examining one's priorities. After the honeymoon, a couple tends to settle down to the business of making money, striving for a bigger house or saving up for a better vehicle. This can become so all-consuming that years down the road, when the couple has successfully acquired all these signs of success, they wake up one day to the awful realization that they are living with a complete stranger. Just like Becky and John in chapter 1, love has been sacrificed for material gain. What a tragedy! The therapist will try to re-focus a couple's priorities so that their love once again becomes their primary goal, while all other objectives are given a proper secondary importance. Love was the reason for the marriage in the first place and if it is not nurtured, then in the midst of later affluence, the marriage is slowly dying.

The best way to achieve success in marriage counselling is to promote a real change of attitude in the husband and wife towards themselves and towards each other. If a spouse insists on seeing the other as malicious or as an enemy out to destroy his or her happiness, where is the hope in that? If, on the other hand, a spouse chooses to see his partner as well-meaning, desiring happiness as much as he does, and like him, given to low moods, then his attitude towards her behaviour becomes more understanding and more gracious. As a result of this healthy change in attitude, a wife can see her husband behaving badly, can hear him saying hurtful things, but instead of allowing these behaviours to wound her, she is immediately aware of her husband's insecurity and responds with compassion.

The basis of this style of counselling is the belief that couples can get a fresh start. It rightly emphasises that the problems in a marriage are not the cause of the marital discord, but are merely the symptoms. It emphasises that when two people are in a state of healthy psychological functioning, they will feel warmly towards each other and capable of loving acts. The good news is that healthy psychological functioning can be taught. As a result of learning about healthy thinking, moods, mind-sets and feelings, a couple begins to see the innocence in each other. The couple will learn how to forgive, how to overlook irritable behaviour in a spouse, and how to bring out the best in each other. A very important principle of high mood therapy is that when we are in a high mood we are like the good Dr. Jekyll. We are magnanimous, understanding, patient, forgiving and joyful. But when we are in a low mood, we are the horrible Mr. Hyde, aggressive or complaining, childish or mean. We are at our worst. If Mr. Hyde learns not to be drawn into his low moods, but wisely waits for his higher mood to return, he will automatically recover his real Dr. Jekyll self.

For marriage therapy to be effective, it is obviously ideal if both partners begin to change, but the surprising fact is that wonderful things can happen even if only one makes the effort. If one spouse decides to become the very best wife or husband possible and begins to live out the marriage vows as God intended, then miracles of change will usually occur in the other spouse. There is a very good adage in therapy. "If you want to change your spouse, change yourself." It only takes one Dr. Jekyll to move a marriage towards health. Nevertheless, I still find it a lot easier when both partners genuinely desire change.

If we are really honest, then the very things which irritate us today about our spouse are the very things which often attracted us to him or her in our courting days. For example, now I see my spouse as aggressive where only a few years ago I loved him or her for being confident and assertive. I can't stand my spouse for being critical yet not long ago I admired her for being so truthful. What is slovenly today was relaxed and laid back yesterday. The smothering intimacy I hate today was yesterday's wonderful loving hugs. What has happened here? Nothing has really changed except for my own attitude. I am seeing my spouse differently and that is my problem, not hers. The marvellous truth is that I can change my attitude in the blink of an eye. I can get in touch once again with my first love for her and re-claim my former appreciation for her qualities.

Bearing in mind that men and women come from "different planets" why should it surprise young married couples that they have different opinions on just about everything? If my attitude towards this discovery is that we are *incompatible*, then I will be despondent, maintain myself in a low mood and so I will be constantly poised for an argument. If my attitude is one of *excitement* at my wife's way of seeing the world, I will be in a high mood, constantly stimulated by her ideas and never threatened by them. It becomes a joy to discover the ways in which she sees the world. Instead of an irritant, her opinion stimulates me to reconsider my own opinion. Our life is then filled with interesting discussions. In the first scenario, I believe that my wife's contrary opinion accuses me of being wrong. Therefore I must prove that I am right and she is wrong. The battle is on. In the second scenario, I know that opinions are not important, that instead of one being right and the other wrong, we could easily both be right or both be wrong. It does not matter to me, because I love my wife and we enjoy the process of knowing each other more and more each day. Because it is exciting, the idea of fighting over it never enters our minds.

Our attitude towards a troublesome event changes the way we think and the way we feel.

ATTITUDE	THOUGHTS	FEELING
1. A tragedy.	This is terrible.	Depression/despair.
2. A big problem.	I can't cope.	Stressed out.
3. A challenge.	I can handle it.	Interested.
4. A lesson.	I needed this.	Grateful.
5. An opportunity.	I love this.	Exhilarated.

Dr. George Pransky, a practising psychologist, recounts a story which demonstrates how our attitude influences our thinking. "The scene is the lobby of a movie theatre. You are standing in line to buy tickets. Suddenly a burly man walks in front of you and steps on your toe. He offers no apology. In fact, he acts like you don't exist. Anger builds in you. Suddenly your anger turns to chagrin. You just noticed his white cane and black glasses. Turning to the man behind you, you relate your mistake. He laughs and says he knows this alleged blind man. "That man is not blind" he reports. "He's just a sadist who pretends to be blind to avoid punishment for his sadistic acts." Your embarrassment instantly turns to outrage. You ask yourself, "How could anyone be that low?" You consider taking a punch at him despite his size. An older man pulls you aside. He tells you that the man behind you is the sadist and the burly man actually is blind. Your outrage turns to confusion and then to levity when a middle-aged, bald-headed man comes over and says, "Smile, you're on Candid Camera!"

Notice how the man in the story romped through a variety of different feelings depending on the attitude he had at any given moment towards the blind man. Marriage is like that too. Therefore, we need to discard useless attitudes which breed conflict and take on a more philosophical attitude which leads us to warm feelings about our spouse.

We need to rise above our problems instead of fretting about them. If I have a sore on my arm, the last thing I should do is pick on it. Fretting about problems and giving them undue attention is like picking at a sore. It will never heal. For example, disagreement over money is a very common cause of marriage breakdown. Yet money seems to be a problem for some couples and not for others. This has nothing to do with whether the couple is wealthy or poor. It has to do with attitude. When financial matters are not a problem for a couple, they simply do not spend much time on it. Husband and wife share their resources without petty squabbles about "mine and yours." If they have the cash, they buy the item they always wanted. If they are short, they have no difficulty in refraining from a purchase. Money is not important to them. But if another couple sees money as a problem then the very thought of money fills them with insecurity. Any mention of the word "money" is a source of anxiety or despondency for the couple and sets them up for fights and an exchange of blame.

A perceived problem is in fact a *state of mind* which can manufacture a problem out of anything or even out of nothing. It is my attitude that will decide whether a life's issue is a problem for me or not. Certainly a major tragedy is a problem. That is not in dispute, but even there, my attitude will have a big impact on how well I handle it. If my bank collapses and I lose all my savings I can tell myself, "This is the end. My family will starve to death. I wish I were dead." I could equally well say, "What a mess. Well, we are not going to roll over and die. We can start over again."

Understanding is a powerful tool for saving a marriage. It is in fact the stimulus to a *change of heart* which is so necessary if we are to cast off previous hurtful behaviours. As a rule, people convince themselves that they cannot change. If that were true, then there is no hope either for our own personal salvation (I am a drunkard, or an adulterer. That is the way I am and I cannot change it), or for our marriages (I know you don't like me going out with the boys so much, but I can't help it). Believing one cannot change is a cop-out from mature Christian living.

Everyone has the ability to change. Change takes place when I act out of my real self, rather than out of my conditioning. If I feel insecure, I tend to fall back into my conditioned personality, which is full of bad habits. For example, if I was raised in a home where there was a lot of violence, then I have been conditioned to be violent. As a result, whenever I feel insecure (criticised, threatened, irritated, anxious), then I will be strongly tempted to fall into the old habit of violence. It is not however, a foregone conclusion. I can experience a change of heart whereby I renounce violence, see the wisdom of becoming a peacemaker and I become more understanding, tolerant and gentle. The way to facilitate a change of heart is to treat people with understanding and goodwill. Goodwill relieves insecurity. It invites my spouse to drop her old defence mechanisms and to become her authentic self. As a result, she quickly regains her built-in qualities of wisdom, creativity, humour and compassion.

As Dr. Pransky again writes "When Jim gets insecure at work he puts on an armour called 'frenetic.' By the time he gets home to Elaine he is wound up like a spring. She reacts to this tension by becoming irritable, forcing him deeper into his shell of tension. When Elaine sees that insecurity is causing Jim's freneticism, she becomes compassionate and warm toward him. He relaxes and the tension starts to dissipate. Soon, the contrast between his relaxed feeling at home and his overwrought feeling at work helps him to get his perspective. Gradually, he learns to keep his bearings under pressure. A human being can be likened to a flower. In a climate of emotional well-being a person grows towards his or her potential. Understanding and goodwill are the food and water that nourish the blossom."

All of this can be taught by a good therapist. In high mood therapy, the focus is on showing a couple that their behaviour so often depends on their thinking, their moods, their mind-sets and their old habits. It teaches healthy psychological functioning, how to think, how to deal with low moods and how to tap into our own natural resources of wisdom, understanding and creativity. Once a couple takes this teaching to heart, then a change of heart automatically follows. It may surprise many couples to be told, that regardless of years of bad habits and destructive behaviour, there is within each of us a perfectly natural mechanism for healthy psychological functioning. It is still there even if it is not being used and it can be activated at any time. All it takes is a teacher-therapist to show how to tap into your own built-in health resources and a willingness to learn on your part. As one learns how to think creatively, one automatically becomes more compassionate, more understanding and more gracious in dealing with one's spouse. My new psychological equilibrium leads to the same thing in my spouse.

For a Catholic, a change of heart means even more than simply mental and emotional health. It means more than a change in personal habits. It calls me to a higher *spiritual* change of heart, the kind of change which works miracles both in myself and in my spouse. This is the massive change of heart which prompts me to "lay down my life" for the other. Such a leap from the merely worldly to the sublime can only occur with the direct help of the Holy Spirit. It is, in other words, *conversion.* Conversion is not a once-in-a-life-time event. It is an on-going daily transformation by which we submit our lives and our will to the will of God. It means accepting Jesus Christ as my personal Lord and Saviour and following in his footsteps, carrying the cross. For this to occur, sanctifying grace is needed and that comes through the power of the Sacraments. As married couples, we can lay claim to the vast graces of Matrimony which are ours for the asking and we can receive an increase in grace as we attend regular Confession and frequent Holy Communion. Conversion, or a holy change of heart, transforms the ordinary, worldly, dual relationship of man and woman into the extraordinary, supernatural, three-way relationship of man, woman and God. All it takes is a decision by the couple to allow God to rule in their home and in their hearts.

As a result of such conversion, a husband learns to become a real man, while a wife becomes a real woman. "Real" in this context refers to the real world of the life of grace, not the illusory world of money, work and pleasure, which the majority of people mistakenly call real today.

The beauty and joy of this conversion lies in the fact that the husband begins to live for his wife instead of for himself, while his wife begins to live for him, rather than for herself. If I "lay down my life" for my wife and live for her happiness, I need never worry, since it is very likely that she will do the same thing in turn for me. The result is that my wife's needs will be met and my needs will also be met. Instead of living a self-centred life, I live an other-centred life, and I am empowered to do this because I live for God first. "If there is any encouragement in Christ, any solace in love, any participation in the Spirit, any compassion and mercy, complete my joy by being of the same mind, with the same love, united in heart, thinking one thing. Do nothing out of selfishness or vainglory; rather humbly regard others as more important than yourselves, each looking out not for his own interests, but everyone for those of others" (Phil. 2:1-4). This is the formula for a long, happy and satisfying marriage. It requires dying to self but the rewards are guaranteed by the Word of God. It is the royal road to real communion as a couple.

The truth is that we should discard all false notions of "incompatibility." That is a myth created by secular psychologists and psychiatrists. It is simply a feeble excuse to avoid real commitment and is a passport to separation and divorce when the going gets rough. Christianity does not teach incompatibility. In fact, it recognises and rejoices in the countless successful marriages where couples would never have been considered compatible by secular standards. Yet they found excitement in one another and stood by one another throughout a lifetime. Christians can love anyone whether they are compatible or not in the eyes of the world.

If your marriage seems troubled, do not give up. It is more than possible, if you both want it, to be transformed from conflict to lasting communion. "In everything you do, act without grumbling or arguing. Prove yourselves innocent and straight forward, children of God without reproach" (Phil. 2:14-15). God is the best of all marriage counsellors.

CHAPTER 7

Children: The Fruit of Love

"He blesses the children
within you."

(Ps. 147:13)

Children are the fruit of our love as husband and wife. Husband, wife and child form an earthly Trinity, contained in the mind of the Divine Trinity. As such, the family is created in the image and likeness of God (vol. 2, chap. 14). Just as God the Holy Spirit proceeds from the love between God the Father and God the Son, so also the child proceeds from the love between his father and mother. It is a sublime and wondrous mystery that God has given to human beings the privilege of co-creating new souls for his kingdom. Such a joy was not given to the angels and yet we, who are inferior to them, can help God to fill up heaven with holy souls. Surely this is the highest of all callings, to give life and to nurture it towards its supreme good, which is God himself. Priesthood is of course the most perfect of all vocations, but there would be no priests at all without fathers and mothers who first loved one another.

Children, being the fruit of love, therefore also thrive on love. Since they are created out of love, they feed on love and are made to love in return. Some argue that a child is not always created out of love but, rather, could be conceived in violence, drunkenness or lust and that the resultant child is not a fruit of love. This is not true. Even where a conception has occurred in disorder, the child is still created out of ***God's love***, since God cannot be unfaithful to his covenant with humanity, even if we are unfaithful to our covenant with him. "If we are unfaithful, he remains faithful, for he cannot deny himself" (2 Tim. 2:13). That is why there is no such thing as an unwanted child. A child may be unwanted by his selfish parents but he is always wanted by God. "Yahweh called me when I was in the womb, before my birth he had pronounced my name" (Isa. 49:1).

Children are a blessing from God. "He blesses the children within you" (Ps. 147:13). "And their children become a blessing" (Ps. 37:26). When God blesses, he bestows grace and so children are, as it were, grace incarnate. The child playing before us is an embodiment of grace, a sign of God's delight in our love. As such, the child is both a blessing and a responsibility, for grace always imposes the responsibility of nurturing it. Parents, therefore, are expected by God to cherish their child as a most precious gift from the heart of God, and are expected to devote themselves to the welfare of that child. This obligation of promoting welfare applies not simply to the basic bodily demands for food, clothing and shelter, but includes the higher demands for love, teaching, discipline and, above all, training in godliness. The last is indeed the first in importance, since eternal life for a child depends upon it. All the others foster earthly life and even quality of life, but without godliness, all our efforts will be wasted.

Children become what they learn. If they are taught about Jesus and his Blessed Mother and the truths of their faith from the cradle, they will become disciples of Christ. It is true that in the first flush of freedom from parental control, as young adults, they may decide to test the dark waters of sin, but they will not be able to fully escape from their training in the ways of goodness. Sooner or later, they will waken up to the fact that they have engineered their own misery, and they will turn back to the wisdom of their childhood joy in the Lord. This turning back, however, will depend on the nature of their faith experience when they were little. If all they received was cold, harsh religion, then religion will never be life-giving to them. If, on the other hand, they learned the love of God and the warmth of prayer and worship, then like a powerful magnet, it will always draw them back.

The most beautiful and endearing quality of a child is innocence. To God, innocence is his greatest delight since innocence does not know sin. A child has the ability to simply be. He is what he is. He is like a flower which blooms and gives off a marvellous perfume and without knowing it, gives us delight. He laughs, he plays, he explores, he falls down and always gets up again. If parents try to see the world through their child's eyes, they too will recapture the wonder, the awe and the excitement of all things. To a child all things are new and marvellous and the world has not yet taken on the dust-covered layers of experience and boredom.

One of the great attributes of a child is his curiosity. Children are delightfully curious about every thing. G. K. Chesterton wrote, "The most childlike thing about a child is his curiosity and his appetite and his power to wonder at the world." Children remind us that the very things we adults now take for granted are the very signature of God. The world around us is saturated with the love of God, crying out to us to see the handwriting of its Maker. The proof of the existence of God lies in his works and that idea is so simple to a child that it need not be questioned. It is adults who try to explain away the mystery of the universe as some cosmic accident, but in so doing, they rob themselves of their own meaning. God gives meaning to all things, especially to the lives of his people, and the childlike heart rejoices in it.

Innocence means freedom from corruption by evil. A child enjoys this innocence until the age of reason and it is then that he comes to that dreaded milestone of "knowing good and evil" (Gen. 3:5). It is at this point that his innocence is in grave danger, just as the innocence of Adam and Eve was corrupted by this "knowing." It is true that a very young child can be self-centred, even wilful, but that is not actual sin. As the Church teaches, actual sin is not possible until the child reaches the age of reason, which occurs when he attains the age of seven or thereabouts. From then onwards, he is accountable for his actions, thoughts and decisions. Wise parents understand this transition and so they are diligent in their duty to guide the child in the ways of holiness.

One day, when Jesus was in Judea on the far side of the Jordan, many loving parents brought their children to Jesus asking him to lay his hands on them and to pray over them. The disciples, full of their own importance and desiring to protect Jesus from such irritation, scolded the parents. It is amusing to imagine the apostles shooing the children away and telling them not to be pestering this important man. After all, Jesus had a mission to get on with and children would simply be a bother and a distraction from his real work. They were in for a shock. Jesus, without scolding his disciples, simply said with great love "Let the little children alone, and do not stop them from coming to me; for it is to such as these that the kingdom of heaven belongs" (Matt. 19:14). What a gentle and wonderful lesson Jesus taught us that day. God's love of innocence is so great that the kingdom of heaven belongs to children, that is to say, to the childlike heart.

"So he called a little child to him whom he set among them. Then he said, 'In truth I tell you, unless you change and become like little children, you will never enter the kingdom of heaven. And so the one who makes himself as little as this little child is the greatest in the kingdom of heaven'" (Matt. 18:2-4). We, as adults, are called to scrape off the barnacles of our sophistication and to rediscover the heart of a child within us, full of love, wonder, and simple acceptance of the mysteries of God.

Jesus went even farther in this discourse when he said, "Anyone who welcomes one little child like this in my name welcomes me" (Matt. 18:5). In other words we are to revere children as God's blessing, as the fruit of love, and in so-doing, we are giving honour to Jesus himself. In fact, Jesus is teaching that no one on earth is a closer facsimile to the mind of Christ than a little child and so childhood demands our respect and holy imitation. Therefore, we are bound to love all children in a very special way, for they are very special to God. No child should be deprived or starved or treated cruelly, otherwise we will be held to account. Strangely enough, our sinful society agrees with that statement and then uses it to justify the abortion of so-called unwanted children, as if killing a child were not the ultimate in cruelty.

To God, the innocence of a child is so precious that Jesus was compelled to indicate the dreadful consequences for anyone who violates that innocence. "Whoever causes one of these little ones who believe in me to sin, it would be better for him to have a great millstone hung around his neck and to be drowned in the depths of the sea" (Matt. 18:6). Therefore sexual abuse, physical abuse, mental cruelty and any other sin against innocence is one of the very worst crimes one can commit. Such corruption of the child also occurs when parents allow their little ones to watch immoral videos, to listen to music with satanic or evil lyrics or to keep bad company with their peer group. These sins mutilate the sacredness of a child and the consequences are terrible. The child loses his or her innocence, since it has now been breached, and so grows up to be distorted, disturbed and disconnected. The perpetrator, of course, is now horribly disfigured in his own spirit, and while he need not be damned if he repents, he must shoulder an enormous debt for atonement. Yet atonement is by far preferable to a millstone.

By the very fact of their innocence, little children seem to have no problem with the mysteries of God. Adults grapple with the things which are beyond their power to understand. Little children never do this but rather enjoy the wonderful ability to hear the truth and accept it no matter how profound. The critical factor for this acceptance is the degree to which they trust the person who tells them this truth. For a little child, the resurrection of Jesus from the dead is quite simple. He or she sees no difficulty with that idea whatsoever. The fact that volumes, if not libraries of books, have been written for and against the mystery of the Resurrection, is of no interest to the child. Jesus rose from the dead. Mother said so. Therefore it is true.

One day, St. Augustine was pondering upon the mystery of the Trinity while walking along the seashore. Suddenly, he noticed a little boy dipping a thimble into the ocean, then emptying it out on the beach. The child was very intent on this activity and repeated it over and over again. Finally the theologian asked him, "What are you doing my child?" The boy, without stopping his serious task replied, "I am emptying the ocean." The theologian smiled condescendingly and said, "Son, it is impossible for you to empty the ocean." The child quietly said, "Not nearly as impossible as you trying to understand the Trinity." He then disappeared. I love that story since it shrinks our proud adult ego down to its proper size, which is minuscule in the affairs of God, and the shrinking was done by a little child. "And a little child shall lead them" (Isa. 11:6).

This does not mean that in becoming like a little child, an adult must also become uninformed and renounce his experience and learning, but it does mean that an adult must become de-programmed from all his years of worldly conditioning. He needs to be bleached from the accumulated dirt of duplicity, guile, self-centeredness, pride and above all, the arrogant reliance on his puny reason as the only way by which he can *know* anything. "When I was a child, I spoke like a child, I thought like a child, I reasoned like a child; when I became a man, I gave up childish ways" (1 Cor. 13:11). Therefore, when Jesus tells us that we will lose the kingdom of heaven unless we become like a little child, he is not telling us to become *childish.* He is reminding us that so much of what we think of as adult and sophisticated is in fact childish and stupid. It is when we learn from our experience of life, grow in wisdom and *marvel* at the mysteries of God that we become like a little child, and thereby delight our Father-God. This childlikeness means facing our own limitations with fearless honesty, and that is humility. It also means an abiding gratitude to God for absolutely everything.

It is as though life is a kind of circle. We are born as infants and raised to adulthood by our earthly parents. Once released from their authority, we then allow ourselves to be raised by our heavenly parents who are God the Father and Mary the Mother. If we are docile to their discipline, they in turn will raise us to become children once more, true children of the kingdom. We have come full circle, from child to adult, to child again. In the spiritual sense, our adult is childish and our child is childlike and God desires all of us to embrace this childlikeness. "All your children shall be taught by the Lord and great shall be the prosperity of your children" (Isa. 54:13). It was Solomon, the man of wisdom, who prayed "And now, O Lord my God, you have made your servant king in the place of David my father, although I am but a little child; I do not know how to go out or come in" (1 Kings 3:7). Solomon asked Yahweh for the gift of wisdom, for it is wisdom which distinguishes the true child of God from the merely childish. "A wise child makes a glad father" (Prov. 15:20).

As soon as our child has language skills, we should teach him that he has a guardian angel specially appointed by God to be his constant companion. The child should come to know and believe that even when mother and father are out of his sight, he is never alone. His guardian angel is an unseen presence, hovering over him and protecting his soul. Wherever the child goes, his angel goes with him. Whatever the child thinks, his angel knows his thoughts. Whatever the child does, his angel observes it. The child must believe that his angel is not a parent and certainly not some kind of policeman, but is his very best friend who cares for his goodness and welfare. His angel is really a teacher as well as a guardian, and the child should come to a relaxed familiarity with his angel. He should be encouraged to give his angel a name and the angel will joyfully accept that name and wear it with love. It does not matter to the angel if the name is male or female since angels are not distinguished by sexual differences. The angel simply rejoices in whatever name is given, since it signifies that the child acknowledges him and desires to have an intimate relationship with him.

The child should be instructed never to do anything which will make his angel sad, and of course it is sin which saddens our angels. Jesus tells us, "See that you do not despise one of these little ones; for I tell you that in heaven their angels always behold the face of my Father who is in heaven" (Matt. 18:10-11). This is the ultimate testimony to the great innocence and sinlessness of a little child, that his guardian angel is given the privilege of constantly beholding the face of the Father. How sad that we usually lose that innocence, and thereby our angel is no longer able to gaze upon the face of the Father. If a child understands this truth, surely he will try not to hurt his best friend in this way, but will make every effort to avoid the sin which deprives his angel of the ultimate privilege. "My son, give me your heart and let your eyes observe my ways" (Prov. 23:26). This could equally well apply to our guardian angel, who strongly desires that we observe his ways, which are God's ways.

Apart from direct instruction from his parents, a child learns most of his skills from play. The child rehearses by meaningful role playing and hones his abilities by repetitive practice. In other words, he learns by imitating his parents or by imitating other heroes to whom he has been exposed. This is why parents must be very anxious to give the child holy and wholesome heroes, such as the great saints of the Church. He also learns physical dexterity by exercising his body, repeating the same manoeuvre over and over again until he gets it right. Once more, the parents must quietly observe these play activities and direct the child into good practices, and firmly distract him from those that are sinful, reprehensible or dangerous.

A child needs to play. Naturally, he needs also to learn how to work, and that will be discussed in more detail in chapter 9 of this volume. But he must be allowed to be a child. Adult knowledge should *never* be given to him before his time, since that is a sure way to corrupt his childhood. His innocence should be as valuable and precious to parents as it is to God himself. There is no place in a Catholic family for so-called sex education of a little child.

A very important concept for all of us, is that we desperately need the *Father's blessing.* This includes not only the blessing from God our heavenly Father but also the blessing from our earthly father. Gary Smalley in his book, *The Blessing,* explains this vital built-in need within every person. For both sons and daughters in the Old Testament, the father's blessing was a momentous event. Esau in his misery at selling his birthright for "a mess of potage" cries out "Bless me, even also, O my father" (Gen. 27:34). In losing the father's blessing, Esau realised that he had lost everything.

A father's blessing indicates that the child is highly valued, and it also denotes an abiding confidence by the parent in the child's unique future. It is both a blessing and a sign of trust. All of us desperately need this blessing even if we are not aware of it. So many children are never given the blessing and so they grow up to feel unworthy. They deem themselves to be flawed in the estimation of their parents, themselves and others. Because they were cheated of their earthly father's blessing, they believe they can never have their heavenly Father's blessing. This destitution leads to a fruitless search for acceptance and that can mean acceptance by anyone at all, so long as it is some kind of blessing, no matter how disordered. The result is, that so many of our teenagers, being starved for blessing, will associate with a sinful peer group and even fall into drugs, drunkenness and debauchery. The need to be accepted is so powerful that a child will accept a counterfeit blessing rather than none at all. Many grow up into adulthood and become workaholics and perfectionists, or withdrawn and dependent, or wallow in self-hatred, frantically searching for the blessing they never had. How hard it is to believe in the loving, gentle fatherhood of God when we were robbed of blessing by our own earthly father.

Esau was so devastated by his loss that he pleaded with Isaac, "Do you have only one blessing, my father?" (Gen. 27:38). The ancient Jewish custom was to reserve the father's blessing to a special time only, and it was usually reserved to the eldest son. Thankfully, this exclusive blessing has been transformed by Jesus in the New Testament to include all of God's children. All of us deserve blessing as our birthright by baptism, and all of us crave for it. Not only that, but this privilege of bestowing the blessing is no longer reserved to earthly fathers alone, but is a prerogative of both parents. We need our mother's blessing as much as we need that of our father. Do we Catholics not desire the gentle blessing of our Mother Mary as well as that of our God-Father? Likewise, we desire, deserve and desperately need the blessing of both our earthly parents. This is the fullness of blessing, which gives us the secure knowledge that we are the treasured offspring of our mother, our father and God. The blessing of the new covenant is so much more affirming than the old.

Today, there are so many cults seducing our children. These cults are very good at offering a counterfeit blessing to our children and those who have not known genuine blessing are very vulnerable to it. The cults provide a false sense of family, attention, affection and affirmation and that is very alluring indeed. Yet these are the very gifts which ought to have been bestowed by the child's own parents in the first place.

The family blessing also prepares the young adult for a true commitment to marriage. "For this reason a man shall leave his father and his mother and shall cleave to his wife" (Gen. 2:24). By dint of being blessed, the growing child is affirmed and is capable of leaving the comfort and security of his parental home and is empowered to love a marriage partner in a mature and holy way. Unblessed adults may ultimately leave home to marry, but they never emotionally leave it. They continue to be chained to their parents, constantly seeking blessing and therefore never able to enjoy a wholesome, committed intimacy with their spouse. If a man or woman feels unworthy, how can he or she feel that a spouse would value their total giving of self? The self is not worthy and so the gift of self is a worthless gift in its own estimation. Not only that, but if the parents themselves were unblessed, then they find it impossible to let their children go and they neurotically continue to disapprove of their child's freedom, of his choice of partner for life, and interfere sinfully in their child's marriage.

The solution is not so difficult. Parents must decide to bless their children and this blessing should be offered daily. It is so beautiful for parents to ask their child to kneel down at bedtime and receive a brief prayer of blessing, along with a reverent sign of the cross on his or her forehead. The little child feels the solemnity of that blessing and feels so affirmed by it, that he would not dream of going to bed without it. For the older child, it takes on the additional quality of trust. When I was a teenager and a university student, I earned my tuition fees by playing piano in a band. Naturally, that placed me in a regular atmosphere of late nights, revelry, drinking and opportunities for sexual adventure. Before I went off in my tuxedo to play, my father would place his big carpenter's hands on my shoulders, look me in the eye and say "Son, I trust you. I know you will not bring shame to the McDonald name." Whenever the opportunity for sin arose, my father's words would come back to haunt me and I remembered his holy trust. He did not try to stop me from encountering the world, but with his trust he stopped me from being seduced by it. I was a beneficiary of my father's blessing. Even when I did fall into sin, I had to first deliberately suppress my father's wise words, and then afterwards, I invariably was overwhelmed by remorse, which led to repentance, which led to confession of my sin, which led to atonement, which led to once more bathing in the blessing of my two fathers, my dad and my Abba-God.

The family blessing consists of meaningful touch, a spoken message, attaching a high value to the one being blessed, picturing a special future for the child, and an active commitment to help the child fulfil the blessing. The latter means that the parents need to be diligent in encouraging their child to realize all the potential of his being. This means the consistent interest in and involvement in the dreams and aspirations of the child, both in the world and in the

life of faith. Blessing is the key to becoming a lover oneself in the
holiest sense, and a lover of God and neighbour.

I am not sure who wrote the following poem, but it says so
much about childhood. It is entitled *Little Jesus.*

Little Jesus, wast thou shy
Once, and just so small as I?
And what did it feel like to be
Out of Heaven and just like me?
Didst thou sometimes think of *there,*
And ask where all the angels were?
I should think that I would cry
For my house all made of sky;
I would look about the air,
And wonder where my angels were;
And at waking 'twould distress me,
Not an angel there to dress me!
Hadst thou ever any toys,
Like us little girls and boys?
And didst thou play in Heaven with all
The angels that were not too tall,
With stars for marbles? Did the things
Play *"Can you see me?"* through their wings?
And did thy Mother let thee spoil
Thy robes, with playing on *our* soil?
How nice to have them always new
In Heaven, because 'twas quite clean blue!

Didst thou kneel at night to pray,
And didst thou join thy hands, this way?
And did they tire sometimes, being young,
And make the prayer seem very long?
And dost thou like it best, that we
Should join our hands to pray to thee?
I used to think, before I knew,
The prayer not said unless we do.
And did thy Mother at the night
Kiss thee, and fold the clothes in right?

And didst thou feel quite good in bed,
Kissed, and sweet, and thy prayers said?
Thou canst not have forgotten all
That it feels like to be small:
And thou know'st I cannot pray
To thee in my father's way —
When thou was so little, say,
Couldst thou talk thy Father's way? —
So, a little Child, come down
And hear a child's tongue like thy own:
Take me by the hand and walk,
And listen to my baby-talk.
To thy Father show my prayer
(He will look, thou art so fair),
And say: "O Father, I, thy Son,
Bring the prayer of a little one."
And he will smile, that children's tongue
Has not changed since thou wast young.

Nothing is more powerful in moving the heart of God than the prayer of a little child. As the poem says, "O Father, I thy son, bring the prayer of a little one." As scripture says, "Your majesty is praised above the heavens; on the lips of children and of babes you have found praise to foil your enemy, to silence the foe and the rebel" (Ps. 8:1-2). It should be the most sublime delight of all parents to know that their child is the fruit of love and is truly God's blessing. If little children and babes can give the Most High God acceptable praise, surely we parents should joyfully protect and bless them as our highest treasure.

In learning what children are, we adults learn what we ought to be.

CHAPTER 8

Parenting: God's Design for Children

> *"Honour your father and your*
> *mother so that you may live*
> *long in the land that Yahweh*
> *your God is giving you."*
> *(Ex. 20:12)*

The most valuable resource for understanding the Catholic family is the new ***Catechism of the Catholic Church***. It is a gold mine of truth and probably Pope John Paul II's greatest legacy to the universal Church. It has much to say about God's design for good and godly parenting and all of it is thoroughly founded upon Scripture and upon the Holy Tradition of the Church.

Paragraph 2205: The Christian family is a communion of persons, a sign and image of the communion of the Father and the Son in the Holy Spirit. In the procreation of children, it reflects the Father's work of creation. It is called to partake of the prayer and sacrifice of Christ. Daily prayer and the reading of the Word of God strengthens it in charity.

Paragraph 2206: The relationships within the family bring an affinity of feelings, affections and interests, arising above all from the members' respect for one another. The family is a privileged community, called to achieve a sharing of thought and common deliberation by the spouses as well as their eager cooperation as parents in the children's upbringing.

Paragraph 2214: The Divine Fatherhood is the source of human fatherhood. This is the foundation of the honour owed to parents. The respect of children, whether minors or adults, for their father and mother is nourished by the natural affection born of the bond uniting them. It is required by God's commandment.

Paragraph 2215: Respect for parents derives from gratitude toward those who, by the gift of life, their love, and their work, have brought their children into the world and enabled them to grow in stature, wisdom and grace.

"With all your heart honour your father and do not forget the birth pangs of your mother. Remember that through your parents you were born; what can you give back to them that equals their gift to you?" (Sir. 7:27-28).

Paragraph 2216: Filial respect is shown by true docility and obedience.

"My son, keep your Father's commandment and forsake not your mother's teaching ... when you walk, they will lead you; when you lie down, they will watch over you; and when you awake, they will talk with you" (Prov. 6:20-22).

Paragraph 2217: As long as a child lives at home with his parents, the child should obey his parents in all that they ask of him, when it is for his good or that of the family.

"Children, obey your parents in everything, for this pleases the Lord" (Col. 3:20).
Children should also obey the reasonable directions of their teachers and all to whom their parents have entrusted them. But if a child is convinced in conscience that it would be morally wrong to obey a particular order, he must not do so. As they grow up, children should continue to respect their parents. They should

anticipate their wishes, willingly seek their advice and accept their just admonitions. Obedience toward parents ceases with the emancipation of the children; not so respect, which is always owed to them. This respect has its roots in the fear of God, one of the gifts of the Holy Spirit.

Paragraph 2221: The fecundity of conjugal love cannot be reduced solely to the procreation of children, but must extend to their moral education and their spiritual formation. The role of parents in education is of such importance that it is almost impossible to provide an adequate substitute. The right and duty of parents to educate their children are primeval and inalienable.

Paragraph 2222: Parents must regard their children as children of God and respect them as human persons. Showing themselves obedient to the will of the Father in Heaven, they educate their children to fulfil God's law.

Paragraph 2223: Parents have the first responsibility for the education of their children. They bear witness to this responsibility first by creating a home where tenderness, forgiveness, respect, fidelity and disinterested service are the rule. The home is well suited for eduction in the virtues. This requires an apprenticeship in self-denial, sound judgement and self-mastery, the preconditions of all true freedom. Parents should teach their children to subordinate the material and instinctual dimensions to interior and spiritual ones. Parents have a grave responsibility to give good example to their children. By knowing how to acknowledge their own failings to their children, parents will be better able to guide and correct them.

"He who loves his son will not spare the rod. He who disciplines his son will profit by him" (Sir. 30:1-2).

Paragraph 2225: Through the grace of the Sacrament of Marriage, parents receive the responsibility and privilege of evangelising their children. Parents should initiate their children at an early age into the mysteries of the faith of which they are the first heralds for their children. They should associate them from their tenderest years with the life of the church.

Paragraph 2226: Education in the faith by the parents should begin in the child's earliest years ... parents have the mission of teaching their children to pray and to discover their vocation as children of God.

Paragraph 2227: Children in turn contribute to the growth in holiness of their parents. Each and everyone should be generous and tireless in forgiving one another for offenses, quarrels, injustices and neglect. Mutual affection suggests this. The charity of Christ demands it.

Paragraph 2229: As those first responsible for the education of their children, parents have the right to choose a school for them which corresponds to their own convictions. This right is fundamental.

Paragraph 2230: When they become adults, children have the right and duty to choose their profession and state of life. They should assume their new responsibilities within a trusting relationship with their parents, willingly asking and receiving their advice and counsel. Parents should be careful not to exert pressure on their children either in their choice of profession or in that of a spouse. This necessary restraint does not prevent them — quite the contrary — from giving their children judicious advice, particularly when they are planning to start a family.

The foregoing paragraphs beautifully give us the foundation of Catholic Family Life. However, it requires some expansion in order to fully appreciate the jewels which the church offers in its inspired wisdom.

Basically the Catechism teaches that *good parenting is God-parenting.* This means that parents must make every effort to teach their children the ways of God. In doing so they will automatically raise their children in virtue, in self-esteem (which is not to be confused with vanity), in responsible behaviour towards others, in tolerance, moderation and love. The ways of God will also include holy discipline and a recognition of the dignity of honest work. The family is expected to be united in prayer and sacrifice for one another. Parents are commissioned by God to joyfully put aside their own selfish needs and to put themselves out for their offspring. This cannot be properly done in the Catholic manner without daily prayer and a firm grounding in the teachings of Jesus. Mutual esteem must exist amongst all of the family members, without any exceptions. There is no place for favouritism in a Christian family. God has no favourites and neither should parents and if they fall into that trap, they create a selfish self-centeredness in one child and destroy the self-esteem of another.

Parenting can be said to pass through four stages or phases:

1. Pregnancy
2. Childhood
3. Teenage Years
4. Releasing the child into the world.

PHASE I. A child is a gift from God and is the incarnation of God's blessing to a couple. As such, the child enjoys a very special place in the Heart of Jesus. "Let the children come to me, and do not prevent them; for the kingdom of heaven belongs to such as these" (Matt. 19:14).

Parental responsibility actually begins with the act of sexual union. Ideally, this should be a moment of total communion, a true act of selfless love between husband and wife, with a generous openness that if God blesses their love with a new life, they will joyfully welcome it. They will accept and love this child whether it be male or female, intelligent or retarded, healthy or disabled. These are the proper dispositions of Catholic parents towards their sexual love and towards their children who are the fruit of that love.

From the moment that the couple is aware of a pregnancy, they should begin the task of parenting their child. This they do by praying together and by praying over the tiny life in the mother's womb, speaking words of love to the baby and planning together for the baby's welcome into the world. A husband has the indispensable manly duty to promote his wife's emotional, physical and spiritual well-being. Her whole being is focussed on the task of carrying the child growing within her. For her to be completely fruitful in her pregnancy, she should be as free as possible from stress and from having to worry about worldly things. She needs to feel protected, nourished and loved by her husband, whose duty it is to allow her to be fully female, fully mother, and fully free to give her whole self to the precious life she carries.

The as-yet-unborn baby should be welcomed as God's blessing with grateful hearts, and a pledge should be given to God by both parents that they will do their utmost to raise this new little soul in the love of God.

PHASE II. Once born, the baby is a blank blackboard, waiting for his or her parents to write on it. Many of the baby's future personality traits, ideas, dreams and most importantly his beliefs, will depend on what his parents will write on that blackboard. The newborn baby is not born angry or proud or jealous, or hate-filled or frightened or a worrier, nor does he loathe himself. These things are all learned from the parents, if that is what they teach him by their example. If mother worries, the child will soon come to worry simply by imitation. If dad is angry, the child will learn that anger is an acceptable response to frustration.

There is nothing more innocent than a newborn baby. The baby simply lies in his or her crib with total helplessness, waiting for his birthright, which is love, food, clothing, warmth, teaching, protection, and discipline. These are parental duties and this total dependence of the baby and the young toddler is *a dependency ordained by God the Father.*

During the first few years of growth, the child assimilates information and data at a phenomenal rate. This is the most important time for the parents to lay the foundations of the child's personality and beliefs. A Jesuit priest once said, "Give me a child from the age of three to seven and he will be a Catholic for the rest of his life." In other words, right from the beginning, the parents must teach their child about God, Mary, angels and the saints, because that teaching will remain deep in his heart for life, even if he chooses to stray later on. They must teach about love, self-esteem, sharing and friendship, not just how to drink from a cup and hold a spoon. These skills are so vital to the little one's subsequent adulthood, how can we hand over this job to a day-care centre? How can your child learn *your* standards and *your* faith from a paid professional? Certainly, once the child is at school, the mother may legitimately go to work if she wishes, but from the moment of conception to school, the child learns family values only from the mother's lap. Today, no stranger can be trusted to put God into your child's heart. Jealously reserve that duty to yourself, just as the Blessed Mother did. It was she who taught little Jesus everything from his first baby steps to God's Holy Scripture. There were no day-care centres in Nazareth. "Wisdom brings up her own children, so become wisdom and do the same" (Sir. 4:11). "Listen my child, to your father's instruction; do not reject your mother's teaching" (Prov. 1:8).

St. John Vianney said, "Virtue passes easily from the hearts of mothers into the hearts of children." How then can a child receive teaching from his mother, if mother is working an eight-hour shift during the child's most productive time of the day? Father's instruction of his child has to be different since he is the family provider and he must work. Therefore his instruction has to take place outside of his working hours. Even so, it is still a vital fatherly duty, and if he fathers in a slovenly manner, he will do untold damage, both to his child and to his own soul. He has so much to teach about life, about work, about practical survival skills and about manhood.

From conception to the age of around nine years, the most important person in a child's life is definitely the mother. But from the age of nine to sixteen years, the most needed person is the father. The child's healthy growth into a healthy sexual being depends on the presence of a loving and manly father. It is he who models the man his son would like to become, and it is he who models the kind of man his daughter will seek out as a future partner.

"Better die childless than have children who are godless" (Sir. 16:3). That says it all. The first and primary duty of parenting is to teach children about God and his truths. Regardless of what that child may choose to do in adult life regarding the faith, if the parents have not planted the seed of faith in his heart as a toddler, this will be held against them as neglect of the worst order. More will be written about this in chapter 10. It is God, then, who gives us the gift of becoming parents, and he expects that we will behave like parents, not like mere custodians. We must father and we must mother. Our model of father is God himself and our model of mother is Mary.

PHASE III. The teenage years have always been the most difficult challenge to parents throughout the entire history of the human race, but in these times, it is a much more difficult challenge.

Chapter 11 will be devoted to this difficult phase of parenting, but it need not be depressing. This can be a most rewarding time for parents who know how to love, who understand the marvellous changes a teenager is experiencing in his or her body, and who appreciate the struggle of coming to a fuller self-knowledge. Wise parents give their growing teenagers more and more good self-determination as they work towards Phase IV and finally leave home. Again, only love will conquer, together with a great deal of prayer for guidance as a parent. I deeply believe in the power of consecration to Jesus through the Immaculate Heart of Mary for the entire family. This is a great force for safe-guarding our young people from worldly temptations. In her locution to Fr. Gobbi of July 23, 1987, Our Lady said that when a family is consecrated to her, she will take care of the children. "When I enter into a family, I immediately look after the children; they become also mine. I take them by the hand; I lead them to walk along the road of the realization of a plan of God, which has from all eternity already been clearly traced out for each one of them. I love them. I never abandon them. They become a precious part of my maternal estate." Every Catholic parent should rejoice in the knowledge that the Blessed Mother is eager to personally help them in parenting their children and teenagers. The act of Consecration engages the Mother of God to do precisely that. We need all the heavenly help we can get, so it is wise to invite Mary to help us in these difficult years.

PHASE IV: The final act of parenting which all of us must accomplish is releasing the grown child into the world, to fend for himself and to take his rightful place as a responsible citizen in society. Many parents find it surprisingly painful to do so, and this is especially true of mothers. Some mothers completely fail to understand that the time for obedience is over and, as the Catechism tells us, while it is right that they continue to command respect from their adult children, they no longer can exercise legitimate *control* over their children. The umbilical cord must be severed. There are mothers who continue to manipulate their sons and daughters long after they have left home, disapproving of their career decisions, jealous of their choice of spouse, and flatly refusing to accept the spouse as a new son or daughter. Some mothers even insist that sons, for example, show more allegiance to them than to their wives. This is sinful behaviour on the part of parents. I am not denying the pain parents will face when the nest becomes empty, but this must be accepted as a part of life's inevitable cycle. It happens to all of us. "A man shall leave his father and mother and be united to his wife and the two shall become one flesh" (Eph. 5:31). He will be united to his wife, not to his mother.

One day, I was looking out of the kitchen window and I saw a female robin perched on the edge of my raised vegetable garden. She was looking intently at a spot on the lawn. When I looked down I saw a very young robin on the ground. He flapped his little wings, trying to fly, and when he got a couple of inches off the ground, mother bird immediately took to the air and hovered about two feet over the little bird, flapping her wings at high speed. He flopped to the ground again, obviously tired, and mother went back to her perch. This went on several times and I realised that she was, first of all, showing him how to fly by the furious flapping of her wings. By hovering over him, she was also making sure he could not get too much height, so that when he became tired and fell he would not be hurt. Then all of a sudden the little bird finally got it. He rose into the air and triumphantly flew to the upper branches of a large tree. And what did mother do? She flew away! Her last act of mothering had been completed. The little bird was now on his own and would have to fend for himself. Why is it that so many human parents do not seem to know what that mother robin obviously knew?

There are two indispensable ingredients for good Catholic parenting. The first is *love* and the second is ***teaching.***

Love is the foundation stone of human parenting, just as it is the foundation stone of God's parenting. Therefore, just as God is love, so also human parents must strive to be love. A child cannot be spoiled with love. It is impossible. Spoiling a child is only done by lack of discipline and indulging his every whim with things. True love is never a sugar-coated indulgence. On the other hand, true love can never be too much. Love given can only result in love returned and love always bears fruit.

As Catherine Doherty said, "The home should be a school of love," that is to say, a place where children are taught what *sacrificial* love is all about. Love is not easy. It requires more than just a natural parental instinct, and it is much more than simple bonding. Love requires time, effort, thought and patience. It often demands sacrifice of our immediate personal needs or desires. A child needs my time, not my money. For a father, that may mean giving time out of his evenings or weekend hours when he might feel justified in taking his own leisure. It may even demand that he give up a promotion in the best interests of his family. A workaholic father is a neglectful father. A true father balances work and family. He recognises his need to be gainfully employed, but he subordinates that to his most important priority, which is his wife and children. He knows he works for them, not for money or a bigger fishing boat.

For a mother, it means long hours of dedication, often having to love even when she is tired and in need of rest. She may have had to give up a promising career in order to devote herself to the more important career of mothering. The career of a nurse or the president of a big company pales before the awesome career of raising godly children to become responsible citizens and evangelisers for Jesus.

Both parents have to love, often when they do not feel like it, and yet, they must have enough love left over to love each other. How is this possible? It can only be done by constantly asking for the graces freely offered by God through their sacrament of Matrimony. Human effort alone is doomed to failure but, "With God all things are possible" (Luke 1:37). Therefore, parental love must be founded on prayer of petition and intercession, holding up the children to the Father of all children, begging for their well-being and especially for their holiness.

Touching is an indispensable part of loving. There can never be enough hugging in a loving family. Mommy's and daddy's lap should be a safe and familiar place to a child. Where better to hide from a scary world and to feel safe than on a parent's knee? Never deny a frightened child the security and love of your physical closeness. Remember, you were frightened yourself once.

Words of love need to be spoken with sincerity and joy, without strings attached. Never tie love to the child's performance, otherwise the child comes to believe he is only loveable if he is good. This was the unhappy experience of John in the story outlined in chapter 1. It is a parent's duty to make sure the child knows he is loved no matter what he may have done. Discipline should be seen by the child as an act of love, not as a vicious act of vengeance.

Parents should always be willing to listen attentively and to show interest in their child's dreams, problems, career choices, boyfriends or girlfriends, activities, their music, and their growing sexuality. Children need to know they can come to their parents with anything, and that it will be heard with love and fairness. This means that they should be able to come to their parents with **absolutely** anything, even something of which they are ashamed.

It is love which fuels all the desirable outcomes which we cherish for our children. Responsible adults were once loved children. If love is not given in this way, we should not be surprised if the children start to look for their love needs elsewhere. They will look for it in someone else's home, with their friends, of whom you may not approve, or later on in drugs and alcohol, and of course in sex, which is so easily confused with love.

Catherine Doherty once wrote this, "I knew a lady whose housekeeping was so impeccable that all the women of the neighbourhood extolled her, and whose cooking was so perfect that all the men wished their wives could cook so well. Yet, the strange thing was that both her husband and her children were seldom home. Mr. X preferred to spend his evenings 'with the boys,' and the children could invariably be found a few doors away, where the lady of the house and her husband, and her brood welcomed them happily, and gave them the front living room for themselves. Mr. & Mrs. Neighbour spent much time in an old fashioned large kitchen, to which everyone eventually gravitated for cookies and milk, of which there was always an inexhaustible supply. Now Mrs. Neighbour was not a perfect housekeeper. How could she be, with youngsters running in and out all day? With records covering the tables, chairs, not to mention skates, sweaters and such. But the whole house smelled of the wondrous cookies she seemed always to be baking. And the lazy big smile of her husband just drew crowds of boys to talk about anything and everything from fishing to dating."

Is this not a wonderful sketch of a home filled with love and with memories a child will cherish for life? A child does not need worldly things for happiness. He needs love, but if the parents are irritable, quarrelsome and led by a materialistic spirit, then the fire of love will simply die out and the family will find itself living in the cold. The cute little toddler will surely grow up to be a problem teenager and ultimately a problem adult.

Teaching children is a major responsibility for parents. "Train a child in the way he should go, and when he is old he will not depart from it" (Prov. 22:6). As Christians, we believe in the mystical Body of Christ, and just as in any body, each individual cell has a specific function. By carrying out that function, each cell contributes to the health and well-being of the body. If, however, a cell rebels, then it becomes a threat to the integrity of the body. Children, as individual cells in the Body of Christ, need to be taught by their parents in order that they will take on full responsibility for their own unique function in the Body of Christ and as future citizens in our society.

Parents must be sensitive to the fact that all of their children are uniquely different, with various gifts according to the will of the Holy Spirit. Parents have the duty to nurture and develop those gifts, respecting the differences between their children, because one child may be studious, another good with his or her hands, another artistic and so on. Parents must beware of imposing their ambitions and desires onto a child. That is a sinful parental dictatorship which will destroy a child's self-image and can easily kill God's gifts to that child. Years ago when I used to take my little boy to hockey practice, I was often shocked to see a father and mother screaming at their own little boy (who clearly had no hockey talent) to score, to body-check and to skate beyond his ability. What an intolerable burden on a child who, deep in his own heart, knows he cannot meet such expectations. He was robbed of his right to find joy in play. In the early days of my son's hockey career, he spent a lot of time falling down but he and I both had a great time. Today, we can both laugh about it, but we also know that he learned a lot about his own abilities and about team spirit. My son knows how not to let the side down in life and he learned this well, precisely because he had fun learning it.

Teaching means thorough instruction in all necessary things, from moral values to good manners. However, the child has to **understand clearly** what is asked of him and must be shown gently how to carry out a command correctly. If the child is confused, then he will blow his assignment and come to think of himself as a failure. A parent has no right to expect good workmanship in a child if the parent does not invest time and effort to instruct him clearly. It will save hours of heartbreak if parents properly train the first one or two children well. The later children will observe the older ones applying themselves, and so they will follow by imitation.

Parents must also teach their children moral values as well as work. **Truthfulness, faith and modesty** are three vital virtues for children. Parents should demonstrate a deep disgust for lying, for unbelief in God, and for immodesty, and instill these principles into their children. Lying is a sin, and children must very quickly come to understand this. Lying arises out of pre-meditation, cunning and cold calculation, and is therefore deserving of a more severe punishment. Satan is the prince of lies, and he must not be allowed a foothold in your child's heart. The truth, and nothing but the truth, must rule in your home.

Children must be taught to have a firm unswerving belief in God and his doctrines. Lack of faith leads to the modern heresy of doubting everything, of scepticism, which is extolled today in our schools and universities. Scepticism is the devil's tool. Faith is our weapon against it. Teach your children to put on the armour of God every morning to protect them from the onslaughts of Satan.

"Stand your ground, with truth a belt around your waist and uprightness for a breastplate, wearing for shoes on your feet the eagerness to spread the gospel of peace and always carrying the shield of faith so that you can use it to quench the burning arrows of the Evil One. And then you must take salvation as your helmet and the sword of the Spirit, that is, the Word of God" (Eph. 6:14-17). Have your child imagine himself putting on this powerful armour every morning and he will likely be strong in the Lord for the rest of the day.

Modesty is under vicious attack these days and it seems people have become shockproof. Young people today embrace the most insulting immodesty in manner of dress, speech, and body language, and they display these on the street, in school, and often in church. This cannot be justified by saying that because the rest of the world is immodest, our youngsters must conform to the world's standards. The world is not interested in modesty. A Christian must swim against the current and establish God's standards of modesty if he is to follow Jesus at all. If the Queen of England were to be introduced to me, would I receive her in cut off shorts and a revealing shirt? More likely I would rush to put on my very best clothes in an effort to be "presentable." How much more, then, should we make a supreme effort to be presentable to the King of kings at all times. If a Christian mother dresses provocatively, which not too long ago was done only by women of loose virtue, then will she be shocked to see her teenage daughter go off to school, inviting boys to lust by her same manner of dress? Does this mother realize the consequences of such immodesty? Her daughter has lost respect for the miracle of her body and so will think very little of losing her virginity, and once that is lost, she may think very little of promiscuity.

Boys, who are so easily aroused and often think that their manhood depends on being a successful sexual hunter, will be only too willing to take advantage of this cheaply available sex-without-responsibility. That sets the scene for venereal disease, H.I.V. infection, illegitimate pregnancy, contraception, abortion, and loss of the Christian vision of each other as holy children of God. It cheapens that vision by reducing women to mere objects of unholy desire and tempts men to use them for their own selfish pleasure.

A Christian household must have rules, but the rules must be reasonable. It is just as destructive to have too many rules as to have none at all. Too many rules confine a child to a rigid stifling environment in which he cannot grow or explore, while no rules create anarchy in the home and violate the divine order. While children may kick against the rules because they want to do as they please (don't we all?), they fail to realize that they depend on their parents to establish order in their lives and to render their world manageable. I often hear nonsense from parents who say, "I can't do anything with little Johnny." Of course they can. What they are really saying is, "I can't do anything with little Johnny because I can't be bothered to do anything with little Johnny. I don't want to put out the effort. I don't want to give up some of my comfort or pleasure. I don't want to be unpopular." Well, take the time and be unpopular now or regret it later. The rewards will be multiplied a thousand-fold in the end. What a child thinks of you when he is being chastised is irrelevant. What the child thinks of you twenty years down the road is much more important.

Here is what one young housewife wrote about her mother (with a lot of tongue in cheek, but a lot of wisdom): "I had the meanest mother in the world. While other kids ate candy for breakfast, I had to have cereal, eggs or toast. When others had cokes and candy for lunch, I had to eat a sandwich. As you can guess, my supper was different from the other kids also. But at least I wasn't alone in my sufferings. My sister and two brothers had the same mean mother as I did. My mother insisted upon knowing where we were at all times. You'd think we were on a chain gang. She had to know who our friends were and what we were doing. She insisted if we said we'd be gone an hour, that we be gone one hour or less, not one hour and one minute. I am really ashamed to admit it, but she actually struck us. Not once, but each time we had a mind of our own and did as we pleased. That poor belt was used more on our seats than it was to hold up daddy's pants. Can you imagine someone actually hitting a child just because he disobeyed? Now you can see how mean she really was. We had to wear clean clothes and take a bath. The other kids always wore their clothes for days. We reached the heights of insult because she made our clothes herself just to save money. Why, oh why, did we have to have a mother who made us feel different from our friends?

"The worst is yet to come. We had to be in bed by nine each night and up at eight the next morning. We couldn't sleep till noon like our friends. So while they slept, my mother actually had the nerve to break the child-labour law. She made us work. We had to wash dishes, make beds, learn to cook and all sorts of cruel things. I believe she lay awake at night thinking up mean things to do to us. She always insisted upon our telling the truth, the whole truth and nothing but the truth, even if it killed us, and it nearly did. By the time we were teenagers, she was much wiser and our life became even more unbearable. None of this tooting of the horn of a car for us to come running. She embarrassed us no end by making our dates and friends come to the door to get us. If I spent the night with a girlfriend, can you imagine she checked on me to see if I were really there? I never had the chance to elope to Mexico. That is if I'd had a boyfriend to elope with. I forgot to mention, while my friends were dating at the mature age of twelve and thirteen, my old-fashioned mother refused to let me date until the age of fifteen and sixteen. Fifteen, that is, if you dated only to go to a school function. And that was maybe twice a year.

"Through the years, things didn't improve a bit. We could not lie in bed 'sick' like our friends did, and miss school. If our friends had a toe-ache, a hang-nail or other serious ailment, they could stay home from school. Our marks in school had to be up to par. Our friends' report cards had beautiful colours on them, black for passing, red for failing. My mother, being as different as she was, would settle for nothing less than ugly black marks. As the years rolled by, first one and then the other of us was put to shame. We were graduated from high school. With our mother behind us, talking, hitting and demanding respect, none of us was allowed the pleasure of being a drop-out.

"My mother was a complete failure as a mother. Out of four children, a couple of us attained some higher education. None of us has ever been arrested, divorced or beaten his mate. Each of my brothers served his time in the service of his country. And whom do we blame for the terrible way we turned out? You're right, our mean mother. Look at all the things we missed. We never got to march in a protest parade, nor to take part in a riot, burn draft cards, and a million and one other things that our friends did. She forced us to grow up into God-fearing, educated, honest adults. Using this as a background, I am trying to raise my three children. I stand a little taller and I am filled with pride when my children call me mean. Because, you see, I thank God, he gave me the meanest mother in the world."

This lady has learned, on looking back to her childhood, just how dedicated, loving, and wise her mother really was. Her negative opinion of her mother, when she was a mere child, did not matter at all. What mattered was that as an adult she was able to appreciate mother's wisdom. Mother did not try to win a popularity contest with her young daughter. She hung in for the long haul and won her daughter's admiration years later. We should take the same delight in raising our children to become responsible citizens and disciples of Jesus Christ.

Catholic parents would do well to remember one most important thing. Many, many parents come to me and complain that their son is alcoholic, or their daughter is living with her boyfriend, or their kids have all left the church. They constantly ask themselves where they went wrong. God left lots of room for free enterprise. He gave us a very wide margin for error. Most of us parent according to our best ability and if I am a bad parent, I know it in my deepest heart. But the vast majority of us are good parents, and we should comfort ourselves with the thought that most of our rebellious teenagers eventually grow up to be responsible people. It is a fact that, no matter how much we have done imperfectly, most kids do grow up. What they have learned as little children usually comes back to them later on, once they have checked out the sinful side of the tracks. So give up feeling guilty. If your children are now of legal age and are choosing rebellion, they are now God's job. All you are asked to do is pray for them. You do not need your child's permission to do that. Call on God to perfect that which we all do imperfectly.

Most parents would like to know how they are doing and how they stack up against other parents. I have printed here a "Spiritual Check-up for the Married." It is not my invention, but it is a wonderful little tool for Catholic couples. It might help some to recognize a flaw and take steps to correct it while there is still time.

Duties Toward God and Each Other:

1. Am I in earnest about saving my soul, as well as my husband's (or wife's) and children's souls?
2. Do I go to Confession and receive Holy communion at least once a month, realizing that it is the best thing I can do to bring happiness and blessing upon my family, because I thereby bring God into it?
3. Do I try to attend Holy Mass and receive Holy communion even on weekdays if it is possible?
4. Do I recite my Rosary daily and invoke the blessing and protection of the Blessed Virgin upon my family?
5. Do I permit mortal sin to harm the peace and happiness of my home and bring down God's judgement upon it by missing Mass on Sundays and holy days, by drunkenness, by giving scandal to my children, by not keeping my marriage chaste and holy?
6. Do I avoid in my language vulgarity and cursing?
7. Do I speak to my husband (or wife) in a way that betokens love, or am I in the habit of nagging, complaining, arguing or refusing to talk?
8. Do I lose my temper easily and frequently, want to have my own way, and always consider myself right?
9. When differences arise, do I discuss them with my husband (or wife) calmly and honestly?
10. Do I overlook the shortcomings of my husband (or wife) or do I hold grudges against him (or her)?
11. Do I discuss the faults of my husband (or wife) with others?
12. Have I made it a point to do those little things for my husband (or wife) which keep love alive in the human heart, or have I given my love to another?
13. Am I neat in appearance to please my husband (or wife)?
14. Do I keep things secret from my husband (or wife) which he (or she) ought to know?
15. Am I happy about sharing the intimacies of married life, or am I selfish and inconsiderate, thinking only of my personal satisfaction?

16. Have I shirked motherhood (or fatherhood) and yet taken the pleasures connected with my state of life, or offended God by the terrible sin of birth prevention?
17. Have I given my husband (or wife) a good example, especially by frequent reception of the Sacraments and prayer?

Duties Toward Their Children:

1. Am I conscious of the sublime dignity of parenthood and its grave responsibility?
2. Do I give my children a good example in the matter of frequenting the Sacraments, praying, keeping from sin?
3. Do my children ever hear me use improper language, tell questionable stories, talk unkindly about others?
4. Am I impatient and irritable in dealing with my children?
5. Am I loving but firm in correcting my children, and do I discuss their development and progress with my husband (or wife)?
6. Do I send my children to a truly Catholic school, if possible, or at least to Catechism classes? If not, do I see to it myself that they are given true Catholic education?
7. Do I know my children's companions, reading, types of recreation?
8. Am I interested in their school work and in preparing them for their future?
9. What would be, or has been, my reaction to a religious vocation in the family?
10. Is my outside work and recreation depriving my children of proper care and protection?
11. Is there any questionable literature in my home?
12. Do I do everything possible to make my home a clean, happy, and pleasant place for my children to live in, or do I waste much of my money and time outside my home?
13. Are my children proud of their mother (or father)?
14. Do I pray fervently each day for my husband (or wife) and children?

If we took this to heart and lived it out, we would be rightfully proud of our children as they grow to become wholesome and holy adults. We would one day be able to stand before Jesus and say, "I was not a perfect parent but, by the grace of God, I was a Catholic parent."

CHAPTER 9

Parenting: God's Discipline for Children

"Children, obey your parents
in the Lord, for this is right."
(Eph. 6:1)

The Oxford Dictionary defines discipline as "instruction, mental and moral training, the maintenance of order, *chastisement and mortification by penance.*" In other words, discipline can be achieved by a variety of strategies such as good example, teaching, explanation, repetition of lessons, encouragement and if necessary, punishment. Punishment can mean different things for different situations and different children.

For today's permissive society, discipline is a forbidden word, and our godless culture naively believes that it can raise disciplined children by giving them no discipline at all. Discipline is fundamental to a Christian. The Bible mentions discipline fifty-eight times, so it can safely be concluded that, since God took the trouble to talk about discipline in fifty-eight different ways, discipline is very important to God's order.

God's order is founded on obedience. It was Jesus who decreed that the Holy Father obey Jesus Christ. The bishops are to obey the Holy Father, the priests obey the bishops, parents obey the priests and children obey their parents. This is the moral hierarchy of obedience. God disciplines us and we in turn discipline our children.

It is very important to appreciate that by disciplining our children we are *not* imposing our *will* upon our children, rather we are being *obedient* to the word of God. As was emphasised in chapter 8, *good-parenting is God-parenting.*

> *"So you must realize that the Lord your God*
> *disciplines you, even as a man disciplines his son."*
>
> (Deut. 8:5)

> *"Whoever loves discipline, loves knowledge. Stupid*
> *are those who hate correction."*
>
> (Prov. 12:1)

> *"Discipline your children while there is hope; Do*
> *not set your heart on their destruction"*
>
> (Prov. 19:18)

From these scripture passages, it is evident that:

1. We discipline because God disciplines.
2. Without discipline, a child can have no worthwhile knowledge. So discipline and learning go hand in hand.
3. We must discipline children while there is hope. That is to say, we must begin to discipline a child at the earliest possible age.
4. The obedience of a child is not *optional.* It is *demanded* by God.

Great care must nevertheless be exercised. While discipline may at times use correction, not all correction is true discipline. Correction or punishment can sometimes be brutal, excessive, and cruel, and that constitutes child abuse. Christian discipline is principally a fatherly prerogative, since it is derived from God the Father, and it is always designed to save, to purify, and to heal. "Not for vengeance did the Lord put them in the crucible to try their hearts, nor has he done so with us. It is by way of *admonition* that he chastises those who are close to him" (Judith 8:27). As it is for God, so it is for Christian parents. Punishment is an act of *love,* not an act of *vengeance.*

"If you wish it my child, you can be taught. Apply yourself and you will become intelligent" (Sir. 6:32). Are these not the words of a loving and gentle Father? Yet, love must not be confused with permissiveness. "Pamper your child and he will terrorise you, play along with him and he will bring you sorrows?" (Sir. 30:9). This is exactly what we are seeing in our society today. We are being terrorised by a whole generation of pampered children. I have seen a family utterly controlled by a five-year-old child running riot. He spits, he stamps his feet, he screams for what he wants, and his distraught parents give it to him. He breaks his toys then throws a tantrum till he gets a replacement. He is in fact a child abused by neglect, who is trying to find the boundaries, but can never reach them because his parents do not give him any. It is so easy for parents to lose or relinquish their legitimate and God-given authority. How can parents take back what has been lost and give back to children what they do not know they have lost? It is accomplished by means of loving discipline and just discipline.

The first and most fundamental prerequisite for just discipline is to *know* your child. All children are unique and different, they come in all shapes and sizes, and what is good discipline for one child may be disastrous for another. A rebellious child may respond to more severe correction, while a sensitive child may be totally crushed by it.

Many parents make the mistake of trying to treat all of their children exactly alike, in the belief that equality is the same thing as justice. It is not. A father once told me that he was disturbed that his two very young daughters seemed always to be fighting with each other. As an experiment he bought them two identical toy cribs with identical little comforters and identical little dolls. He gave one set to Susan and one to Melissa. They were delighted at first, but within a half hour, they were fighting over one crib. Susan screamed, "It is mine!" while Melissa yelled back, "No, it isn't. It is mine." Meanwhile, the other crib was lying over in the corner being ignored. Treating children identically does not work. Their very uniqueness demands individualised parenting.

Only the parents can know their own children and it is the duty of parents to observe their children, to know how sensitive each one is, and to respond accordingly. A day-care attendant cannot understand your child and his special needs. God gave your children to *you*, not to paid professionals.

All of us have moods both good and bad, both high and low, and our children do too. But little children do not understand their low moods, and they will often express their bad feelings with bad behaviour. As grown ups, however, we must understand that hidden behind every low mood there is a temporary insecurity. Whenever we feel insecure, we will experience a low mood, and a low mood tempts us to give in to anger, anxiety, fear, sadness, hurt, jealousy and other negative feelings.

Imagine little Johnny. He is angry. He is sitting on the rug and he is demolishing his dump truck. He is tearing the wheels off it and throwing them away, and is pounding the truck into a shapeless pulp. If all you see when you observe this is his destructive behaviour, then you will feel justified in yelling at him, "Who do you think you are? Don't you know I had to work hard to get the money to buy that dump truck? How dare you show such ingratitude. Well, you are grounded, mister. Go to your room." Little Johnny will have to react to your punishment and he will react by having his mood plummet even lower. He will therefore feel even more insecure, and so he is likely to throw a major, out-of-control tantrum. Instead of attacking his dump truck, he is more likely to start trashing your house! However, if instead of merely judging his behaviour, you look beyond that and see that he is feeling insecure and that what he is doing is expressing his low mood, then you might react very differently.

In the light of this insight, you could distract him from the useless truck demolition enterprise by lifting him up onto your knee. Then you might say, "Johnny. Let's just sit here for a while and let me love you." There is no need for words at this point. A silent hug will speak volumes. Then when Johnny is feeling more secure, you can talk. "Johnny, you were feeling really bad there, weren't you?" "Yes, mom." "You sort of wanted me to know that, right?" "Yes, mom." "Well, do you think that it was a good idea to smash up your dump truck just to let me know how bad you feel, because now you don't have a dump truck to play with any more?" (Notice I did not say that you would rush out and buy him a replacement. He trashed it so he will have to do without. A child must learn that there are consequences to actions.) "No mom." "So what are you upset about Johnny?" "I heard daddy say he was leaving us." "Oh, that's the problem! No, Johnny. Dad is only going away for a couple of days on business. He isn't leaving us. He is coming back on Tuesday. Why don't you and I do something special for daddy when he comes home? So listen, Johnny, the next time you are feeling bad, instead of breaking your toys, why don't you tell me you're feeling bad, and we'll work something out, OK?" "OK, mom." And off he goes to play. First of all, he is reassured about his fear; secondly, he is learning there is a better way to express his insecurity; and thirdly, he has learned that some behaviours merely end up by hurting himself. In this case, he no longer has a dump truck. Naturally, this takes time, but it is time well-spent. It means dropping some agenda of your own in order to listen to your child, but only you, the parent, can understand that what Johnny was doing was not out of malice, but out of a low mood. Another of your children may do the same thing with his dump truck, but you know that with him it is not a mood but *rebellion,* and that must be handled differently.

The second most important tool for discipline is *love*, because effective discipline is loving discipline. There is no other way. It is loving discipline which we receive from our heavenly parent, God the Father, and he expects us to discipline in like manner. "For the Lord disciplines those whom he loves" (Heb. 12:6). Likewise, we who love our children are to discipline them also. In fact, discipline and love go hand-in-glove. Discipline without love is nothing more than tyranny, and love without discipline is indulgence. Loving discipline generates love in the child. Loveless discipline generates fear which renders the child incapable of performing almost any task. Disciplineless love generates disobedience, which reaps the whirlwind of an out-of-control child. Needless to say, this concept of love is so often misunderstood by parents and they wonder why they are raising aliens from outer space, instead of children.

Gary Smallery, a well known counsellor, identifies four types of parents: **Dominant, Neglectful, Permissive, Firm Lovers.**

Dominant parents tend to have excessively high expectations of their children. They expect them to be perfect in everything. They seldom offer warm, loving support and they seldom help the child understand why the rules have to be so rigid. The result is that when the child does not know why something is wrong, he will tend to secretly do that wrong thing. A major study out of Columbia County, New York, found that high aggression in younger children is often caused by overly dominant parents. This aggression usually lasts a lifetime and can lead to major violence. The study also showed that harsh punishment, such as washing out a child's mouth with soap, coupled with rejection will always lead to aggressive behaviour.

Neglectful parents neither give loving support to their children nor do they exercise control over them. They isolate themselves from their children by excessive use of baby-sitters, and they forever indulge in their own selfish activities. Neglect of children in our society occurs for four reasons:

1. Divorce

The current high divorce rate leads to single parent families. The divorce rate has increased seven hundred per cent since the beginning of the century, and as a result a single mother has to be both provider and parent. While it does not absolutely have to happen, it is difficult for a single mother not to be emotionally distant from her children, simply because she is so burdened and exhausted. In spite of that risk, numerous courageous and dedicated single mothers should be applauded for their often awesome commitment to their children. They are heroines in a broken society.

2. Absentee Parents

Dr. Amand Nicholi, a psychiatrist at Harvard Medical School, warns that by going out to work, mothers are less accessible to their young children. One study he quoted shows that American parents spend less time with their children than parents in any other nation in the world, except England. A Russian father said he would not think of spending less than two hours a day with his children. By contrast, the average father in the U.S. spends about thirty-seven seconds a day with his children! I still have difficulty believing that statistic, but there it is, like it or not.

3. Television

Television has become a major child rearing resource, and not for the better. The problem with television is that even though people are physically together in a room, there is no meaningful and emotional interaction going on. As parents neglect their children by watching T.V. or other activities, children experience a powerful emotional loss similar to that of losing a parent through death. The child can come to believe that the reason for this is that he is bad and so his self-esteem is seriously wounded. He needs more than just your physical presence — he needs loving interaction.

4. Frequent Relocation

Society today is increasingly mobile. Moving house every three to five years robs children of a stable, manageable and predictable environment. They become isolated from their extended family and school friends, and if mum and dad are simply dragging their children all over the country without helping them to understand, then the children become insecure and uprooted.

Permissive parents are often warm, supporting persons, but are very weak when it comes to establishing and enforcing rules and limits for their children. They live in fear of confronting their children, not realizing that failure to confront will produce the very things they fear. Good parents know that a certain degree of permissiveness is healthy. They accept that children will be children, that a clean shirt will not stay clean for long, that a mirror is for making faces, and puddles are for splashing. But over-permissiveness cuts children loose, allowing them to beat up other children, to break valuable objects, and to write on walls. The child learns that the rules are not rules at all. They are simply there to be ignored.

Firm loving parents combine loving support with loving discipline. They take time to help their children understand the rules. They are flexible and willing to listen so that they themselves understand fully why their child has done something and, as a result, the child is more content. He has learned to control himself. He is more secure because he knows he is loved. He knows that his parents are investing time and effort in him, that they are strong, and thus he is safe in their care. Study after study confirms that children of loving and firm parents rank highest in self-respect, and obedience to authorities at school, church and society. They also have a greater interest in their parents' faith in God, and a greater tendency not to join a rebellious group. "How blessed are all who fear Yahweh, who walk in his ways. Your own labours will yield you a living, happy and prosperous will you be. Your wife a fruitful vine in the inner places of your house, your children round your table like shoots of an olive tree. Such are the blessings that fall on those who fear Yahweh" (Ps. 128:1-4).

Ed Piorek, who has done a powerful work on the meaning of fatherhood in God's design, tells of a distraught father who came to him one day and said, "Ed, I am at my wits end. My son is out of control. He is into drugs, sex, defying my curfews, you name it! I yell at him, threaten him, and impose bigger and bigger punishments on him, but it is all to no effect. What can I do?" Ed looked at him for a minute in silence, then softly said, "Dan, how has your heavenly Father fathered you?" Dan was stunned. Tears filled his eyes and he said, "God has always graced me. He has always loved me and I have not done this with my son. God forgive me." Dan repented, went off and began to treat his son with love and with respect. He began to *listen* to his son's heart. As a result, the boy began to turn around and come back to the family love he always desired, and which he felt forced to seek outside of his home.

The third tool of discipline is *prayer*. Ask the Holy Spirit to come into your heart in every situation related to your children. The Holy Spirit is available free of charge every moment of every day so why rely on your own limited notions when you can have the inspiration of Wisdom itself? Before you utter a word of correction to your child, breathe a prayer to the Holy Spirit for wisdom in your discipline. You will receive that wisdom. It is promised in Scripture by Jesus himself. "If you, then, who are wicked, know how to give good gifts to your children, how much more will the Father in Heaven give the Holy Spirit to those who ask him?" (Luke 11:13).

The fourth tool of discipline is *example.* There is no use in asking your child to do something if you do not do it yourself. It is pointless to say, "Don't drink, son" while you are slurring your speech with a beer in your hand. Parents must show order in their lives if they are to expect order from their children. If you demand that your little daughter pick up her toys or that your teenage son tidy his room, you must also be a model of tidiness. If you expect your child to obey the ten commandments, you had better be seen to obey them also. If you expect him to go to Mass, you must be faithful to it. But it is not enough just to do those things, you must demonstrate joy in them. Show your child how happy you are in obeying God and the Church. The child will pick up on your enthusiasm and try to please you too. Good example justifies your demands. The message to the child is, "Do as I say, because I also do as I say."

Dr. David Posen, a psychotherapist, recounts how he helped a father who was very anxious about his son's disobedience. The man said, "Doctor, I can't do anything with him. He comes home from school and drops his satchel on the hall floor. No matter how much I tell him, he just will not change his slovenly habit." Dr. Posen thought for a moment and said, "Joe, where do you leave your briefcase when you come home from the office?" Joe's face was a sudden picture of surprise. "Oh no!" he said, "I drop it in the hall and it stays there all night till I go out to work in the morning." The solution was obvious. Dad had to learn to change his bad habit before he had the authority to demand the same from his son.

There are some practical guidelines for effective and loving discipline — for true Christian discipline. In order to do this, I will give examples of how to handle specific situations, but most importantly I want to empower parents with an understanding of the principles in order to gain the best results from a child rather than unwittingly bringing out the worst in him or her.

In the Catholic tradition, the first principle is that liberty for a child means the *freedom to do what is right,* but the child must defer to authority at all times in determining what is wrong. This is fundamental to good Catholic parenting. Parents would do well to write this out, stick it up on the door of the fridge and memorise it. It would avoid many power struggles and pain for both the parents and the child.

A child has the right to do what is pleasing and interesting to him, provided that what he is doing is not wrong or dangerous or destructive to property. Parents often make the mistake of diverting a child from some activity which he finds fascinating, but which the parent sees as useless. In so doing, that parent is choking off the child's initiative to explore his environment and to achieve a task which he believes to be important. For example, dad notices his child is carefully taking a small spoon and scooping up some sand to put it in his bucket. Dad can see that this is going to take hours and hours. The child is totally absorbed in the task, but dad, a) desires to help him and, b) is impatient at the obvious waste of time of this pointless task. So dad, with the best will in the world, goes over, picks up a man-sized shovel and with one scoop fills the bucket. The child collapses in tears of frustration and dad, totally puzzled, becomes angry with the child. "After all," thinks dad, "the object was to fill the bucket and I was only showing him how to do it more quickly." Dad is also thinking how dumb it was for his child to be using a spoon. But dad has missed the point. The object in the child's mind was not to fill the bucket. The object for him was to repeat a complicated manoeuvre over and over again so as to train his muscles, eyes and balance, and to do it well. As an adult, dad was goal-oriented. As a child, little Johnny was method-oriented. Johnny is not yet old enough to figure out the *why.* He is too busy figuring out the *how to.* Johnny had a right to play for hours with the spoon, the sand, and the bucket. He was not doing anything wrong, and he should have been given the freedom to do what was right, even if it seemed pointless to the parent. It is rarely pointless to the child.

The second principle of discipline is that a child must come to gradually understand the difference between ***good and evil.*** That understanding, of course, must become more and more sophisticated as the child grows older. "When I was a child, I spoke like a child, I thought like a child, I reasoned like a child. When I became an adult, I put an end to childish things" (1 Cor. 13:11). Therefore, ***do***

not give adult information to a little child. The child is not ready for these things, and will be seriously damaged by such premature information. That is why I am not a supporter of current sex-education programs in Catholic schools. The children are not ready for the information given. The system completely fails to recognize that children, like little Johnny with the spoon, the sand and the bucket, learn by imitation, by rehearsing and by repetition. A child will try to make sense of this sex-education information by doing it, not by reflecting on it. The sex class becomes a "How-to" class, at least that is how the child will *perceive* it.

This will no doubt shock many Catholic parents, but I believe that *premature sex-education is child sexual abuse.* Everyone agrees that any adult who exposes himself to a little child, or touches a child intimately, or has intercourse with a child, is *sexualizing* that child. That is called sexual abuse. Providing premature sex education to a young child also sexualizes that child, and so it too is a form of sexual abuse. They are little innocents and deep within, they know that their innocence is being violated. Educators do this with the best will in the world, and I am sure many will be offended by what I have written, but these remarks are not meant to be offensive. Rather, they are meant to promote an honest re-assessment of what has become an unchallenged assumption. I believe that the well-intentioned efforts of Catholic educators often betray a sad lack of understanding of child psychology. A child will ask questions when he is ready for the answers. He should not be robbed of his precious childhood.

Illegitimate pregnancy and sexually-transmitted diseases (S.T.D.'s) are not prevented by sex education, but rather are promoted by it. They are prevented only by abstinence and by teaching the child about the virtue of modesty. *Education in modesty is the only sound Catholic sex-education.* It is a frightening fact that illegitimate pregnancies and S.T.D.'s are increasing at an alarming rate in spite of widespread sex-education programs. Is it not possible that these very programs are contributing to this increase? Only by returning to instruction in chastity and the sanctity of the body can we ever hope to protect our cherished children. Wise parents instinctively know how to wait for the right moment, which will be different for each of their children. Only the parents know enough to discern this right moment for their child. But classroom sex education mass-processes children, as though they were all at the same stage of receptivity. Pope John Paul II has solemnly announced his opposition to current sex-education programs and it is encouraging for me as a Catholic therapist to know that my foregoing remarks are in accord with the teaching of the Holy Father.

The third principle is that Christian discipline consists of *silence and activity.* A little child should be given repeated lessons in silence, but in *active silence*, not *forced immobility.* The very young child should be engaged in a game that teaches him how to be silent. Make it an adventure. Ask him to show you how silent he can be so that not a sound or a movement is made. Ask him to listen in the silence to see if he can hear a whispered word or name. Show him how to be silent. This is vital. Do not command him to be quiet and sit still. Show him how to get up without making a sound, without scraping the chair on the floor. Then ask him to do it. Show him how to walk silently. Then ask him to do it. Make it a fun game. This is silence in action, not enforced inertia. Encourage him to repeat these actions till he can be silent and attentive, then congratulate him on a job well done. You will be amazed at how he will learn, not only to hear a whispered or quiet command, but will be delighted to obey it to show you how clever he is. Alternate periods of silence with activity and the child will learn about his body, how to control his movements, and so will learn self-discipline.

He will also learn the value of silence when he comes to meditate later on in prayer. Many young people today are afraid of silence and so they assault their ears continually with blaring music from stereos and radios. Silence is vital if we are ever to contemplate the mysteries of God. Such a child will instinctively feel his success, and will grow in self-esteem as he learns to conquer both himself and his environment and he will come to value his own thoughts.

This kind of discipline should begin at the earliest possible age. A child is never too young. From birth, he is absorbing information at a phenomenal rate. Before he can use language, he is watching you and preparing to imitate you. Apart from the words "mama" and "papa" one of the first words he will learn is "no." If he is doing something harmful or undesirable, no matter how young, let him hear a gentle but firm "No." Then distract him from the undesirable behaviour and into another activity.

Effective discipline must be active. A child is not disciplined who is rendered mute or totally immobile by force. Rather, he is annihilated. A disciplined person is one who has learned to master himself, and who regulates his own conduct. Give him the freedom to move and in so doing, he will learn to perform easily and correctly the simple acts of community and social life. However, the limit or boundary to the child's liberty is the common good. We must check in the child any rough or ill-bred actions, or whatever offends or annoys others. All the rest should be permitted. We often do not appreciate the consequences of suffocating a child's spontaneous action at a time when he is just becoming active.

Believe it or not, a parent has to learn a certain passive role, observing the child's behaviour, rather than dominating it. Parental duty is to discern which are the acts to hinder and which to leave alone. For example, a little girl gathered her friends around her in class and began talking and gesticulating. The teacher rushed forward and told her to be still and to keep quiet. What the teacher did not take the time to find out was that the child was taking the role of teacher and was teaching her friends the Hail Mary and the Sign of the Cross.

Mother is tidying up the living room. The child comes and picks up things. Mother says sternly, "Leave those alone." As a result the child is crushed. He learns that it is not good to try and imitate mummy and to help her. Mother has missed an opportunity to give a lesson in tidiness, a lesson the child was clearly ready for.

A child is watching others. He cannot see what they are doing, so he gets the brilliant idea of bringing over a chair. He intends to climb onto it in order to see. Suddenly a well-meaning adult comes along and lifts him up and says, "There you are. Now you can see." That adult has stifled the child's inventiveness in conquering a problem. Instead, the child is being taught that others will solve all his problems. *The child who does not do, does not know how to do.* How often have you seen a parent dress a child as though the child were a doll or a puppet? Much better to encourage him to experiment with dressing himself, and if he puts the right shoe on the left foot, do not scorn him or ridicule him. Tell him how good he is for trying, then show him the difference between a right shoe and a left one. Mark the shoes with two coloured laces, red for right, yellow for left. He will get the hang of it. He wants to.

The fourth principle is that as soon as possible, it is vital to give your child a sense of *work*. Work was decreed by God, because God himself worked, and God continues to work. In six days, he worked at creating the universe, and he works constantly at his on-going creative process, making new souls and revealing his face to us in research, new knowledge and new discoveries. We must inculcate work into our children right from the beginning. A working child is not getting into mischief. A working teenager is not hanging out on the street corner looking for trouble.

Give the young child a role to play in the organization of the house. He must be shown that you expect him to do his assigned job but, for him to do it well, he must understand what is expected of him. So show him. Do the job yourself and show him how you want it done. Hang in there with him, encouraging him, congratulating him and gently correcting him till he gets it right. This whole exercise of learning a new skill should be made into an exciting adventure. Do not just say, "Do it" and then give him heck when he is confused and messes up. He has no idea, on his own, what is a good performance and what is bad.

While he is learning, do not focus on what he does wrong. Focus, rather on what he does right. Congratulate him and hug him. Show him your pleasure at his efforts. Where he is not doing things quite right, encourage him, show him again and he will put his little heart into it, because instinctively he wants to please you and to be loved by you. Once he masters one job, start him off on another and work at that till he gets that one right, and so on. Work teaches discipline and work is discipline. In taking time to do this, you are teaching your child responsible work habits. Later, as an adult, he will expect to work, he will take pride in his work and he will accept responsibility.

If you inculcate good work habits in your children as soon as you can communicate with them, they will come to accept that responsible behaviour is preferable to sloth, and is a great deal more satisfying. Delinquents have too much free time. As one judge put it, "Football players don't get into trouble during football season. They are too tired at night to do anything but fall into bed. After the season, they start to roam around and some of them turn up at Juvenile Hall." Thelma Hatfield, an educator, once wrote, "Parents, you must teach and train your children so they will like to work or at least when faced with a piece of hard work, be able to get in and do it without suffering oppression. A lazy Christian never did anything for God. When you get your child to do a long and tedious piece of work, do not permit him to dispute and enlarge upon redundant details in order to build obstacles, or to be just generally irritable, because he must work, thinking he will wear you out and soon be able to leave the job undone. If you are not firm here, this spirit will possess him, and when he is an adult and expected to make something of himself, he will fail, because he was trained to avoid and oppose that which is unpleasant."

Note that a lazy adult is only doing what he was allowed to do in his childhood years. A child who is permitted to play, play, play from morning to night for eighteen years will expect to play for the next fifty years. All work and no play will surely make Jack a dull boy, but all play and no work will make him a grown-up slob. How can such a person ever face the challenge of weariness and the duty of the moment? It is too late. "Whatsoever a man sows, that also shall he reap" (Gal. 6:7).

Thelma Hatfield also wrote, "I have in mind a family where the child was not obligated to do anything, but what pleased his fancy. He was made the centre of attraction, and when small, was allowed to indulge in all sorts of wee-sized vandalism throughout the house and grounds. When an interested person saw what was taking place in that child, he tried to speak to the parents. However, they could not be approached. The friend had scarcely broached the subject when he was silenced by their angry and superior attitude. Years later, when this child was the literal embodiment of the Devil, and totally incorrigible, the parents in tears were ready to talk hours on end to the same friend regarding their trouble. The kindly man did not have the heart to shake his finger under their nose and say, 'Remember when I tried to tell you.'"

Work is a holy thing. Play is only holy when it is justified by work.

The fifth principle is that a child needs to know what *goodness* is and that goodness is to be preferred over sin. Take every opportunity to teach the child about goodness, about such things as modesty, consideration for others, his prayers, reverence in Church, and respect for authority. Teach him about Jesus and the Blessed Mother. Tell him how good Jesus was and is, and how obedient he was to his parents. Tell him how much he is loved. Read stories to him about Jesus and about the saints. Ask him never to embarrass his guardian angel.

Keep him away from television, the corrupter of innocent minds. By all means show him a good Christian video, but avoid regular programming. It is disguised to instill worldly values. T.V. is not a baby-sitter. It is an idol, so do not bow down before it. Apart from the actual hypnotic effect of television, which leads the child to uncritically soak in and internalise whatever message is being peddled, there is also the "jolt effect." Any T.V. producer will tell you that for a visual input to be really effective, the picture has to be continually changing. These changes are referred to in the trade as "jolts." The child who is glued to the set is receiving a preplanned number of jolts per minute. As a result he begins to need his jolts. He will start to look for them in his world, in his parents, his siblings, in Church and at school. Since jolts are not built in to these encounters, he becomes bored with them and they lose their power to mould him. He will therefore find Church boring (how many jolts do we receive in a homily?), school becomes a chore, and his parents will lose their authority to command.

The four watch words for discipline, therefore, are: Silence, Activity, Work, and Goodness.

If you have asked a child to do some work, do not sit around idle yourself. That discourages the child. For example, if he is doing homework, at some point make him some hot chocolate and cookies, and get on with a useful task of your own. Do not flop on the couch and watch the ball game. That is a contradictory message.

Imagine that the child is playing in the sand box, and he starts to throw sand around. He is giggling with delight at this exciting new discovery. As a parent, you know this is undesirable and dangerous behaviour, so you must put a stop to it. Since the child is not knowingly doing evil, it is cruel to punish him. Go immediately to him and distract him from his behaviour. You can say, "Johnny, instead of throwing sand around, why don't we dig. Let's dig." If he throws some more then you can explain that this might get sand into someone's eyes and that would hurt a lot. In other words, if you distract him from the undesired behaviour, that is usually enough. This is a good time to tell him a story about a little bird in his nest. Parents are often shocked at this story and think it cruel, but children understand it fully.

"A little bird's mother told him she had to go and look for food and that he must stay in the nest till she got back. He decided not to obey his mother and after she was gone, he climbed out of the nest, fell onto the ground and a big cat came and ate him up." This will not terrify your child. He will listen wide-eyed and immediately get the point. You are teaching Johnny that mummy knows best, and that is a very good lesson for Johnny to learn at an early age.

It is vital to avoid a power struggle. A child will often try to pull you into one, and if he wins you lose. This only leads to more power struggles, because he loses respect for you. If you win, then while you may have control, the child feels weak and defeated. A power struggle is a losing game, so always try to avoid it. The best way to deal with a temper tantrum is to remove yourself. In this way, the child has nobody to perform for. By all means use humour to get him to quit, but never be sarcastic. Watch your language with a power-hungry child. Don't say, "You will go to bed now." That is only setting yourself up. Rather say, "Bedtime in ten minutes, Johnny, so let's play one more game." If he throws his coat on the floor, say, "Oh, you forgot to hang up your coat. Let me show you where it goes." Then show him. The next time he drops his coat on the floor you say, "Johnny, can you show me where your coat goes?" And in so doing, you give the child input into the solution. This is the way to avoid the authority which threatens and to share the authority with the child. Another example is if you want the child to learn how to set a table, you say, "Johnny, I'm having a problem setting the table. How can you and I do this?" Then Johnny may say, "Well, you do the forks, mummy, and I'll do the spoons." In other words respect the child, but use firmness and determination. In this way, the child becomes part of the solution instead of part of the problem.

Children, of course, often get into expressing their need for attention. They can do this passively or actively. Passive attention-getting occurs in the child who says, "I can't do it" or "I'm not good at that." It is his way of saying, "I am discouraged. I don't want to fail again." If you, as a parent find yourself throwing up your hands and saying, "I give up" then you are simply reinforcing his discouragement. Try to build up this child's self-esteem by giving him tasks which you know he can do. He needs to experience some successes in his efforts to conquer his environment. Encourage a lot and try not to criticise him or her since criticism really crushes a child who is in this frame of mind.

The active attention-getter is the child who gets into the power play, and is prone to the classical temper tantrum. This child does not obey the first time, because the payoff is he will get more attention. He will try to get mum and dad involved, or he will refuse to eat or to go to bed, or he will fight other kids. So be firm but kind. Do not pay attention when he is trying to get attention. Instead let him take the consequences of his negative behaviour. Give him good attention, and not self-defeating attention. That is to say, if his behaviour is not in and of itself harmful, then ignore the bad and compliment the good. However, if the behaviour is sinful, then the parent must step in. If the child is destroying property, then it must be stopped and he must clean it up.

An excellent way to deal with deviant behaviour is to isolate the child. Place him where he can see the normal loving activity of the rest of the household. He will calm down eventually and want to return to the warmth and activity of the others. *Always be consistent.* Inconsistency will cause a child to test the limits. A child without boundaries panics and starts to frantically try and find out where these boundaries are. He will simply run out of control, and that is anarchy.

When my son was about six years old, he was sitting very quietly on the rug looking very thoughtful. Suddenly he looked up and said, "Dad, which would you rather be, a frog or a snake?" I replied, "I don't want to be either." He looked disturbed and said, "No dad! You have to choose one. Which do you want?" I said again that I preferred to remain a man, and my son became even more agitated and kept on insisting that I had no choice but to select one of his two options. The idea that there could be other possibilities never seemed to enter his mind. Reflecting on that, I realised that young children can only hold on to two choices at a time. They cannot hold onto three or more options. Use this knowledge when dealing with a disobedient child. Give him two punishment options and let him choose whichever one he wants. For example, if little Johnny spits at you, first of all let him know firmly but kindly that this is not acceptable behaviour. He spits at you again, so you give him a choice. "Alright Johnny, until you are ready to be with people you can either go to your room or you can sit in the corner on that chair. It's up to you." Johnny will instinctively opt for one of the two choices presented. Either way he is being punished. Do not put a time limit on it by saying, "OK, you will sit there for fifteen minutes." That will only set you up for another power struggle. Instead, after a little while you say, "Are you ready now to be with people?" He will say, "yes" or "no." If he says "no" leave him a little while longer, then don't ask again. Just say, "It is time to get up now." If he says "yes" then welcome him back with love.

It is time to address the controversial and difficult problem of physical punishment. Is there a place for it in a Catholic home? The new Catechism seems to imply that at times discipline will demand the rod. In *paragraph 1804*, it places two biblical quotations together. "He who loves his son will not spare the rod" (Sir. 30:1). "Fathers, do not provoke your children to anger, but bring them up in the discipline and instruction of the Lord" (Eph. 6:4).

The Church recognises that parents aren't to choose between the rod of the Old Testament or the love of the New. Rather, we are to seek a Christian balance between the two. The Old Testament was the time of the law and of justice, and so discipline was seen mainly in terms of physical retribution. With the New Testament, we have Christ incarnate and the spirit of the law which is mercy, love and gentleness. Certainly the effects of original sin are there in us, but Baptism makes available God's grace whereby we are able to love God and to more clearly discern what is good.

Two thousand years ago, a child was born and he grew up to say: "Suffer little children to come unto me" (Mark 10:14). "I give you a new commandment: Love one another as I have loved you" (John 13:34). Yet, the same gentle Jesus was capable of being stern when it was called for: "Whoever causes one of these little ones who believe in me to sin, it would be better for him to have a great millstone hung around his neck and to be drowned in the depths of the sea" (Matt. 18:6). Jesus loved innocence so much that he threatened unspeakable punishment on those who would corrupt the little ones. Is this not another very good reason for parents to avoid anything which they know would corrupt their children, or lead them into sin?

"Making a whip out of cord, he drove them all out of the temple, sheep and cattle as well, scattered the money changers' coins, knocked their tables over" (John 2:15). Clearly Jesus was not afraid to discipline those who offended his Father in heaven. We too must not be afraid to discipline our children if they offend God.

"You serpents, brood of vipers, how can you escape being condemned to hell?" (Matt. 23:33). The ultimate punishment from God is to be lost forever. We, as parents, must correct our children while the correcting is good, otherwise, they may grow to a life of offending God with its awful consequences. What parent would choose such an eternity for their child? Therefore, choose now and discipline now. Eternity does depend upon it.

"My son do not disdain the discipline of the Lord or lose heart when reproved by him, for whom the Lord loves, he disciplines. He scourges every son he acknowledges" (Heb. 12:5-6). God's discipline is founded on love and so should ours as parents. Yet God *scourges* his own when they need it. As parents, designated by God, we may also have to show our love in a physical way to our children if they need it.

Bishop Fulton Sheen once said, "A spanking is just a pat on the back that is low enough and hard enough to let the child know you love him." Therefore, the only motivation for spanking is love. It must never be an act of vengeance. A loving parent will use the rod in obedience to the word of God, not as a merciless avenging angel. A child should never be physically punished in anger. Anger always results in harshness and unnecessary pain, and always provokes a child to resentment. ***Physical punishment out of rage is always child abuse.***

One child may need a swat and react well to it. Another may be too easily crushed and be totally defeated. Only a parent can truly know his or her own child well enough to punish appropriately. Let the rod be reserved as a last resort, and only for outright rebellion. The parent must be sure that the child is deliberately and with malice choosing to rebel, to tell lies, to take the name of the Lord in vain, to be stealing, or breaking any of the other commandments. The rod is reserved for open rebellion against God.

The discipline must be administered immediately. There must be a direct connection in the child's mind between his action and the consequences. Do not say, "Well, just you wait till your father gets home. You're going to get it then." This makes no sense to a child. Do it and do it there and then. "Because sentence against an evil told is not executed speedily, the heart of the sons of men is fully set to do evil" (Eccl. 8:11). A threat of punishment followed by no punishment is a waste of breath. Absolutely never use threats that cannot be carried out. Some parents make threats which would make one's hair stand on end, but the child is clever enough to know that this will never happen, so he ignores them. Never scream or yell or get out of control. A child soon learns to tune you out, and all you will achieve is high blood pressure. The child will also learn that it must be acceptable for him to scream and yell in order to get what he wants. Meanwhile, the child continues blithely to do whatever he was doing which irritated you in the first place. It is far better to remain serene and demand what you want from the child in a calm, quiet, but firm voice. If you have taught him silence he will already be primed to hear a quiet command. If that is ignored, then as Scripture tells us, punishment should be immediate. Never ask a child over and over again to do something. He soon learns that he can safely ignore the first dozen or so commands. Ask once only and then act. Thereby, the child soon learns to obey a request immediately. Punishment should be administered in a calm, quiet and firm manner. Scriptural discipline with the rod is not child abuse. Today's misguided "authorities" try to tell us that discipline is child abuse, but that is absurd. *Lack* of discipline is child abuse.

Always bear in mind the size of the child who is about to be spanked. The size of the rod must match the size of the child! A firm tap on the back of the hand for a three year old will get his attention and get the message across. A nine year old may need something more convincing. If you are firm and loving and you discipline your child right from the beginning, you will soon realize that you do not have to get physical with your child as time goes on. A slap on the wrist at age two will avoid dozens of ineffective blows later on. Your word simply becomes a corrective presence in the back of your child's mind. He now carries in him a memory of discipline, and his instinct is to continue to obey a quiet command right away. He knows that if he ignores the first command there will not be a second.

This is the best way to discipline effectively. Ask the child to do what you want him to do. If he does not, then punish him *appropriately and immediately.* Appropriate punishment, more often than not, means being banished from the family for a while or being deprived of some privilege or other. If, however, the child's behaviour is outright rebellion, then it is valid to use a physical attention-getter. Rebellion must not be tolerated. After the punishment is over, and a short time is allowed for the child to think about it, that is the moment to kneel down with him and ask him to ask God for forgiveness. After all, he must know that it is God whom he has offended here. You are only being obedient to God by punishing him. You are imposing God's will on him, not your own. After he has repented before God, then you pray over him, thanking God for giving you such a wonderful gift in this child. Tell God and the child how much you love him. Then it is time to hug and kiss and put the whole incident into the past. The prodigal son or daughter is welcomed back to the love of the family.

My father spanked me only twice in my life. The first occurred when I was seven years old, when I had refused to stop interrupting him when he was in serious conversation with his brother-in-law. The second time was when I was caught out in a deliberate and flagrant lie. When it was over, I was left to lick my wounds and I was given a little time to reflect on my sins. Then my father came and apologised for having had to resort to this, but he insisted that before God, he had no choice. He then hugged me. He said, "The pain will go away, but the lesson you have learned never will." He was right.

For a teenager, spanking time is definitely over. It is ludicrous. They are usually bigger than you are. All you can do is let them know what you expect and what God expects. It is vital that their actions be directly linked with the consequences. The consequences usually become longer-term, since the adolescent is capable of understanding more. It should take the form of some kind of deprivation, such as not going to a dance, or not going out for a bike ride. You have the keys to the car, not your child. You have the money, not the child. You can ground your child. He cannot ground you. You pay for the mortgage, not your child, and so you can refuse to accept certain types of behaviour in your home. In fact, it is a duty of parents, commanded by God, that you must not allow mortal sin to occur under your roof. If a young man wants to bring his girlfriend home to sleep with her, the answer is very simple. You may not be able to control a lot of what he does outside of the home, but you surely can control what goes on inside it. He might get drunk in someone else's house, but never in yours.

Never try to be a buddy or a pal to your teenager, or try to win a popularity contest with him. You will regret it. You are a parent and you owe it to your child always to be a parent. The Catechism tells you to command both respect and obedience from your child. If you are only a pal, then I may respect my pal, but I need never be obedient to him. So watch for this trap. God the Father will always be a loving Father to us, never a buddy.

A tired teenager cannot get into trouble. So tire him out! He has limitless stores of energy and if allowed to become bored or idle, he will find some mischief with which to relieve it. In addition to his school work and homework, involve him in extra-curricular activities which interest him, such as sports or camping. During the summer vacation, encourage him to find a job. Whatever you do keep him busy. He needs it and it will save you and him from the grief which is born of boredom.

If a teenager is being disobedient in a major way, then something was wrong with his childhood discipline. Thomas Millar in his book, *The Strong-willed Child,* states that in the old days parents were strong on discipline and weak on affection. The child grew up to be strong in character but unhappy. Modern parents, on the other hand, are strong on affection and weak on discipline, so the child grows up happy with his own disorder, but also unmotivated and irresponsible. Real parenting gives a child both affection and discipline. This does not mean that it is hopeless to try and discipline an unruly teenager. God and you can do anything, but it is just harder!

Good, non-threatening, civilised communication is essential. Take time to *listen* to your teenager and to offer good advice. Emphasize his choices and give him more control of his life. Help him to choose his friends, or if you have problems with that, at least stop him from having bad friends. Encourage him to bring his friends to the house so you can observe them. Encourage the good. Forbid the bad. Let your home be a place of welcome to his friends. Talk to them and let them feel accepted.

One day recently, I was seeing a young man in my office. His girlfriend sat in the waiting room talking to my wife. At one point the girl admitted that most of the teenagers in her high school were into crime, drugs, sex, alcohol and defying curfews. Rita asked her why she thought this was so. The girl replied, "Because their parents do not love them." Rita said, "But they have everything, the best of running shoes, leather jackets, cars, and spending money." "Yes" said the girl, "Their parents are just buying them off."

Another tenth-grade girl said to me, "There is violence in my school. But that is because parents either don't care or are too strict. We need limits. I have limits, but I have a lot of freedom within my limits."

So it is a question of balance — balance between permissiveness and stifling control. Moderation will have far better results.

All of the foregoing material has been directed at the "normal" child who is by nature disobedient, but who will respond to love and balanced discipline. There are two abnormal situations, however, which must be mentioned and understood. The first concerns those children who suffer from Attention-Deficit Disorder (ADD), Depression or Fetal Alcohol Syndrome. Such children will be often angry, exhibit very poor concentration, perhaps be aggressive, and certainly will always be disobedient. They will be unresponsive to the frantic efforts of their parents to bring order into their lives. In fact, the more the parents discipline, whether by stern admonition or physical punishment or both, the child will react by becoming even more unmanageable. His energy for resistance seems to feed on punishment. These are very unhappy children, and because they are dysfunctional, punishment becomes unjust and ineffective. They need help. The good news is that these conditions are treatable. They should be referred by a family doctor to a child psychiatrist for confirmation of the diagnosis, and then excellent results can be expected from good therapy. I have treated a number of such children, and it is a cause for praise to God to see many of them become calm, reasonable, manageable and functioning well in their studies and in their relationships. If you have an unmanageable child, then have him checked out by a professional. He or she may have a treatable disorder. You will not regret it.

The second situation is a very disturbing phenomenon which has surfaced in our modern society and is, to say the least, extremely alarming. "You must understand this, that in the last days, distressing times will come. For people will be lovers of themselves, lovers of money, boasters, arrogant, abusive, *disobedient* to their parents" (2 Tim. 3:1-2). These are words of prophecy from St. Paul. Why would he mention children being disobedient to their parents? After all, ever since Cain and Abel, children have always tried to be disobedient to their parents at times. St. Paul emphasises this because he foresaw that in the last days, a new kind of disobedience would show itself. It would be total and very widespread and not curable by ordinary disciplinary measures. Is this not what we are witnessing in our own day? Little children are running riot and big children are into sex, drugs, alcohol and sinful pleasure. It seems that practically a whole generation is now defying discipline, and it is making them into very miserable souls indeed.

I was talking recently to a distraught couple in my office. They began to suspect that their fifteen-year-old daughter was sneaking out of the house during the night, and they had no idea what she was up to. These were very intelligent, very loving, and very holy Catholic parents. Eventually they found out that the girl was using marijuana. They found a supply of birth control pills and condoms in her satchel. When they searched her bedroom, they found Satanic posters, and they discovered that the music she listened to was full of lyrics encouraging suicide, mutilation of women, and worship of evil. To their horror they also found a box in which was concealed black candles, incense and other paraphernalia for witchcraft rituals. They also found a book on how to practice Wicca.

Mother and father confronted the girl and were devastated to find that instead of repenting or feeling ashamed or desiring to be accepted back into the love of the family, she took on a cold, mask-like look. It was a look they had never seen before on her face. It was then that they realised that their daughter did not want to be taken back into the love of the family and into goodness. She *wanted* evil.

This scenario is much more common than Catholic parents realize. I advise all parents of teenagers to exercise their rights to go into and to search their youngster's bedroom. They must listen carefully to the music the child is listening to and trash anything Satanic or evil. The teenager's bedroom should never be allowed to be locked. Parents have a right to know what is going on in that room. Never allow a television set in a teenager's bedroom. How can you know what they are watching? Beware of the Internet. Pornography of all kinds is easily available, and it is a parent's duty to know which web sites are being visited by their teenagers. Their bedroom should be a bedroom, not a place where they can hide away for hours and do dark things. If a teenager is bringing Satan into his or her bedroom, then Satan is being allowed into your home. This must be stopped at all costs. Satan, given a foothold, will do everything possible to destroy family peace, harmony and love.

Naturally, the good parents of that girl asked me what they could do. They wanted their daughter back, knowing that she no longer wanted goodness and love, and that she had chosen the very opposite of all that was good. I told them that ordinary, reasonable discipline would no longer be effective. There were only two things they could do, and it was Jesus himself who told us, "This kind can only be driven out by *prayer and fasting*" (Mark 9:29). I told these worried parents that their child was beyond the reach of their love and wisdom. She could only be helped by a dedicated program of prayer and fasting. Needless to say, her parents were praying, but in such a case, prayer alone would never be enough. It needed the powerful sacrifice of regular fasting by the parents on behalf of their daughter.

Fasting can be done in a variety of ways. We can fast for an extended period or we can fast one day a week. The nature of the fast also varies. One may fast on bread and water, on water only, or on fruit juices and so on. Fasting, however, need not simply be confined to depriving ourselves of food. It can be a decision to avoid other things which we find pleasurable. We could abstain from smoking, alcohol, entertainments, and other pleasures. Some couples I know abstain from sexual intercourse, and offer that up as a holy gift to the Lord. Whatever way you choose, do it with love and if possible with joy, and during the fasting period pray like you have never prayed before. I can think of no other weapon against this new type of disobedience, which is sweeping our society today.

The police department in Houston, Texas once drew up a list of twelve rules for raising *delinquent* children! Follow these and you can be guaranteed that you will suffer from the tyranny of a problem teenager.

1. Begin with infancy to give the child everything he wants. In this way he will grow up to believe the world owes him a living.
2. When he picks up bad words, laugh at him. This will make him think he is cute. It will also encourage him to pick up "cuter" phrases that will blow off the top of your head later.
3. Never give him any spiritual training. Wait till he is twenty-one, and then let him "decide for himself."
4. Avoid the use of the word "wrong." He may develop a guilt complex. This will condition him to believe later, when he is arrested for stealing a car, that society is against him and he is being persecuted.
5. Pick up everything he leaves lying around, books, shoes and clothing. Do everything for him so he will be experienced in throwing all responsibility onto others.
6. Let him read any printed matter he can get his hands on. Be careful that the silverware and drinking glasses are sterilised, but let his mind feast on garbage.
7. Quarrel frequently in the presence of your children. In this way they will not be too shocked when the home is broken up later.
8. Give a child all the spending money he wants. Never let him earn his own. Why should he have things as tough as you had them?

9. Satisfy his every craving for food, drink and comfort. See that every sensual desire is gratified. Denial may lead to harmful frustration.
10. Take his part against neighbours, teachers and policemen. They are all prejudiced against your child.
11. When he gets into real trouble, apologize for yourself by saying, "I never could do anything with him."
12. Prepare for a life of grief. *You are likely to get it!*

There is no such thing as perfect parenting, so it is a futile exercise to beat up on yourselves for mistakes. God does not expect you to be perfect parents, but you are the best parents for your children because God gave them to you and not to anyone else. The only perfect parenting ever accomplished on the earth was done by Mary and St. Joseph in the Holy Family. Nobody else is a perfect parent and no one else has all the answers. So relax.

God parents the universe. The Holy Father parents the Church. The bishop parents the Diocese. The priest parents the parish. Parents parent their children, while single adults also parent, in that they are to bring life and love and give birth to Jesus in the community around them. Parenting is for all of us, and so it is vital that we study God's plan for parenting and live it out. God's design for parenting is the only design which will work.

CHAPTER 10

Parenting: God's Instruction in the Faith

"Take to heart these words
I enjoin on you today. Drill
them into your children.
Speak of them at home and
abroad, whether you are
busy or at rest."

(Deut. 6:6-7)

The Catholic Catechism states,

Paragraph 2223: Parents have the first responsibility for the education of their children. They bear witness to this responsibility first by creating a home where tenderness, forgiveness, respect, fidelity and disinterested service are the rule. The home is well suited for education in the virtues. This requires an apprenticeship in self-denial, sound judgement and self-mastery, the preconditions of all true freedom. Parents should teach their children to subordinate the material and instinctual dimensions to interior and spiritual ones. Parents have a grave responsibility to give good example to their children. By knowing how to acknowledge their own failings to their children, parents will be better able to guide and correct them.

Paragraph 2225: Through the grace of the Sacrament of Marriage, parents receive the responsibility and privilege of evangelising their children. Parents should initiate their children at an **early age** into the mysteries of the faith of which they are the **first heralds** for their children. They should associate them from their tenderest years with the life of the Church.

Paragraph 2226: Education in the faith should begin in the child's earliest years. Parents have the mission of teaching their children to pray and to discover their vocation as children of God.

Paragraph 2227: Children, in turn, contribute to the growth in holiness of their parents. Each and everyone should be generous and tireless in forgiving one another for offenses, quarrels, injustices and neglect. Mutual affection suggests this. The charity of Christ demands it.

Paragraph 2229: As those first responsible for the education of their children, parents have the right to choose a school for them which corresponds to their own convictions. This right is fundamental.

This is the framework for understanding how to impart the faith to our children. But it must not be confused with the mindless teaching of cold religion. Many parents believe that by merely delivering religious facts to their children, they are doing their duty. This is wrong. Anybody can hand a child a Penny Catechism and have him recite it by rote, but this does not nourish a lively faith. It is true that the child has to learn facts about Jesus and the salvific mandate of the Church, but if that is all he is given, then later on, when he is attracted to the sinful trinkets and glitter of the world (as we all are at some point), he will be likely to abandon the faith. The word of God will have fallen on shallow soil and the weeds of the world will find it easy to choke it. Rearing children in the faith is a much more awesome responsibility than some might think. It is not just classroom pedagogy. *It is a way of life.* The faith has to be something in which the child is immersed. He must swim in the faith, he must breathe the faith, and he must find the Catholic faith to be in front of him, behind him, to his right and his left, above and below him. Only by this can the child be immunised against the plagues of the world and its allurements. The faith must be brought to life in his heart, must be nurtured in his heart, and the child must be constantly encouraged to grow towards that perfection which is union with Jesus Christ. "You must be perfect as your heavenly Father is perfect" (Matt. 5:48).

To parents falls the wondrous task of this evangelisation. But how can good parents, who desire this result with all their hearts, help their little ones to pulsate with the spirit of God? At first glance this can appear too daunting, and could lead to a throwing up of the hands in discouragement. Many parents do just that. They look at the desired end-point, see it as too lofty an ideal, and then, aware of their own deficiencies, give up before they even begin. This is a defeatist posture and defeatism comes from listening to Satan's lies. He wants to discourage us, and he puts a lot of effort into it because, by getting parents to give up, he is assuring himself of yet another soul or souls who will grow up with little or no faith.

God built in a lot of margin for error in our parenting. While we may not be perfect parents, we should take heart in knowing that for our children, we are the best parents possible. God decreed it to be so. God has faith in you and so you should have faith in you, and you can be sure that your child has faith in you. You are not alone, for the simple reason that God is with you. You are Catholics, so you have access to sanctifying grace through the Sacraments. You are not raising your children with your own limited human strengths. On the contrary, you are only able to fulfil this mission by your human weakness, for as St. Paul reminds us, "For power is made perfect in weakness" (2 Cor. 12:9). God did not give you this assignment without also giving you all that you need to do it. You have each other and parents should come together with other parents to provide mutual support, praying together, encouraging one another and exchanging those useful ideas which you have discovered, about which no educator could ever tell you.

When a child is born, he has intrauterine memories and has already been formed by events which had an impact on him while he was in the womb. It may come as a surprise to realise that teaching religion to your child should ideally begin at the moment of conception. This means that even if you are not aware of your pregnancy for a few weeks, you should already be living out your faith, faithfully. You should always be ready to welcome new life. Your sexual loving should be ever holy and self-giving, one to the other, not tarnished by lust or drunkenness or violence. Then the womb in which the new life will be placed is at all times a holy place, ready to impart holiness to that tiny single cell. As soon as they become aware of the pregnancy, both mom and dad should know that they are now parents. So often, pregnant couples say, "We are going to be parents." This is erroneous thinking. They are *already* parents, and should immediately begin a lifelong campaign of prayer for their child. This should be prayer of thanksgiving and gratitude to God, the Father of all children, and to Mary, the mother of all children. It should also be prayer of supplication and intercession for the holiness of the child. Parents would do well, as soon as possible, to consecrate that new little life to Jesus through the Immaculate Heart of Mary. In this way, the Blessed Mother will be given permission to regard this child as her own, and she will take that task very seriously indeed. She will then orchestrate the child's life, always drawing him or her ever closer to the Sacred Heart of her Son Jesus. She will do all in her power to protect her little consecrated one from the snares of the Devil.

As stated in chapter 9, every day of the pregnancy, mom and dad should pray over that tiny growing life for its protection and to minimise one of the effects of original sin, which is the trauma of labour pains to the mother and the trauma of painful progress through the birth canal for the baby. This daily habit of prayer should be maintained after birth, every day of the child's life, by praying over him, and by praying together for him even when he is absent from the home.

I believe that raising a child in the faith can only be done well by *prayer and fasting.* If Jesus has shown us that fasting can cast a demon out from someone who is possessed, can fasting not also keep Satan away from our children, fortify them against daily temptations, and protect them from the poisonous influence of their peer group and the world? It can and it does. The power of fasting in dealing with a very disturbed child has already been addressed in chapter 9. The Church calls parents to empty themselves for their children. What could be more powerful than to fast for their souls?

Fasting, quite simply, is giving up something good in order to experience a higher good. Obviously we are to fast from all that is bad. We should fast from sin. But while it is good to eat food, or to enjoy a holiday, it is a higher good to deny ourselves some of these things, because such fasting not only storms heaven to grant our request, it also strengthens our spiritual muscles, giving us the virtues of fortitude and perseverance. Fasting is spiritual gold, both for our children and for our personal sanctity. If you are feeling discouraged in your efforts as regards teaching the faith to your child, then begin to pray and fast, asking Jesus and Mary to change things around. They will. Jesus promised it and he always keeps his promises. Never be afraid to remind Jesus of his promises for he loves to be reminded. He loves a confident faith. If you are willing to offer him the rather small gift of your mortification and penance, he in turn, will refuse to be outdone in generosity and so will respond with a "good measure pressed down, shaken together and running over" (Luke 6:38).

Once the baby is born, he or she enters a new phase of education in the faith. A newborn baby will learn at a rate which will never be matched again as he grows older. Now is the time to instill holy things into the baby's mind. For example, he should consistently hear and feel mom and dad praying over him as he lies in his crib. Prayer is a harmonic rhythm which penetrates and affects the subconscious. Even if the baby cannot understand your words, he can absorb the holy and peaceful vibrations of his parent's prayer. He will make deep and rich interior connections between the energy of prayer and his own inner sense of peace and love and security. His guardian angel will be empowered by prayer to protect him more effectively. Likewise sing hymns to your baby instead of lullabies. Baby will again make profound associations of tranquillity with the music of praise to God. He cannot help it. He was built that way by a loving Father. It is in his very nature to absorb holy things. As parents, you will never have more power than during your child's infancy to be a sanctifying influence for him, and of course you must convey love. You cannot love enough. The child needs touching and soothing. The more you do this, the more the child will recognize you as his source of love and the more credence he will give later on to your instructions in the faith. He will be able to accept that God is the source of all love, even the very love he is receiving from his parents.

The most important principle of all in religious education is that you yourselves must live it. The child must see you practising what you preach. That is what makes your commands authentic and believable. You cannot tell him not to be angry if you yell and scream at each other whenever you have a disagreement. You cannot direct your child away from lust or promiscuous sex if you have pornographic magazines lying around the house. You cannot demand that your child pick up his toys if you are a disorganized slob. You cannot ask him to give up television and do his homework if you spend hours in front of the one-eyed monster watching ball games and immoral sitcoms. Your most powerful educational tool is your example. Let your lives be a living homily and your children will eagerly imitate you. In fact, during the child's earlier years, he will eagerly imitate you anyway, so beware of what you role model. The manner of your life will instruct your child more surely than instruction itself.

When you see your child misbehaving, ask yourself if you are not doing the same thing. Observe your child and you will be amazed at how perfectly he imitates your behaviour in word, gesture, action and play. If one of your gestures is a clenched fist, do not be surprised that your child clenches his fist. If one of your gestures is the Sign of the Cross, you should not be surprised that your child readily and joyfully does the same. Long before you are able to explain to him that the Sign of the Cross is the sign of our faith and a ritual of blessing, your child will somehow know that it is a powerful and solemn thing to do. He knows in his heart much much more than you think he does.

Many of today's fathers have a very impoverished view of what their function should be. That is not God's opinion. It may come as a surprise to fathers to know that to a very young child, dad is god. To an older child dad is all men. In fact, the role of father in the religious education of children ought to be paramount. It is not a responsibility to slough off onto mothers. As fathers, we reflect the fatherhood of God, and for this reason we are required to father our children as God fathers us. Certainly fathers are providers and protectors of the family entrusted to them, but fathering means much more than that. As fathers we carry the awesome responsibility of the moral authority over our family, and this is no mean duty. We must model tenderness, gentleness, manly firmness, generosity and willingness to listen to our children. The children must see mother deferring to dad's authority in holy things. That does not mean that wives must obey when dad wants to quit his job for no good reason, nor must she buy him alcohol when he is going to get drunk.

St. Paul is very clear on this. "Husbands should love their wives just as Christ loved the Church and sacrificed himself for her to make her holy" (Eph. 5:25). Therefore husbands must be like Jesus to their families. Fathers must serve their wives and their children, they must instruct their little "domestic church" in the faith, and they must lay down their lives for it. Fathers cannot and must not abdicate their vocation as religious and life-educators for their children. They must be involved, and they must do it in one mind and one heart with their wives. This is God's order, and if we ignore it, we create disorder.

Whatever image a father portrays, that is exactly the image a young child will have of God. In fact, one child psychologist has said that if you could creep into your child's mind while he is saying his night prayers and see the visual image of the God he is praying to, you would find your own face there. A father is the only way a child can relate to God in his early years. Therefore, if dad is stern and aloof and unaffectionate, the child will have a problem believing that God is loving and merciful. If dad is a rigid and punitive disciplinarian, then the child will see God as a giant cruel policeman waiting to punish him. If dad is a strict controller, the child will see God as the great controller, who is responsible for the death of his pet dog or the rain that ruined his day at the beach. If dad is an indulgent weakling who spoils his children they will grow up to be moral weaklings also. They will see God as "nice" and believe that he would never censure them for doing as they please, even if it is sinful.

If, on the other hand, dad is gentle, kind, playful, considerate and forgiving, then the child's vision of God will be true and good. While mother is the constant presence to the young child, and dad has to be out at work all day, nevertheless, dad is present because his spirit orchestrates the family and he role-models for God. Many dads *play* god in their families, instead of *reflecting* God to their families. Fathers, therefore, should take back their God-given role as religious educators of their children, by leading their families in prayer. They should insist on God's discipline in their homes, and their wives will find their efforts blessed as they too play their part in teaching the faith.

The most powerful educational tool that we can use with children is the story. Jesus modelled that perfectly for us by teaching his disciples by means of parables. "Give ear, oh my people, to my teaching: incline your ears to the words of my mouth. I will open my mouth in a parable, (The N.A.B. renders this, 'I will open my mouth in story.') I will utter dark sayings from of old, things that we have heard and known, that our ancestors have told us. We will not hide them from their children: we will tell to the coming generation, the glorious deeds of the Lord, and his might, and the wonders that he has done. He established a decree in Jacob, and appointed a law in Israel, which he commanded our ancestors to teach to their children: that the next generation might know them, the children yet unborn, and rise up and tell them to their children, so that they should set their hope in God, and not forget the works of God, but keep his commandments" (Psalm 78:1-7).

God therefore, wishes us to teach our children with parables and stories, just as he himself does, and as Jesus his obedient Son did. He knew that people remember stories much better than facts, and so he used powerful, beautiful and captivating stories to make his doctrinal points. We only have to think of the parable, of the prodigal son and the good Samaritan in order to realize the power of the story. By means of these, all of us understand the forgiveness and love of the Father even when we have squandered our inheritance in sin, and we also learn the way in which we are to act towards our neighbour who is in pain. The moral theological point could not have been so well remembered if it had not been delivered in story format. In my own preaching I always try to find or to write a story which will emphasize the readings of the day. There is no doubt that people's hearts ring with the truth if they can link it up with a narrative. They remember the story first and then infer the moral after.

So it is with children. They, even more than adults, love a story. Not only do they love it, but they eagerly demand that it be repeated over and over. Children learn by repetition and so we as parents should be ever willing to tell good stories as many times as the children want to hear them. When they have assimilated the point of the story, they will drop their demands and move on to the next one. But it is not just the story itself which has power: *Story-telling* has power. The children love to cuddle up close to mom or dad and feel connected, intimate and loved. Story-time is a source of warm memories well into adulthood. My own grown up children still reminisce with me about my stories when they were little, as though they need to recapture the warmth and security of those days. Tell your children the stories of the Bible. Tell them about the lives of real heroes — the saints of the Church. Never mind sports idols or movie stars. They are hardly role models for a good moral life, nor even of achievement in life, apart from those who have remained strong in their faith. If we teach our children to look up to the saints who lived and died heroically, our children will inevitably try to model their own lives to their favourite saint. This firmly puts them onto the path of their own call to sainthood.

Another exciting method with which to re-enforce a story is through activities. In this way the child learns to take what he has heard in the story and "make it his own." Naturally the activities, whether discussion, drawing, dramatizing or writing, should be selected according to the age and ability of the child. A very young child finds it much easier to express himself with drawing than with verbalising. As he retells the story with crayons, he is thinking through the story again, mulling it over and interpreting what he has heard from his parents. Also, a parent will be able to assess what the child has learned when he is asked to talk about his picture.

For example, after reading the story of the prodigal son, ask the child to answer the following questions:

a) How was the younger son selfish?
b) How did the father show love for his son throughout the whole story?
c) What do we learn about our Father God from this story?
d) When are we like the prodigal son?

Ask the child to draw the main characters in the story. Then cut them out and paste each one onto a popsicle stick. These can then be used as puppets, and the child can retell the story by acting it out in his own puppet play.

If the day's theme is Baptism, then after talking about the Sacrament, you could show your child photographs, slides or a home video of his Baptism. Tell him about his Baptismal day, who was there, the priest who baptised him, who his Godparents were and what they said. Compare his birth and growth in your own family to birth and growth in the family of God. Help him to understand the responsibility each member has towards the others if there is to be peace and harmony in the family. Tell him how happy you were on that great day, and why it was the greatest day in the life of his soul. Have him mark the date of his Baptismal anniversary on the calendar. Plan with him how you will celebrate that day. His Baptismal candle could be the centrepiece for the family meal. The child should be given the privilege of saying grace, and the family can thank God for the gift of this child and that they all have been admitted through Baptism to God's family. Ask him to draw a picture of his Baptism and have him send it along with a note of gratitude to his Godparents.

I did not think up these activities. I took them from a wonderful little book called, ***Will Religion Make Sense to Your Child?*** by Earnest Larsen and Patricia Gavin. If you could locate a copy, you would find it most helpful in teaching your child about the faith.

As pointed out earlier, religious training is not just the imparting of facts or doctrinal truths, but is a way of life. The child must therefore be immersed in the faith, he must be made to see that the faith affects everything in his life, and he must see that it works, as opposed to all the other systems to which he will be exposed in life. All of us are a man or woman, a spouse, a parent, an aunt or uncle, a cousin and a son or daughter, but we are much more than that. We are a ***Catholic*** man or woman, a Catholic spouse, a Catholic parent, a Catholic aunt or uncle, a Catholic son or daughter. That makes all the difference in the world, and your child must come to know why. A Catholic parent should never be indistinguishable from a pagan parent. A Catholic teenager should never be a clone of his non-Catholic peers. Everything we do, and everything we teach our children to do, must be stamped with a unique Catholic character.

To become effective teachers of the faith, parents must educate themselves as to what it means to be Catholics and followers of Jesus Christ. They must show their children how mommy and daddy love each other, and they must show their children that they too are humble of heart, mutually forgiving and obedient to their master, Jesus Christ. Ideally they avoid harsh words, anger and yelling when trying to resolve disputes. They should show the children that differences of opinion are exciting opportunities to learn about each other. They demonstrate by action that it is better to find peaceful and respectful ways to come to loving closure of an issue. They should always, of course, show that there can be no compromise in matters of faith or morals.

Do not judge your success as parents by the results. Parents understandably get down on themselves when their children later abandon the faith of Jesus. By the time a child is old enough to choose to abandon the Church, he is old enough to take the consequences. The parental power in this matter has been taken out of their hands. All that is left is prayer and fasting, beseeching God to keep your grown-up children solidly in the Faith or to bring them back to it if they have fallen away.

Finally, since religious education is preparation for Catholic life, the child must come to think of church as his extended home. He must be taken to Church often, shown how to be reverent, shown the beautiful works of art in the Church, encouraged to walk the stations of the Cross, to recognize the True Presence of Jesus in the Tabernacle, and to take part in the Sacramental and Liturgical Life of the Church. A beautiful practice with a pre-communion child is to have him come up to the priest with you at Communion time, to cross his arms over his heart and to receive a blessing from the priest. This teaches a holy disposition and prepares the child to look forward to the wonderful day when he will be able to receive Jesus, Body, Blood, Soul and Divinity along with his parents and older brothers and sisters. When a child finds love, peace, joy, encouragement and friendship in Church and family, he will be eager to learn his faith and he will develop a proper sense of the holy. His heart will resonate with a deeper and deeper sweet chord of wonder and awe at God's perfect plan and he will find it impossible to imagine that anything outside of the faith could be life-giving. True religion is life. Give your child life, and God in turn, will give you eternal life.

CHAPTER 11

Teenagers: From Caterpillar to Butterfly

*"God, you have taught me from
my youth. To this day I proclaim
your wondrous deeds."*
(Ps. 71:17)

When I was a teenager, which according to my children was sometime before the Flood, but which to me seems like only yesterday, it never entered my head that God had "taught me from my youth." I was caught up in my own pain like a caterpillar writhing in its chrysalis, convinced I would never make a butterfly. On the one hand, I was arrogantly convinced of my own opinions on just about everything. On the other hand, I felt threatened and buffeted about by events beyond my control. My teenage life was a mix of youthful exuberance, periods of depression, moments of exultation, bouts of anxiety, feelings of dread, and self-loathing, alternating with intense conceit, a hormonal roller-coaster. And yet I was also imbued with a deep sense of destiny. I believed that I had a future and that belief probably saved my life. It is not that I had experienced a bad childhood. On the contrary, in spite of World War II and the sense of insecurity that went with those years, I was deeply loved by my parents and my extended family. We were poor but I really never knew that. I accepted my lot in life because that was just the way things were, and all my friends were equally poor. I was raised in the Catholic faith by a mother who was a convert and a holy woman, and by a hard working father who knew how to discipline with fairness.

The teenage years, however, exploded upon me, and like most teenagers, I was not ready. In spite of the fact that I was an "A" student and the high school sports champion, I mostly agonized over my perceived physical defects and was constantly preoccupied with being accepted by my peers. My self-esteem was near zero on a scale of one to ten, and I would have given anything to be me in a different body. What I did not realize at the time, and nobody pointed it out to me, was that *all* of my classmates felt exactly the same way. To me they looked self-assured, happy and confident and I longed to be like them, but if by some miracle I could have become one of them, I would have found the same pain, the same self-hatred and the same deep-seated insecurity.

It is very important for parents to understand that, while the teenagers of today are no different from the teenagers of yesterday, there is a huge difference in the environment within which they are being raised. In today's society, Christian parents are out-manned and out-gunned by the peer group and by a pagan culture. Teens are bombarded by a sex-obsessed environment, by friends who use drugs, by sin-filled messages on television, by pornographic magazines handed around by so-called friends and by satanic messages of rape, violence and suicide in today's heavy-metal music, punk rock and acid-rock. They are seduced by anti-Catholic articles in newspapers, by a self-centred consumerism, and by the New Age message that we are gods and so we do not need God, that sin does not exist and that whatever feels good must be good. How can parents combat this barrage of corrupting influences on their teenagers?

The teen years are the most morally vulnerable phase of their lives. They are not quite out of childhood and not quite into adulthood. They do not want to be children anymore but do not know how to be adults. They want to be treated like adults but are afraid of the responsibility which goes with being adult. They struggle with powerful sexual urges, yet emotionally are not mature enough to cope. They are amazingly impulsive and may fall into horrifying sin on a mere whim. Their egos are huge yet they are overly sensitive to rejection. They can spend hours grooming themselves and admiring themselves in front of a mirror. Yet they almost all hate some perceived minor physical imperfection. They feel too fat, too thin, their nose is too big or not big enough. They would rather have brown eyes instead of blue, blonde hair instead of red. They wish they were taller or shorter. The appearance of a single pimple on the chin is a life-threatening event. Enormous amounts of energy are expended on looking good on the outside, while they cover up their agonizing emotional pain on the inside. They feel they cannot confide in their parents because they believe that parents would never understand. So they confide in their peers and risk betrayal, or they secretly write their dark thoughts in a diary. They desperately need an outlet for their innermost angst and if they cannot find a healthy outlet, they will be drawn into destructive behaviour such as sex, drugs or alcohol.

There are numerous self-help books about raising teenagers. Many of them focus on problems and offer all kinds of strategies with which to deal with rebellion, defiance and deviant behaviour. These are all well and good, but such reading can lead us to believe that all teenagers are bad and need to be reined in ruthlessly. It is as though a perfectly good child is destined to become a teenage monster and parents must therefore become more like prison guards than parents if they are to survive the teen years. Teenage deviance is a stark reality, but we can get mired in pessimism if we focus solely upon it. I prefer to look at the wonderful potential of our youth and call them to find their true selves and therefore their true happiness in the love of God.

There is a wonderful light within teenagers which must be appreciated and which parents should always encourage. Teens are not all doom, gloom, sin and defiance. They are the adults of tomorrow and, as such, are bursting with potential. They are the scholars, statesmen, priests, sisters, marriage partners and parents of the near future. They are the Church. They are gifted by God with wonderful talents and are searching for ways to use these to the fullest advantage. At first, they will tend to use their gifts for their own vanity, as I did, but eventually they will realize the truth that these were given by God to be used for the building up of the community and the Church. Once they reach that moment of insight, it is then that they shed their adolescence and become mature, responsible, Christian citizens. They enjoy the energy and vigour of youthful life, discovering a bigger world than the one they have known. They test themselves against the demands of their expanding environment, often with a fearlessness that we adults have lost. Naturally they make mistakes but they do learn from the consequences. Adults never seem to comprehend why teenagers refuse to learn from the wisdom and experience of their elders, forgetting that they too learned in much the same way. It is as though each generation is a fresh new human creation driven to its own maturity by the process of trial and error. It would save a lot of pain and hurt for our youth if they did learn from their elders, but all of human history proves that for the most part they do not. They must dive into the shark-infested waters and find out for themselves. We adults can warn them about the sharks and pray that they will not test the waters, but to our dismay and hurt, we so often find our advice being ignored.

What is absolutely vital, however, is that when a teenager is bitten and comes home wounded, we never react with rage, self-righteous indignation or "I told you so," and absolutely never with sarcasm. We must be there like the Father for the Prodigal Son, to receive him, tend his wounds and be prepared to listen to what he has learned from his reckless adventure. This is not the same thing as condoning what he has done. Wrong is wrong and sin is sin. In spite of the urge of youth to find out the hard way, we must continue to offer our wisdom, to try to protect them from needless pain and especially from soul-destroying sin, but as in all things, we were not given the right to judge the sinner. We adults, no matter how difficult it may be, must put on the mind of Christ and respond as he would respond to the wayward child. That means love, compassion and firm admonition, always welcoming the prodigal son back into the family.

It would be well for parents to meditate on the parable of the Prodigal Son with especial emphasis on the way in which the Father behaved towards his self-willed son. The boy arrogantly demanded his share of the inheritance. He wanted it immediately and was not willing to wait until his father died. The Father did not hesitate. He did not demand to know what the lad was going to do with the money. He did not ask for any guarantees. He acknowledged his son's gift of free will and simply handed it over, which is to say he *blessed* his son, silently expressing his trust in the boy's future. The son, as is well known, squandered every penny on debauchery and lustful indulgence. Now it was time for the consequences. He had dived into the shark-infested waters and been badly mauled. Now he was forced to feed the pigs, the most humiliating job that any Jew could be made to perform. For a Jew, just being near pigs was to be ritually unclean. The son was brought so low, that his fall from grace was even worse than having to merely feed the pigs. He even longed to eat pig-food, he was so hungry. It was only when he had reached this most wretched state that he finally repented. Only when he had scraped the bottom and could not be degraded any further, did he turn around and decide to return to his Father's house. All pride was gone, and he resolved to beg that he be accepted as a servant in his Father's household. He did not believe for one moment that he could be reinstated as a son ever again.

Scripture tells us, "While he was still a long way off, his Father saw him and was moved with pity. He ran to the boy, clasped him in his arms and kissed him" (Luke 15:20). This is a most wonderful passage. The good father saw him from a long way off and so he must have been looking down the road every day, hoping and praying that his son would come home. He had given his son his freedom, even the freedom to renounce all the traditions of his family, but he still never gave up hope. When the longed-for day came, the father did not stand with his fists on his hips, a stern look on his face and wait for the boy to stagger up to him. Instead "he *ran* to the boy" and in his love he hugged him and kissed him. He did not indulge in righteous anger or recriminations nor did he ask his son to recount his humiliations and sins. He already knew that his son was defeated and so he simply welcomed him back.

The son of course launched into his prepared speech but his father would have none of it. He called for the best robe, the sign of wealth, he put the family ring on his finger, the sign of family authority, and he put sandals on his feet, the sign of a free man and not a slave. Then he killed the fatted calf and held a feast to let the entire community know that this son was fully reinstated into the family. "And when he found it, would he not joyfully take it on his shoulders and then, when he got home, call together his friends and neighbours, saying to them, 'Rejoice with me, I have found my sheep that was lost.' In the same way, I tell you, there will be more rejoicing in heaven over one sinner repenting than over ninety-nine upright people who have no need of repentance" (Luke 15:5-7).

Jesus wanted to teach us about the love of his heavenly Father and, by means of this new understanding, to teach earthly fathers how to father their own youth. Fathers must learn to love and to welcome a wayward teenager back into the household. It is useless to indulge in recriminations. The teenager is already punished and humiliated enough by the consequences of his foolishness and he needs to find his sure-point once more. He needs to know that there is one place where he can stand in security and safety and that must be in his father's house. "Yahweh is my rock and my fortress, my deliverer is my God. I take refuge in him, my rock, my shield, my saving strength, my stronghold, my place of refuge" (Ps. 18:2).

Naturally loving Catholic parents desire to save their adolescents from all avoidable harm, and it is right that they should make every effort in their power to do so. For there to be any hope of real success, this effort must begin at the moment of conception. It is a little too late to start doing this when the child has become a teenager. Parents have amazing power over a child during its dependent years and it is then that firm foundations of goodness and holiness must be laid down. Parents who teach a child what love really is, who inculcate good work habits, who discipline with fairness and who live out their own call to virtue and holiness, will prepare that child for the turbulence of adolescence. Such a child will be less likely to wander far from the narrow road of goodness when he is older and tempted by the sin of the world. An undisciplined child will become a nightmare teenager and trying to correct him at that point is like closing the stable door after the horse has bolted. This does not mean that it is too late to do anything fruitful with a teenager who has lost his way, but it is a thousand times more difficult. A teenager is a product of his childhood. As the poet Wordsworth wrote, "The child is the father of the man."

Many parents would agree that there is some kind of communication vacuum between them and their teenagers. They are convinced that youth does not listen to their advice, wisdom and commands. It may come as a surprise to know that teenagers feel exactly the same way. They believe that parents never listen to their ideas, thoughts and dreams. The truth is, that even well-meaning parents who want the very best for their youngsters fail to realize that they are no longer raising a child, but nurturing a fledgling adult. As a result they continue to talk down to the teenager, fully expecting him to obey everything without question, as though he were still in diapers. This is a parent problem, not a teenager problem.

As Father Hampsch put it, "What we think is dialogue is really an interrupted monologue." That is to say, parents often do not talk **with** their adolescents. They talk **at** them or worse still talk **down to** them. The result is that our youth, who are bursting with ideas and insights which are new to them but old-hat to us, feel they are discounted. They cannot get a word in, and even if they do, they know their parents do not hear it. Parents can so easily fall into the trap of talking and not listening. Therefore, they often unjustly assume that the youngster is wrong and they are right. Meanwhile the teenager is equally convinced that he is right and the parents are wrong.

Parents must begin to understand that their teenagers are intensely passionate on just about everything. They are constantly forming opinions about God, about themselves, about the world and about relationships and have a right to question their elders about their values. This is a built-in vital part of growing up. They recoil at the idea of being mindless clones of the past and desperately need to discover their own uniqueness. Parents usually do not like to be challenged by their own offspring but good parents accept it. They recognize that if a young man or woman is to grow to his or her fullness, it is healthy to question, to sift out the dross, to reject what is phony and adhere to what is true.

Young people must question our truths. They will not accept them simply because we say they are true. Teenagers are very sensitive to anything that is phony. In fact the worst insult a teenager can receive from his friends is to be called a phony. So he in turn, despises anything within his parents that is not honest and true. Therefore again, so much in successful parenting boils down to good example, consistently lived out. It takes a good and humble parent to accept an honest criticism from his teenager, to see the simple truth in it, to admit that he is wrong and to try to correct it. In doing so, he demonstrates respect for the teenager's perception and silently teaches him that he too can be wrong and correct it. This is very hard to do but it is just.

However, a parent will not hear these kinds of ideas if he does not listen. Teenagehood should be the automatic signal for parents to change gears. From a more or less autocratic power over the little child, they must now parent in a whole new way. They must shift into the adventure of *listening* and *guiding*. Failure to do so results in the futile attempt to enjoy their former unquestioned authority, and now the irresistible force comes up against the immovable object. That results in a battle of wills in which both the parents and the teenager lose.

Wise parents make the gear-shift as effortlessly as possible and enter this phase of raising their teenager by means of the new tools of listening and guiding. They are willing to sit down and truly listen to what the teenager is trying to say. They let him know that they *want* to understand even if they may not agree in the end. They do not treat him like a fool. They accord him the respect that is due to one who is trying to think for himself. They enjoy true dialogue which is the honest exchange of ideas between people who, though not yet equal in status, nevertheless respect each other. In this way, the teenager eagerly latches on to the respect he is accorded and feels like a significant contributor to the family. This is listening with an *open mind*.

A teenager may have ideas which are not yet refined and matured but they are his ideas nonetheless. That is why guidance is so invaluable. Adolescents do want *authority* but they do not want *authoritarianism*. If they feel that their parents are being authoritarian, they know that there is no hope for dialogue and so they will simply switch off. The well-meaning orders from above will be ignored and will not achieve the desired result. Teenagers, however, will be likely to respond to guidance. If they know they are being heard, they in turn will listen and will be more likely to accept wisdom and to see the sense in it.

They hunger for stability and inner security but they also have a fearlessness about truth. They do not want a raw statement about what is true. They need to know *why* it is true and they challenge parents to show why it is true. It is not enough to baldly state that God loves them. Teenagers will simply come back with ideas which question God's love. "If he loves us then why does he allow a child to die of leukaemia? If he loves us, why does he permit the atrocities of war?" Parents may not like this challenge to their most cherished of truths, but they must learn to transmit them in a way that meets the demands of young inquiring minds. A good response is to let the teenager express his doubts and questions and then to express your understanding as to how he might feel that way. Admit that it is not a simple issue. It is very complex and worthy of their examination. Direct them to relevant reading material which addresses their challenge.

Parents are not walking encyclopaedias and so must never try to pretend that they have all the answers. Teenagers spot that lie very quickly. It is far better to exchange views and together to search out wisdom from experts on the subject. It will never satisfy a teenager if you close the subject by saying, "The Church says so, so there!" To a teenager that is intellectual cowardice. Therefore, we must feed his hunger for a dynamic truth which he can confidently believe in. If our teenager is unafraid of truth, why should we parents be afraid? If parents do not guide in this way, then the adolescent will take his search for truth elsewhere. He will read books which lead him into false doctrine and he will absorb the worldly errors of his peers.

The teenager, being as yet immature emotionally and socially, is less interested in principles than in particular issues. He is passionate about issues. They may not be eager to learn about Church dogma but they do want to know what the Church is doing about the poor, war, justice and unequal distribution of wealth. I remember speaking with a group of teenagers at a well-known Catholic high school for boys. One outspoken young man challenged me by asking, "What is the Church doing for the poor? The Church is rich and yet there are so many poor in the world." It was a very good question. I did not respond by saying that the Catholic Church is the largest charitable organization in the world. I simply replied with another question. I asked, "What are *you* doing about the poor?" He stopped dead in his tracks, thought for a moment and said, "I am being a phony, aren't I?" He had the courage to admit his own dishonesty and all I needed to say further was, "Perhaps. But the important thing to realize is that you are the Church. You reach out to the poor in your own world and I will reach out to the poor in mine." That was listening, that was dialogue and that was guidance.

If there is any trick to this at all, it is to convince the teenager that he is forming himself rather than the parent forming him. Parents almost all love their teenagers but not all love is good. There are two ways by which love can be something disordered. Love can be over-possessive or it can be over-permissive. Over-possessive love imposes excessive restraints and so the teenager cannot breathe. He is suffocated by stupid rigid rules and so he has only two choices. Firstly, he can fight back, which results in a never-ending clash of wills. The more pressure the parents apply, the greater the resistance from the adolescent. As Sir Isaac Newton proved, "To every action there is an equal and opposite reaction." Secondly, he can choose to become overly compliant, stifling his own originality, and grow up to be timid and afraid.

Over-permissive love has no rules whatsoever. A teenager in such a home panics. He can never find the boundaries and so he tests for them by becoming more and more out of control. He searches for authority and finds none and so he becomes deviant, reckless and self-indulgent. In his destructive behaviour, he is crying for help but no one hears him. His parents have opted out.

This cry for help is a very important signal for parents to recognise. If all that parents focus on is the bad behaviour of their teenager then they will tend to react with shock, anger and punishment. If on the other hand, they see beyond the behaviour to the insecurity that the teenager is feeling, then they are more likely to respond with compassion, a desire to listen, talk it out and come up with helpful guidance. A teenager knows when he has betrayed the family honour. He feels shame and wants acceptance, but he will dig his heels in if he feels rejected. Rejection will only propel him into further deviant behaviour.

Another useless strategy is to tell a teenager what it was like to be a teenager in your own day. This is meaningless to him. He is not interested in past history. He is too interested in his present pain. I recall telling my youngsters, "When I was your age, I had to get up at six in the morning, get on my bicycle and ride two miles to Church for morning Mass. Then I had to ride home again to have breakfast and go off to school. You kids have it too easy." Needless to say, my son and daughters merely looked at me as though I had sprouted another head. They saw it as irrelevant to their present reality. Later, as they became adults, I could share these historical facts and they would enjoy hearing about them and even rib me about them, but as teenagers they saw it as utterly pointless.

While little children are very intuitive about whether they are loved or not, teenagers are equally intuitive about control. They know if parents are trying to restructure them or manipulate them. Parents often give out a contradictory message. On the one hand, they demand that teenagers "act their age" which means "act like an adult" yet at the same time they demand absolute obedience which means "act like a child." A teenager cannot cope with the contradiction. He needs to know what is expected of him and that his blundering efforts at adult behaviour are not being scorned.

Parents therefore must be helpful, not controlling. They must respect the adolescent's individuality and gifts and be available for loving listening, guidance and help. Teenagers are often too embarrassed to be open and to share feelings. Parents therefore can help by demonstrating openness first. They can share their feelings and dreams with their teenagers and they, in turn, will learn that it is safe to do likewise. Not only that, but the teenager will feel privileged and included in the family, being recognised as a person who has much to contribute. If such an atmosphere of acceptance pervades the home, then if the teenager gets into trouble, he will be likely to confess it to his parents, which is far better than struggling with it himself.

Sooner or later, it is likely that an adolescent will have to own up to some sin or other. This is when the parental reaction is crucial. Explosion, rage and condemnation will simply ensure that in future, the teenager will absolutely keep his secrets to himself. The only way to handle it is to acknowledge it as serious, to sit down and talk about it and see what can be done *together*. The teenager knows he has to take the consequences of his behaviour, but he will do that more bravely if he knows his parents will stand by him. My father always told me, "Son, if you have something coming to you, take it on the chin. Don't let them have to shoot you in the back." He meant that I should face up to the consequences of my actions and not run away like a coward. It helped enormously though, to know that my father would always be by my side. He never tried to bail me out, which would have ruined the lesson I needed to learn, but he had his manly hand on my shoulder when I faced the music. "You did it, you got caught, you've had your punishment, it is over, so move on." My father never raked up my past sins. He put them behind him and he expected me to do the same.

"Rejoice, o young man while you are young and let your heart be glad in the days of your youth. Follow the ways of your heart and the vision of your eyes, yet understand that as regards all this God will bring you to judgement" (Eccles. 11:9). Our loving Father-God blesses the vigour and excitement of youth, but like a good father, he firmly reminds them that he will call them to account for all that they decide to do with that energy. Parents should pray daily for their teenagers to direct their enthusiasm in the pathways of God, for therein lies true blessing. In fact, without prayer it is difficult to imagine that parenting of teenagers could ever hope to be successful. During this phase, the wisdom of Solomon is not enough. Parents need the wisdom of the Holy Spirit.

Many parents take on unnecessary guilt for the sins of their young people. They understandably blame themselves for their teenager's transgressions. There is no need for such self-flagellation. Parents would do well to remind themselves that teenagers are far beyond the age of reason and are fully accountable to God for their own decisions, both good and bad. "A son is not to bear his father's guilt, nor a father his son's guilt. The upright will be credited with his uprightness and the wicked with his wickedness" (Ezek. 18:20). Therefore an adolescent's sins may be a source of grief to his parents, but never a source of guilt. God will place the responsibility where it properly belongs. Surely this has to be of some small comfort to worried parents, who are scourging themselves for the bad behaviour of their young people.

Above all, parents must let their teenager know that they *believe* in him or her. This, in fact, is the natural continuation of the Blessing of the Child mentioned in chapter 7. Teenagers want your trust and they want to live up to it, but they can only do that if they believe in themselves, and that can never happen without the parents first believing in them. This declaration of trust is basic to the healthy future of the teenager. When he knows he is trusted to carry the family honour he will be a lot less likely to sully the family name. If he ever does, he will be a lot more likely to feel good honest shame at his actions and shame is the beginning of repentance and repentance is the beginning of a resolve not to repeat that behaviour.

The father and the mother must always be ready to embrace the Prodigal Son or the Prodigal Daughter. That is what Catholic family is all about. It is the desire to imitate the love of Jesus Christ, to counsel and instruct just as he did, to love just as he did, to listen and guide just as he did, to forgive always just as he did, and to assure our teenagers that their parents are willing to die for them just as he did.

The following poem was written by an anonymous poet, but it beautifully describes the teenage experience:

Please Hear What I'm Not Saying

Don't be fooled by me.
Don't be fooled by the face I wear.
For I wear a mask, a thousand masks,
masks that I'm afraid to take off,
and none of them is me.
Pretending is an art that's second nature to me,
but don't be fooled.
For God's sake don't be fooled.
I give you the impression that I'm secure,
that confidence is my name and coolness is my game,
that the water's calm and I'm in command,
and that I need no one.
But don't believe me.
My surface may seem smooth but my surface
is my mask, ever-varying and ever-concealing.
Beneath lies no complacence.
Beneath lies confusion and fear and aloneness.
But I hide this. I don't want anybody to know it.

I panic at the thought of my weakness and fear being exposed.
That's why I frantically create a mask to hide behind,
a nonchalant sophisticated facade, to help me pretend,
to shield me from the glance that knows.
But such a glance is precisely my salvation.
My only hope, and I know it.
That is, if it's followed by acceptance,
if it's followed by love.
It's the only thing that can liberate me from myself,
from my own self-built prison walls,
from the barriers I so painstakingly erect.
It's the only thing that will assure me
of what I can't assure myself,
that I'm really worth something.
I don't like to hide.
I don't like to play superficial phony games.
I want to stop playing them.
I want to be genuine and spontaneous and me,
but you've got to help me.
You've got to hold out your hand
even when that's the last thing I seem to want.
Only you can wipe away from my eyes
the bland stare of the breathing dead.
Only you can call me into aliveness.

Each time you're kind and gentle and encouraging,
each time you try to understand because you really care,
my heart begins to grow wings, very small wings,
very feeble wings,
but wings!
With your power to touch me into feeling
you can breathe life into me.
I want you to know that.

Who am I, you may wonder.
I am someone you know very well.
For I am every man you meet,
and I am every woman you meet.

"After this, I shall pour out my spirit on all humanity. Your sons and daughters shall prophesy, your old people shall dream dreams, and your young people see visions" (Joel 2:28). It is God's order for families that the elders will dream dreams and share them with the young, and that the young be allowed to have their visions for a better world. Teenagers may still be immature in so many ways, but they do have visions of their own. Parents must impart their wisdom (dreams) in such a way that the young can grow to realize their own visions. God says they shall prophesy which means to speak the Word of God, and it takes wise parents who know how to listen to hear the prophecies of their young.

One fine day your caterpillar will become a wondrous butterfly.

CHAPTER 12

Growing Older in Years:
Growing Bolder in Christ

*"In old age they will still bear
fruit, will remain fresh and
green to proclaim Yahweh's
integrity."*

(Ps. 92:14-15)

Perhaps the biggest problem the elderly face is that they are stereotyped by a society which has lost its reverence for old age. Strangely enough this is a relatively new phenomenon. Throughout history, the elderly were usually treated with respect for their advanced years and with respect for their wisdom and experience of life. The young were encouraged to consult their elders for advice and wise counsel. In many societies, it was the elderly who governed, who made the decisions for the community and who were consulted in times of crisis. Most villages had a council of elders who were given the last word on village affairs. If ever there was a very, very old person living in the community, that person was often held in some kind of awe, being regarded as "the ancient" and therefore to be accorded the utmost respect and deference. In the tradition of the Jewish people of the Old Testament, old age was regarded as a sure sign of God's favour. "For your part, you will join your ancestors in peace; you will be buried at a happy old age" (Gen. 15:15). Growing old and remaining happy and content were gifts given by God to his righteous ones.

As society has become more materialistic, more taken up with leisure and pleasure, more dependent upon technology and less religious, this respect for older citizens has dwindled. Instead of commanding more esteem from society, they are being regarded as "over the hill" and as economically unproductive. Society today is so obsessed with productivity and profit that anyone who is not productive and who is not generating profit for himself or for the corporation is relegated to the status of inferior or even useless. This disdain, of course, applies not only to the retired elderly but also to younger persons caught in the poverty trap. Unhappily, such an attitude is on the increase, since the number of elderly is growing as a percentage of the general population. The result is that fewer and fewer persons are working and providing the tax base to take care of those in retirement. Because of this shrinking tax base, governments are paring back the numbers of available hospital beds and other medical services necessary to an aging society. Social services such as home care, so vital for many elderly to remain independent in their own homes, are forced to be more concerned with their budgets than with the real needs of older citizens. Perhaps the most alarming development of all is the increasing erosion of respect for human life, reflected in the euthanasia debate. The high sounding words of compassion from those who advocate mercy-killing are nothing more than a front for the unspoken motive of eliminating unproductive and dependent citizens. The needy elderly are a challenge to society's capacity to love and to sacrifice, while the euthanasia movement is really about a refusal to love regardless of its protests to the contrary.

The fact is that a whole new education is needed to bring about a change of attitude towards our seniors. Society needs to rediscover the wonderful truth of what it means to grow older and the elderly need to show to the world what it means to grow bolder in Christ.

For a start, the general notion of aging is that it mysteriously begins somewhere around the age of forty to fifty years. This is untrue. As one gerontologist put it, "Aging refers to the process of change in the organism from the time of fertilisation of the ovum until the death of the individual." In other words from the moment of conception, life is a continuity of aging. So-called old age is nothing more than an advanced stage of the aging process.

Stereotyping is a major hindrance to the understanding of the elderly as unique and valuable persons. Human beings seem to find it much easier to cope when they cluster people into groups, rather than accepting each individual on his or her merits. This is the foundation of prejudice. The result is a whole list of beliefs about the elderly which are completely untrue.

Some of the common misconceptions are:

- "Most of the aged are sick or disabled."
- "Most of the aged are senile and useless."
- "Older workers produce less than younger workers."
- "Older people are like children and need to be treated that way."
- "Older people should be herded into their own group. They cannot relate to anyone younger."
- "Older people are totally dependent."
- "Older people cannot function effectively."
- "Older people cannot learn."

Given these kinds of convictions, it is little wonder that society has lost its way in caring for its elders, and the elders in turn, have lost the respected status they once enjoyed.

The truth needs to be proclaimed and the truth is that most elderly people are physically and mentally able to function well. It is true that many older persons may have to cope with chronic disorders such as arthritis, heart disease or diabetes, but they not only cope, they demonstrate the wonderful courage of the human spirit. If younger persons would take the trouble to acquaint themselves with their elders, they would learn a vital lesson in how to be uncomplaining, to live with physical losses and even to be joyful and at peace with these losses. The vast majority of the elderly are not senile. They enjoy mental and intellectual clarity throughout their lives, able to love, to laugh, to pray and to be of help to the younger generations. Happy elderly are those who, in spite of being forced to retire at the arbitrary age of sixty-five, are still productive and active, still full of purpose in their lives and still creating goals.

Such elderly do not retire and then sit down to await death. They view retirement as the end of one career and the beginning of a new one. Long before retirement has taken place, they have been planning ahead, setting objectives for this exciting new phase of their lives. They may decide to take on part-time work in a different field, they may at last indulge in a hobby which was impossible while they were working at their job, they may now donate their skills and expertise to community groups or take up volunteer work. Many become even more productive after so-called retirement than they ever were in the drudgery of their previous career. At last, they have the time and the freedom to take up crafts, woodworking, landscaping and countless other stimulating projects. The possibilities are endless. What matters is that the retirement stage must be embraced as a fascinating opportunity for new life rather than the beginning of the end.

Jean Maxwell in her book ***Centres for Older People*** states, "Aging is universal, aging is normal, aging is variable, dying is normal and inevitable, aging and illness are not necessarily coincidental, older people can and do learn, older people want to be more self-directing and older people are vital human beings."

Clark Tibbits, a gerontologist, described five needs which should be met if one is to grow old gracefully: the need for relationships and association with others; the need for creativity; the need for security; the need for individuality and recognition; and the need for an intellectual frame of reference. I would add to that a sixth need, which is the deepest need of the human heart. It is the need to have faith in something higher and more reliable than oneself. It is the need to believe that life persists after death. Old age must have meaning. This is the time when many people who have, till now, distracted themselves from any spiritual life because of the pursuit of career and the quest for material things are willing to ask themselves serious questions about God and eternity.

The elderly know that death is closer than it has ever been and so they are more likely to reflect on what death really means. Is it the end of all consciousness or is it the doorway to new life? The first option brings terror. The second option creates hope. Actually, these six needs apply to all human beings regardless of age, but they are more pressing and more immanent for the elderly.

It is not the intention here to imply that aging does not bring problems with it. Two researchers, Clark and Anderson, reported on their study of older people and concluded that there were seven main challenges for them.

1. A change in physical appearance.
2. Partial or total retirement from active duties.
3. Lower energy level.
4. Greater possibility of ill health.
5. Greater possibility of need of help.
6. Changes in cognitive and intellectual functioning.
7. Greater uncertainty about the duration of life.

Again, I would add an eighth problem. It is the problem of *homeostasis*. This is a medical term which refers to the natural ability of the body to keep everything in balance. For example, if a person's blood pressure goes up and is sustained for many years without treatment, the heart will compensate by growing larger, in order to more effectively pump the blood throughout the body. With aging this capacity for homeostasis becomes less and less efficient. The result is that a stress which might have been easily shrugged off in a younger person can be a major challenge to the elderly body systems. Since the major organs are deteriorating as one gets older, even a trivial stress, such as a cold, can trigger a domino effect whereby one organ after another collapses and goes into failure, possibly resulting in death. In other words, one of the problems of advancing age is that one is less resilient in reacting to a stressful event.

Most specialists in the field of gerontology define the problems of aging in terms of loss. As each person grows older, losses both small and large begin to occur and continue. Some of these losses are: loss of physical faculties, such as hearing and vision, loss of one's valued role in society usually through compulsory retirement, loss of prestige due to failing faculties, loss of authority with one's children, loss of close ties with loved ones due to death or relocation, loss of home and independence, and often loss of former optimum health due to heart disease, arthritis or organic brain disease.

These losses lead to one of the most difficult problems of aging, which is increasing dependency. For an aging person to remain in his or her own home as long as possible, there has to be a courageous acceptance of dependency needs. To deny the relentless and progressive loss of independence is to expose oneself to greater and greater risk of accidents in the home, or to the tragedy of falling ill without anyone regularly stopping by to see that all is well. Since there is often some loss of mobility, elderly persons will sometimes neglect grocery shopping due to the effort involved. Even where they are able to bring in their own groceries, they will often find cooking for one to be too irksome, and so they become malnourished and suffer from vitamin and mineral deficiencies.

Increasing dependency must be faced as a reality, especially since it is possible thereby to arrange for others to provide what one can no longer provide for oneself. For example, the home can be rendered safer by some simple adjustments such as a grab-bar in the bathroom, removal of slippery rugs, a speaker phone for the deaf, a raised toilet, or a more user-friendly kitchen where commonly used utensils are stored in the lower cupboards rather than high up out of reach. Where possible, arrangements should be made to have a neighbour, relative, or a caring church member undertake to check up on a senior by daily telephone calls or even visits. Too often an elderly person suffers a stroke and then lies on the floor for days before anyone thinks to call and check. This is easily avoided.

Where necessary, a healthy younger adult can do the grocery shopping. If one is becoming more disabled, then he or she may need to connect with the numerous available social services such as Meals-on-Wheels, home nursing, occupational therapy, physiotherapy and provision of house cleaning. Such strategies should not be seen by the elderly as "cold charity" or as a sign that one is a nuisance to others. These are common-sense solutions which prevent one from "being a nuisance" and help maintain one's independent living for as long as possible. The ultimate in dependency is when so many factors break down to the point where one cannot continue to live at home any longer, even with home-care services. That is when one may have no other choice but institutionalisation. Certainly, this last resort option is the final challenge to one's humility, to become completely dependent on nursing-home personnel for everything, from personal hygiene to food and laundry. As a practising family doctor, I never ceased to marvel at the cheerfulness and the humble resignation of so many of my aged patients who could no longer enjoy even a private bedroom, but who had to share with someone they would never have befriended in their earlier life. How adaptable and how courageous the human spirit can be.

Loneliness is a terrible reality for many elderly people. As mentioned earlier, all people need social interaction and relationships, and this applies just as much to older persons. We are gregarious by nature and so we crave for community. Until recently, families stayed together. It was not unusual for three generations to live together in the same house. As a result, grand-children had easy access to grandparents and vice versa. The little ones revered their eldest relatives and also knew that they could go to grandma or grandpa for advice, for acceptance, and most of all for love. Grandparents are not responsible for the outcome in raising grandchildren. That is the burden of the parents and so grandparents could afford to be indulgent, understanding and caring without anxiety. In addition, they were available as built-in baby-sitters, thereby allowing the parents to take time out for each other, and to escape from the relentless demands of parenting, for a few hours or even for a weekend. Such families, while they probably had their moments of frustration and personality clashes, nevertheless learned to live with one another and to enjoy the balance of having a three-generation household.

Much of that stability has been lost. Career demands have created increasing mobility. So often parents and children have to relocate to new or better paying jobs, leaving the grandparents behind. Although most elderly would never dream of complaining, and indeed would outwardly rejoice at their own children's good fortune, they feel a deep sense of loss of their dear ones. The family may do all in their power to maintain contact through phone calls and even visits on special holidays, but for most of the time, the grandparents feel isolated and lonely. They grieve and usually do it silently.

When I was a young doctor, I emigrated to Canada from Scotland, leaving my parents behind. I visited them every year until their deaths. For at least six months prior to my visit, they lived in excited anticipation and for the next six months they grieved over my departure. To this day I am haunted by the sad look on my mother's face and the stoic look of my father when I said my annual farewell at the airport. Each time, I know they wondered if they would ever see me again.

God is a family, a Trinity, and in creating us in his own image and likeness, he decreed that we too, should live in families. We need family as children, we create new families in marriage, and we still need family in our old age. Mother Teresa of Calcutta once wrote "Loneliness is only Jesus calling us to a deeper union with him. Perhaps then, we need to experience a loneliness for us to turn towards the only reliable remedy for it, which is Jesus Christ who will never stray from us. He is our constant companion if only we invite him into our hearts." "God gives the lonely a home to live in" (Ps. 68:6).

In view of this pain of loneliness and its devastating effects on the elderly, there are two solutions. The first is to have family nearby or even to be living with family. This, however, is a more and more rare phenomenon in today's society. The second strategy is for the elderly to create their own social contacts. They may belong to a senior citizens organization where social activities are available and varied. They may seek out friendships. They may choose to visit those who are also isolated, the sick, the poor or the marginalised. They may get involved in volunteer work, such as the food banks or driving others to hospital appointments. They can become more involved in Church as lay ministers, Eucharistic ministers, members of the Catholic Women's League or the Knights of Columbus. Since they usually have time, they can become more active in the Corporal and Spiritual Works of Mercy.

The Corporal Works of Mercy are:

1. To feed the hungry.
2. To give drink to the thirsty.
3. To clothe the naked.
4. To shelter the homeless.
5. To comfort the imprisoned.
6. To visit the sick.
7. To bury the dead.

Is it not true that our elders are in a wonderful position to do all of these things? They are no longer required to focus on an eight-to-five job. They are usually at a point in their lives where they have fewer wants. They have learned to be content with less and do not feel the former drive to get a bigger house or a bigger boat. Therefore, they are more able to share what they have with those who have less. They may well take someone into their home for the sake of a person in need, but also for their own need of relationship. They have time to visit the homeless and even the imprisoned if they feel called to that generous ministry. As to burying the dead, the elderly can reach out to grieving families with love, in practical support such as providing food for the funeral meal and most importantly in prayer.

The Spiritual Works of Mercy are:

1. To admonish sinners.
2. To instruct the uninformed.
3. To counsel the doubtful.
4. To comfort the sorrowful.
5. To be patient with those in error.
6. To forgive offenses.
7. To pray for the living and the dead.

Once more, the elders are in an excellent position to perform these works for the Body of Christ and for God. By dint of their long life's experience, they have learned so much in the way of wisdom, which they should be eager to share with the young. They can, with the authority of their years, lovingly call sinners to a higher way of life. They can give wise counsel to those who are troubled and give timely instruction to teenagers. They have had to face tragedy in their own lives, and so are well equipped to comfort others in their tragedy. Patience comes with wisdom and the elderly can astound us with their forbearance towards their own infirmities and towards the flaws of others. As to forgiving offenses, how many elderly go out of their way to look for the good in others, to overlook their faults and to excuse members of the family who never visit them? Old age is the last trumpet call from Jesus to grow in love.

The two greatest commandments are for us to love God above all and to love our neighbour as ourselves. Love is everything, and life's hard knocks not only challenge us to love more, but temper us in the crucible of love. The elderly have suffered and it is suffering which melts and expands the human heart to become patient, accepting, forgiving, compassionate and motivated by love.

One of the most powerful duties of the elderly is the seventh spiritual work of mercy, which is to pray for the living and the dead. "But a woman who is really widowed and left on her own has set her hope on God and perseveres night and day in petitions and prayer. The one who thinks only of pleasure is already dead while she is still alive" (1 Tim. 5:5-6). St. Paul is emphatically stating that those who are retired from the work force, whether widowed or not, now have a new job. They are called by the Lord to take up prayer in a committed and more powerful way. They have the time and the wisdom to devote themselves to the task of interceding for souls. Our grown-up sons and daughters are inevitably caught up in making their way in the world and in raising their own children. While it is expected that they will still attend Mass, receive the Sacraments and pray daily, they do not have the same time freedom which the elders have. The world is in desperate need of prayer of intercession and the causes are endless. We need to pray for an end to abortion, for the conversion of sinners, for the spiritual and material well-being of our young family members, for peace in the world and for equal distribution of food and resources to the poor. In days gone by, there were numerous cloistered orders of monks and nuns who offered continuous prayer of intercession for their nearby communities and for the world. These communities benefited incalculably from the graces called down by these holy contemplatives. Most of us do not enjoy the fruits of such prayer today, due to the regrettable decline of monastic life, and so more than ever, the world needs an army of elderly people who have the time, the generosity and the prayer power to bombard heaven on our behalf. The rosary should become a part of their right hand, constantly being offered up through the Blessed Mother to her Son Jesus for the benefit of the world. "Pray without ceasing" (1 Thess. 5:17). "The end of all things is near, so keep your minds calm and sober for prayer" (1 Pet. 4:7).

How many of today's elderly have grandchildren or, for that matter, children, who have left the Church? How many grandchildren are living with their partners without the blessing of marriage? How many grandchildren are being seduced by the world and led astray into drugs, alcohol and selfishness? There is no shortage of things to pray for. God gives to his holy elders the power to evangelise, and to convert the hearts of the young. They should therefore not give in to weariness but should battle on, proclaiming the truth, gently calling the young ones back to a moral life because, of all people, it is the elderly who know that only in an upright life, can peace of mind ever be found.

So often, society dismisses the aged as less than useful with the result that many seniors buy into that lie and think of themselves as useless. That is a treacherous deception. Old age can and should become the most spiritually powerful and effective phase of one's entire life. It is there for the taking.

As we grow older we are at an ever-increasing risk of the disease which is commonly called depression and this condition will be discussed at greater length in volume two, but at this point, it is helpful to know that if depression is confirmed it is treatable. Modern therapy can bring about very gratifying relief and can prevent the tragedy of suicide, which, sad to say, is on the increase in our elderly population. If after reading the chapter on depression, a person identifies with the symptoms or believes that an elderly relative has those symptoms, then a visit to the doctor is well worthwhile. The patient can be restored from the darkness of the disease and into the light of their normal outlook on life. Failure to recognize the disorder or a refusal to seek out medical help could result in an otherwise preventable loss of life.

"The young girl will then take pleasure in dance and young men and old alike. I shall change their mourning into gladness, comfort them and give them joy after their trouble" (Jer. 31:13). The mourning of depression can be changed into the gladness of health and this is a promise of God who guarantees a wonderful reward to those who remain faithful to him into their old age.

"After this, I shall pour out my spirit on all humanity. Your sons and daughters shall prophesy, your old people shall dream dreams" (Joel 2:28). What a wonderful grace to pray for. God is promising that he will transform the Church to the point where our young people will abandon sin and enjoy the gift of speaking God's word to the world. The elderly meanwhile, will dream dreams, which means they will expect to have a future, an eternal future, that for now we can only "dream about."

One of the beautiful traditions of the Catholic spiritual life is that we pray for the Holy Souls in Purgatory. Judas Maccabeus considered it profitable and good to pray for the dead. "For had he not expected the fallen to rise again, it would have been superfluous and foolish to pray for the dead, whereas if he had in view the splendid recompense reserved for those who make a pious end, the thought was holy and devout. Hence he had this expiatory sacrifice offered for the dead, so that they might be released from their sin" (2 Macc. 12:44-45).

We Catholics believe in the Communion of Saints and so we are called to pray for the souls in Purgatory, that their suffering will be shortened and relieved, and that they might sooner enter into the joys of Paradise. They cannot pray for themselves but they constantly pray for us on earth that we might not have to undergo their torment. Therefore, should we not in turn pray for them, especially for those who have no one to pray for them?

The elderly in their generosity can "adopt-a-soul" and direct much of their daily prayer energy towards his or her earlier release into heaven. In fact, very few Catholics realize that they can obtain a Plenary Indulgence every day. A Plenary Indulgence is a privilege granted by the Church whereby, if certain conditions are met, we can obtain the complete and instant cancellation of all punishment due to a soul who is suffering in Purgatory. The conditions are not all that stringent:

1. I must go to Mass on the day that I obtain the indulgence and receive Jesus in Holy Eucharist.
2. I must go to the Sacrament of Reconciliation within one week on either side of the day of indulgence. Therefore, if I went to Confession once every two weeks, I could obtain a Plenary Indulgence every day.
3. In addition to these two, I must either read Scripture for thirty minutes or say a Rosary or spend thirty minutes before the

Blessed Sacrament and I must add an Our Father, Hail Mary and Glory Be for the Pope's intentions.

That is all! For the elderly who are mobile and can attend Mass, surely these are not too difficult to perform. In truth, we could release a soul from Purgatory three hundred and sixty-five times a year.

Such is the generosity of the Church and such is the generosity of Jesus who promised, "Whatever you bind on earth shall be bound in heaven" (Matt. 16:19). In other words, since it was the Church which developed the privilege of indulgence, Jesus keeps his promise and honours that same privilege in heaven. Therefore, our Catholic elderly should never consider themselves to be retired. They can now be employed full-time in praying for the kingdom of God. As one wit put it, "The pay is not very good but the retirement benefits are terrific." This is highlighted by the Psalmist who wrote, "In old age, they will still bear fruit, will remain fresh and green to proclaim Yahweh's integrity" (Ps. 92:14-15). It is prayer which bears fruit and it is good works which proclaim God's integrity.

One of the most beautiful images of old age is to be found in the book of Zechariah, "Yahweh Sabaoth says this: Aged men and women will once again sit in the squares of Jerusalem, each with a stick to lean on because of their great age. And the squares of the city will be full of boys and girls playing there" (Zech. 8:4-5). What a marvellous image this is of holy community life. How wonderful it is for the old to watch the young at play, and how secure it is for the young to be watched over by the old. God promises us a great old age and he promises us the peace to enjoy it. It is holiness which secures it.

The New Testament also promises abundant life in old age. When the Angel Gabriel spoke to Mary, he said, "Your cousin Elizabeth also, in her old age, has conceived a son and she whom people called barren is now in her sixth month, for nothing is impossible to God" (Luke 1:36-37). This miraculous pregnancy was given to us, not solely to bring John the Baptist into history, but also to prove that God can do anything. It also confirmed that God loves his holy elderly people enough to work wonders through them. How many of today's elderly truly believe that? How many trust in the power of God to do great things in their own lives and in the lives of their loved ones? It is never too late to trust in God. Scripture says that *nothing* is impossible to God.

St. Paul echoes this theme when he writes, "It was equally by faith that Sarah, in spite of being past the age, was made able to conceive, because she believed that he who had made the promise was faithful to it. Because of this there came from one man (Abraham) and one who already had the mark of death on him, descendants as numerous as the stars of heaven and the grains of sand on the seashore which cannot be counted" (Heb. 11:11-12). God honours his friends and he honours his elderly who are faithful to his word. Sometimes though, the problem is that we do not have a generous enough picture of what God can do. We limit him by our own human limits and do not ask him for great things. We have to believe in miracles for miracles to occur.

A factor which is too often underplayed, especially by the youth of today and even by the elderly themselves, is that being old demands respect. "Listen to your father from whom you are sprung, do not despise your mother in her old age" (Prov. 23:22). This is a serious demand by God. He expects us to treat our elders with respect, honour and deference, acknowledging their venerable age. This does not mean that children, teenagers, and young adults only owe respect to those elderly who are clever or wise or competent. This respect is owed simply because a person is old and has survived many years of joy and sorrow, health and sickness, prosperity and grief. Old age is to be revered because God says so.

The fourth commandment of the Decalogue states, "Honour your father and your mother" (Ex. 20:12). We therefore are called upon to honour our elderly, for they are all our mothers and fathers. We honour them by our love, respect, tolerance, patience, kindness, caring and a willingness to give them our time.

Sadly, very few younger people seem to do this today, because they have been seduced by the myth of the "generation-gap" but that is no reason for discouragement. The world may shirk its obligation, but God at least, will always glorify his older friends and will always love and honour them. They will not be lacking in what is their right of seniority before him. "Never speak sharply to a man older than yourself but appeal to him as you would to your own father: treat younger men as brothers, older women as mothers and young women as sisters in all purity" (1 Tim. 5:1-2). Therefore, while it is a tragedy that seniors are so often neglected or relegated to loneliness, it is a major catastrophe for the adults and youth who reject them. God in his holy word is commanding us to treat all elders as though they were our very own fathers and mothers. Violation of this ordinance is a serious refusal to love. The Old Testament Jews understood this principle, even if the Pharisees and wealthy landowners often did not practice it. Jews always addressed an elderly woman as mother and an old man as father, even if they were meeting them for the first time. How transforming it would be if our society would adopt the same custom. As soon as I refer to someone as mother or father, I immediately display an attitude of reverence for their age and speak with respect, as I would to my own parents.

Yet, such a reclaiming of one's dignity as an elder is unlikely to happen if the elderly merely sit around hoping for it. If older persons become passive then this only convinces younger persons that indeed the elderly are good-for-nothing and should be set aside. Therefore it is time for our senior citizens to take back their dignity. It is time for seniors to learn where their dignity lies in order to become what they are in truth. Contrary to what is believed by some radical segments of society, the dignity of our elders will not be reclaimed by militant action or protests or the demanding of rights. True holy change can only occur through true and holy people. Seniors must first learn who they are before God and how the Almighty wants them to behave. By becoming a holy people, they will find to their amazement that God will provide in marvellous ways.

"Older men should be reserved, dignified, moderate, sound in faith and love and perseverance. Similarly older women should behave as befits religious people with no scandal-mongering and no addiction to wine; they must be teachers of right behaviour and show younger women how they must love their husbands and love their children, how they must be sensible and chaste, and how to work in their homes and be gentle and obey their husbands so that the message of God is not disgraced" (Titus 2:2-5).

This is a superb sketch of what God expects of his faithful elderly. With a few strokes of the pen, St. Paul describes an older man as one who should be manly in every way. He acts in a dignified manner. He is moderate in all things and therefore not a drunkard or a glutton and shows proper reserve in company. He has learned self-control, he believes in the truth of God and shows manly perseverance in that truth. Naturally, all that he does is prompted by love. It is as though St. Paul is suggesting that the hot-headedness, the anger, the pride and the violence of youth have all been laid aside, and that maturity has at last brought true freedom, the freedom to be a loving and peaceful man.

Elderly women are expected by the Lord to be more like religious in their behaviour than like women of the world. With age there should come the wisdom to know that malicious gossip and excessive drinking are never satisfying, and always do major evil. In addition to temperance and self-control, they also can, where possible, teach younger women in the family (or outside the family if the young girls will listen) how to be pure and good, how to love their husbands and how to nurture their children. What a privilege we have that God would give us the health and the grace to grow to a ripe old age. What a privilege it is to become a mother or a father to all the younger generations. What a joy it is to share one's experience, wisdom, time and skills with those in need. What a privilege it is to have the time to pray for souls, to attend daily Mass, to visit Jesus in the Blessed Sacrament, and to make one's eternal reward a top priority.

It is absolutely true that society has serious obligations with regard to the elderly and it is a tragedy that, for the most part, society is revoking these obligations. There is an erosion of respect for our elders. There is a regrettable tendency for modern society to banish the troublesome elderly into institutions, and no doubt the euthanasia debate will not go away. Nevertheless, if our older citizens could really learn to believe in who they are before God, if they would take up their cross and follow Jesus, if they would live a life of peace, moderation, faith and love, then not only will the elders themselves feel content and at peace, but society will slowly be transformed into a new vision of old age. Once more the elders will be given the respect and deference that is their due. It is not enough to grow older in years. It is necessary to grow bolder in Christ, for seniors to discover themselves and for society to rediscover them.

CHAPTER 13

Death and Dying: The Doorway to Life

> *"Death is swallowed up in victory. Death, where is your victory? Death, where is your sting?"*
>
> (1 Cor.15:54-55)

A friend of mine once attended a meeting of psychologists in a major city. During one of the presentations everyone was asked to write down what they would try to accomplish if they knew that they were going to die in five years time. Everyone wrote eagerly about their dreams, unfinished projects, trips they would like to take and so on. Then the professor asked them to write down their priorities if they knew they were going to die tomorrow. The effect was electrifying. Everyone soon realised that their priority list was totally different. The immediacy of death changed all. There were no more long-term projects. Instead, most realised they needed to gather their loved ones together, to speak the words that had not been spoken, to ask for and to give forgiveness, and to express love and gratitude to them. It was a powerful demonstration of the sad fact that we rarely live as though we would die one day and that death could come sooner than we think. In fact it would seem that death always comes sooner than we think.

Christians are reminded by the Church that death is a reality and that if we are in a state of grace it need not be feared. In fact it can be a peaceful if not a joyful experience as we confidently go to Jesus. "Look, I am old and do not know when I may die" (Gen. 27:2). This not-knowing does not postpone the appointed day and certainly denying death will not prevent it. As followers of Jesus, we can both live and die with hope. We know as no one else can that death is only a change of address. Death is not the end, but is the beginning of a new life and as such is really only a continuation of life into eternity.

"Precious in the eyes of the Lord is the death of his faithful ones" (Ps. 116:15). For God, death is not the tragedy that we consider it to be. For his Divine Heart, it is a moment of greatest joy for he can then delight in giving us our eternal reward in Heaven. The only time that it is painful to God's way of thinking is when we die in our sins. "Would I take pleasure in the death of the wicked, declares the Lord Yahweh, and not prefer to see him renounce his wickedness and live?" (Ezek. 18:23). Most of us, then, look upon death very differently from God. If only we knew what was waiting for us as disciples of Jesus, we would look forward with holy expectancy to see and experience the joy of our Creator God.

Most Christians already know all this, but when it comes right down to it, we really fear dying more than death. Death is not so bad since we can appreciate that it is an end to pain, the moment of final release from suffering. Dying however is a very different matter and all of us are uneasy about that. Naturally very few people, except for some exceptionally holy Christians, relish the idea of terminal suffering and pain. It is only natural to wish to avoid it or even to fear it, but this can lead us to miss an important truth. I very often hear people say something like, "When I go I want to go instantly and suddenly." This is understandable in that they do not desire to suffer, but to be honest, I am personally horrified at the thought of a sudden death. Should that happen to me, would I have any time to prepare my soul for God? Would I have time to tell Jesus I am sorry for my sins? Would I even have time to call upon the name of Jesus? This is a very important concept for me. I pray that I do not have an instantaneous death. On the contrary I pray that the Lord will grant me the grace of a *happy* death, one by which I am prepared and ready to meet him, a death which is preceded by the time needed to put my immortal soul in order.

Every day I pray a little prayer which I was taught as a child. It is the prayer for a happy death.

"Jesus, Mary and Joseph, I give you my heart and my soul.
Jesus, Mary and Joseph, assist me in my last agony.
Jesus, Mary and Joseph, may I breathe forth my soul in peace
with you." Amen.

Some may regard that as a selfish desire. After all, someone else will have to nurse me in my last illness and my illness would cost the taxpayer a lot of money in health care. My only answer is that I, for my part, am prepared to nurse any of my loved ones who are dying, and eternal life is worth it. Also, my salvation is of infinite worth to me and certainly much more than mere dollars and cents.

Having laid the spiritual groundwork, it is important to discuss dying and to promote some understanding of its effects both on the patient and upon his or her family. For this I am indebted to the wonderful work of Therese Rando, a clinical psychologist, who has devoted her life to the care of the dying and those who are grieving.

It is difficult to imagine a more devastating moment in anyone's life than to be told by the doctor that one has a fatal disease. All of a sudden, all illusions of immortality are stripped away and death is close at hand. It becomes real and the patient will be forced to deal with it one way or another. Understandably he or she will have a major emotional reaction, which will consist of initial shock followed by bargaining, anger, depression and ultimately acceptance. These reactions do not necessarily occur in that sequence and people will move in and out of any one of these at any given time. One moment she may feel angry, at another sad, then back to anger again or into a state of shock. It is a time of confused coming to terms with a deadly reality.

The stage of shock is marked by a sense of disbelief at the diagnosis. It causes an emotional numbness and the patient is in a kind of stunned daze unable to really accept that death is staring her in the face. She tends to have such thoughts as "This is not happening to *me*. The doctor has made a mistake."

The bargaining phase is an attempt by the patient to find a way out of her terrible reality. She may bargain with the doctor. "If I give up smoking now, surely that would cure the cancer" or she may completely reject the offer of conventional medical help. She may then latch on to magical concoctions which guarantee more than they can deliver, or worse still she may be duped by charlatans who offer phony miraculous cures. How many desperate people with cancer have ruined themselves financially by rushing off to Mexico for treatment with the new "wonder drug" which was nothing more than extract of apricot pits? No one can blame the patient who is only too ready to grasp at straws, but we should certainly despise those who cheat them.

While it is a good and holy thing to pray for a cure to Almighty God, nevertheless it can also take the form of bargaining with God. "If you heal me Lord then I promise to give up drinking. I will stop being nasty to my wife and children. I will go to daily Mass from now on." This is not so bad and certainly God understands one's desperation, but we must also allow God to be God and humbly accept his perfect will for us, otherwise we risk becoming unjustly angry with him or even blaming him for our plight.

Anger is of course a natural response to devastating news. The patient may have such thoughts as "Why me?" "What have I ever done to deserve this?" It can be directed towards others. "Why has this not happened to Amy? I am a better person than she is. Where is the justice?" When this anger is directed at God, we may find ourselves asking such questions as, "Why has God done this to me." "God does not love me." "There is no God." Family members must never rebuke their loved one for expressing such thoughts. At this time they must understand that it is a frantic effort to cope and it is a cry for help and for hope. The family needs to be there, to accept and to love. It is not the time for deep discussions about death and the afterlife. That may be appropriate later on but during the anger phase, the patient needs acceptance and hope, not doom and gloom.

At any point, the patient can plunge into a severe depression. This is a form of grieving for oneself and it is a deep sense of loss for one's former health and vigour. The patient mourns over her previous enjoyment of life, may regret not having lived it more fully and is anticipating her own death, seeing it as a tragedy. She is unable to see any hope. She may feel guilty over past transgressions and may become so overwhelmed that she feels condemned by God.

During this time, the family must allow the loved one to express her feelings, without judging them and to foster within her an attitude of hope. They need to emphasize that the patient is not dead yet, that there is time to realize some ambitions and that the patient still has some control over how events will unfold. All of us are frightened of losing control and a dying person needs to feel that, while control is shrinking, it is not all gone.

Hope is vital to a dying patient, but as the illness progresses, the hope has to change its focus. As hope of a longer life fades, it must be replaced by an increasing hope of life hereafter. This is absolutely fundamental to a Catholic. The key to a worthy death lies in the hope that there is a God and that Jesus will keep his promise to us of eternal salvation.

The last phase of emotional adjustment is acceptance. This is the time when the patient finally faces reality. The patient knows she is going to die and is at peace with it. She is now able to plan the time she may have left, to attend to her affairs, to communicate with her family and to prepare her soul for God. It is a relief to the patient. It is also a great relief to the family. There is no more need for pretend games. The family can now freely talk about the death of their loved one, about funeral arrangements, about the music for the Mass of the Resurrection and the many other details which the patient may wish to be carried out. In planning her own funeral, she is being given a necessary sense of control over her final rites. It is a way of holding onto dignity.

When the patient has been allowed to proceed through the initial emotional sequence, it is now time for her to face certain very important tasks. Again she should be given as much control as possible.

The first task is to cope with the progressive symptoms of the illness itself. All of us are afraid of pain and so the patient needs to understand that her pain can be relieved very effectively and still leave her in complete possession of her faculties. She can expect to have pain control and continue in a warm and realistic relationship with her family. She can expect to retain her full awareness and intellect. Patients do fear that they will be heavily drugged and thereby out of touch with their loved ones. This does not happen with modern palliative care. Not only that, but medical science can offer relief from distressing symptoms other than pain, such as vomiting or diarrhoea. Nevertheless, there is still going to be suffering in the sense of knowing that one is losing ground daily. There will likely be a drastic change in one's appearance if weight loss occurs, and ultimately, one may become confined to bed. Even though the patient may have reached a good acceptance level of reality following the initial shock of the diagnosis, nevertheless she has to adjust to each loss as it comes along, whether it be loss of former beauty or loss of ability.

The second task is dealing with the demands of often dramatic treatment interventions. The patient may have to face hospitals, medical personnel, chemotherapy, radiation, surgery and prosthetic devices. All of these put new demands on the patient to adapt. Adaptation requires energy and a dying person is losing energy. It is a major challenge and can only be met by means of spirit and sheer courage. Again, family is so vital in supporting the patient through these ordeals, driving her to appointments, being in the waiting room during surgery and helping her with medications.

The third task is to develop a good relationship with medical personnel. So often a patient feels helpless. For her, it is as though her body does not belong to her anymore. She feels at the mercy of the doctors and nurses who "do things to her body" as though it was their property and not hers. There is no need for this. The patient has the right to exercise her own unique dignity, and medical personnel need to understand that it is a profound privilege for them to be allowed to even lay a hand on a patient. Good doctors and nurses understand this, the patient automatically senses it and so she feels confident in placing herself into their care. Unfortunately, this is an ideal not always present since it seems to depend upon the philosophy and the sensitivity (or lack of it) on the part of the caregivers.

Two physicians by the name of Moos and Tsu wrote, "Consider the questions patients may ask themselves: Can I express my anger at the doctor for not coming to see me? How can I ask for additional medication for pain when I need it? How can I deal with the disagreements among different physicians regarding how I should be treated? How can I handle the condescension and pity I sense in the nurses who care for me? How can I tell the physical therapist not to give up on me even though my progress is disappointingly slow? How can I engage my doctor in a meaningful discussion of how I wish to be treated if I am incapacitated and near death? These are problems which plague patients and their families. The frequent turnover and change in personnel, particularly those staff who come into more direct contact with the patient, makes this an unusually complicated set of tasks."

The fourth task is to cope with feelings. As has already been mentioned, this is best done by fostering a sense of hope even where the hope is limited by the realities of the illness. Hope prolongs life, as the work of many researchers has shown and it prolongs quality of life, which is even more important. Loss of hope is despair and that only leads to withdrawal from life. Such a patient merely curls up and dies, which is a major and unnecessary tragedy. The family and the priest are vital agents of hope to a dying Catholic.

The fifth task is to preserve an acceptable self-image and to maintain some sense of control over events no matter how increasingly limited that control may become. For example, a patient may continue to have her hair done regularly. She may decide to have her bed moved downstairs so she can interact with her family. She may refuse to accept the offer of certain chemotherapy, because the side-effects may be unacceptable. She may decide to make a last trip. She may decide to write her life story as a legacy for her loved ones.

The sixth task is to preserve and to deepen family relationships and friendships. A dying patient really needs continued contact with loved ones in spite of the isolation caused by hospitalisation or the reluctance of others to be close to someone who is sick or dying. This is really more of a challenge to the family than it is to the patient. The patient needs this contact but having no control over others, she is dependent upon the love and caring of family and friends, to visit and talk or simply to be by the bedside. We all fear dying alone and no one should ever have to. This task falls onto the family's shoulders.

The seventh task is, if there is time, to put one's affairs into order. That means making sure the will is made out according to the patient's wishes and is properly legal and binding. Perhaps debts need to be paid and insurance policies checked on. Many persons choose to write letters to family, friends and co-workers to be opened only after their death.

The eighth task is spiritual. For a Catholic, death is the beginning of the great eternal adventure and so dying demands preparation of the soul. Arrangements should be made for the priest to visit regularly, to pray over the person, to hear her confession, to bring her Holy Communion and to administer the Sacrament of the Sick. The priest should encourage the patient to talk about life after death and to share with her the truths of Jesus about the promised resurrection. The family should gather around their loved one to pray the Rosary, asking the Mother of God to be present to receive her soul at the appointed time. St. Joseph is the patron saint of a happy death and so he too should be asked to be present at the moment of death so that both he and his spouse, Mary, can lead the soul with joy to Jesus. This is not pious pablum. This is raw spiritual truth.

I have had the privilege of being present many times at the death of a Catholic who, having had time to prepare, joyfully received the last rites. It was heart-warming to see the family gathered around the death-bed and praying the Rosary. On occasion I even heard the patient exclaim that she could see Mary, Jesus or St. Joseph waiting for her expectantly, and then she closed her eyes and died. Such Catholics experienced a truly happy death. I have seen other deaths which I can only describe as fear and terror-filled and it was a harrowing thing for me to witness their refusal to accept Jesus right to the last. They did not die in the peace of Christ, at least it did not appear so. I have always believed that our last hours are Satan's last chance to tempt us. This is the critical time when he makes his last frantic attempt to snatch our soul from heaven's grasp. Therefore it is critical that a patient be surrounded by family, friends and hopefully a priest, to fervently pray for the protection of the soul from this final onslaught. The Chaplet of the Divine Mercy has been proven over and over again to be a powerful weapon against Satan and his demons during this last battle.

The most difficult death for anyone to cope with is the death of a child. The reasons for this are not too difficult to understand. The death of a child is considered a greater loss because the child has not had the opportunity to live a full life as compared to an adult. The life of a child has great social value. We are moved by his or her childlike helplessness and we grieve for the loss of an innocent. Also, we find it very hard to see why a child should have to die. It may even lead us to question God. How can a loving God allow an innocent child to die of cancer or in an accident? The death of a child, even one we have never known, affects us all.

Until recently, families and care-givers alike have tended to withhold from the child the awful fact that she was dying. The adults around her understandably wanted to protect her from unnecessary hurt and they felt confirmed in that attitude by the fact that the child refrained from asking any disturbing questions. This approach is no longer considered to be appropriate. Recent research has shown that children, no matter how young, are very aware that they are dying. They do not ask questions because they quickly pick up on the pain of the adults around them and realize that it would hurt them to talk about death. The brave little soul sacrifices her own need to understand, out of consideration for her parents and family.

Nevertheless, the child suffers from fear of the unknown and really needs to be allowed to ask questions and receive answers. Any professional today, who works with dying children, will agree that children do have an awareness of their own condition and experience grief and anxiety as a result of it. Therefore communication with the child is indispensable. Naturally, parents who may be willing to communicate honestly will worry about how much the child can understand, especially if the child is very young. Again research has shown that terminally ill children can understand their dying in terms previously thought of as possible only in older children and that, surprisingly enough, their ideas and concepts are much more sophisticated than those of healthy children (Bluebond-Langrer 1977).

Fr. Kavanaugh in his book *Facing Death* wrote, "of the many children I visited near death, Tildy affected me the most. Burned beyond repair, her obvious pain and severe disfigurement were instrumental in keeping many friends away. I am ashamed at how frequently I manufactured excuses until she shared with me in our huddled confession her perplexity about how to handle her parents. This loveable nine-year-old could not tell them how much she knew and they would not tell her. Together, Tildy and I kept her secret. Only days before she died, she took my hand and said with smiling pride, 'We did it, Father, we did it! I don't think they know that I know.'" We often do not give our children the credit for their knowledge, insight and great courage.

Dr. Spinetta, writing in 1980, provides a list of topics which should be raised with a dying child and discussed at a level appropriate to the child's age. The care-giver should use the child's own language and should encourage the child to express her own worries, fears and concerns. This allows the parent, doctor or nurse to address the real struggles within the child. There are fourteen points. The first eleven points can be raised when the child may have months or years of life still ahead even though the diagnosis of a fatal disease has been established. It is recommended that points twelve through fourteen should be reserved for the time when the child is very close to death. I will paraphrase the fourteen points from the Catholic perspective.

1. Death is part of nature. In fact it is a part of life.
2. The death of the child is very important to her and it is very important to her family and friends.
3. Not only will the child lose those who are left behind but those left behind also lose her.
4. Death is not the end. The child will live on in the arms of Jesus in the most wonderful joy and she can help mom and dad and her brothers and sisters by asking Jesus to help them. She can also look forward to the day when her family will also die and they can all be reunited in heaven.
5. The child will not have to die alone. Her loved ones will be by her side praying with her and holding her hand.
6. The child needs to know that her life has had a purpose. Parents need to tell her what a precious gift she is from God to them and how much she has brought joy into their lives.
7. It is all right to cry and feel sad.
8. It is all right to sometimes be angry about dying.
9. It is all right not to want to talk about it anymore for a while.
10. When the child is ready to talk about it again, the adult will be there to listen and support. This is crucial.
11. It is all right to feel confused or to say things which you think are silly. Adults say silly things too.

12. Death will not hurt. Dying might be painful and the doctor will do everything possible to take the pain away, but death stops the pain. Children need to know that the pain will stop.

13. When someone you love dies it is important for you to be able to say good-bye. "So we parents will need to say good-bye to you and we do that at the funeral Mass where we give you to Jesus. This is very important for your mother and father and your brothers and sisters. So I hope you don't mind. You will be with Jesus in the joy of Heaven, but we have to stay here for a while longer."

14. The child needs to know that it is also hard for her family to face the separation of death. "If we talk to the doctor a lot and cry afterwards or if we cry when we talk to you about your illness, it is only because we love you and it will be hard to get along without you around, but we will always be with you. We won't be able to hear you talk to us from heaven but guess what! You will be able to hear us talk to you. That is the way it is in heaven so you will know when we are thinking of you and that will be a lot."

Gabrielle was a tiny, elderly, courageous lady who was a patient of mine many years ago. Right from the start, she insisted that I call her Gabby, so Gabby it was. She had been raised in a Catholic home, but had abandoned the Church a long time before I met her.

Shortly after I began to look after her, her husband developed a serious illness and it soon became clear that he was going to die soon. He became house-bound, then chair-bound, then bed-ridden and finally he passed away, leaving Gabby alone in the world. She did have a sick sister who lived too far away to visit. All during that time, Gabby nursed her husband with great love and tenderness. No task, no matter how intimate, was beneath her and she never uttered one single word of complaint.

During her husband's last days, I would make many house-calls, attend to her husband's needs and then Gabby and I would sit down to a cup of tea. I was able to talk to her about death, about life after death, about prayer and the love of God. Not long after her husband's death, she asked me to come and talk some more about the faith. I did, and one day I asked her outright if she was ready to make a long-overdue confession and return to the Church. She said a joyful "yes" and I arranged for her to see a good priest. She was instantly transformed and her natural exuberance for life became a joy that sparkled in her eyes.

After that I would take the Holy Eucharist to her when I made my house-calls and, whenever she received Jesus, she seemed so peaceful and happy. Her face would light up at the sight of the Sacred Host and she would say, "Oh! I am the luckiest girl in the whole world!" Some time later, Gabby's sister died and in her will she left Gabby a single dinner place-setting of Limoges china. For Gabby, who was very poor, this was a priceless treasure and it was with great excitement and pleasure that she carefully unwrapped it to show it to me. In all innocence she said, "Now my dream is to sit down at a table with my place-setting and to enjoy a tender filet mignon with mashed potatoes and garden peas, and maybe even a sip of good wine."

When I returned home that night, I told my wife, Rita, of Gabby's dream and it was no surprise to me that Rita immediately set about making the dream come true. A week later I picked up Gabby and her Limoges china and we went home, where Rita lovingly set out the china on the dining table and all three of us had a marvellous dinner with the filet mignon and all the trimmings and Gabby even had that sip of good wine. I do not know how many times she said, "Oh! I am the luckiest girl in the whole world!"

Not too long after that, Gabby began to complain of some very ominous-sounding symptoms. An X-ray revealed a rapidly growing cancer in her large bowel. She was so tiny and elderly and fragile that the surgeon wisely refused to be aggressive with treatment. So Gabby came home to face death. I continued to see her regularly and to bring her Holy Communion and I did all I could to keep her as comfortable as possible. Christmas was coming and so Rita and I invited her to share Christmas dinner with us. She was so excited, she kept on talking about it, telling all her neighbours in her apartment building. She could hardly wait for the big day. However, it did not work out as we had planned.

Around five o'clock in the afternoon of Christmas Eve, she called me in great pain. I went round to find her in complete bowel obstruction and I had no choice but to take her to hospital right away. She was so crestfallen that she would miss her longed-for Christmas with us, but we were not beaten yet. The next day, Rita and I loaded her presents into a colourful shopping bag and off we went to visit Gabby in the ward. Rita had bought about twenty little gifts, all beautifully wrapped and she piled the lot onto Gabby's bed. Needless to say, Gabby had already captured the hearts of all the doctors and nurses on the ward and soon they all gathered round to enjoy the big unwrapping ceremony. Again and again Gabby kept declaring, "I'm the luckiest girl in the whole world!"

The good doctors were able to temporarily relieve the bowel obstruction and so Gabby was allowed home for a little time. Her prayer life became more and more beautiful and fervent. She said her Rosary faithfully and continued to receive the Sacraments. However, it was clear that she was failing fast, losing weight and becoming weaker.

It was in March of the year that I had to admit her to hospital for the last time. When Rita and I went to see her, she humbly whispered to us that she was embarrassed to have to wear a hospital gown. She did not have a gown of her own. That was enough for Rita, who promptly took off to the shopping mall and purchased an exquisite white satin nightdress for Gabby. When Rita took it in to the hospital I could not be there but Rita reported to me that Gabby was beside herself with excitement and joy. She put it on and looked like a little bride, which is exactly what she was. She was a pure and holy little bride of Jesus.

While visiting, Rita noticed that some of Gabby's flowers were wilting badly and she innocently reached over to remove them. Gabby look up and said, "No! Leave them alone. They are not dead yet." Rita knew that Gabby was really saying, "Don't count me out. I'm not dead yet, either." So Rita just smiled and gently left well enough alone.

The following day, Gabby knew I was coming in to see her and so she put on her new gown, wanting to look her very best. Unknown to me, she also refused to take any morphine shots that day so that she could be fully alert for my visit. She looked like a little porcelain doll sitting up in bed. She must have been in severe pain but she never let out a whimper. She had received the Sacrament of the Sick and she told me quite matter-of-factly that she was ready to meet Jesus. She promised that she would pray for Rita and me when she got to Heaven. Before I left, she took my hand and whispered, "I'm the luckiest girl in the whole world!" I kissed her and said good-bye. She died the next day.

Little Gabby taught me more than years of study with books. She taught by her wonderful spirit of thanksgiving and gratitude to God for all her blessings. She thanked God for her life, for her Limoges china, for her filet mignon, for her friendship with Rita, but most of all she thanked God for calling her back to the rich life of the Church. She truly considered herself to be the luckiest girl in the whole world even in the midst of dying. Above all, I thank God for Gabby and for her happy death. She will never be canonised by the Church. She was too tiny to be noticed, but she is in heaven. "Remain faithful unto death and I will give you the crown of life" (Rev. 2:10).

Dying is not easy but it is the doorway to life.

CHAPTER 14

Grief: My World is Empty Without You

> *"We want you to be quite*
> *certain, brothers, about those*
> *who have fallen asleep, to*
> *make sure that you do not*
> *grieve for them, as others do*
> *who have no hope."*
> (1 Thess. 4:13)

The virtue of hope is vital to every human being and it is hope which gives us the fortitude to bear our worst tragedies. It is indispensable to the person facing a terminal illness and it is indispensable to anyone who is grieving over a loved one. It should go hand in hand with being a Catholic, and that is why the funeral Mass is called the Mass of the Resurrection. The Church calls us at the time of death to remember that Jesus conquered death, to tap into our hope and to look to the heavenly reward which our relative or friend is now enjoying. It urges us to find our own joy in the fact that she who has died is now free from pain of any kind and is in the arms of the Lord. The Church also reminds us that our time of separation will be short and one day we will be reunited in Heaven in unspeakable joy. "Eye has not seen nor ear heard what God has prepared for those who love him" (1 Cor. 2:9).

While this message of joy is absolutely true, we still cannot escape from grief over the loss. All of us, in one way or another, will enter into a time of mourning which is painful, and for some it will be very prolonged indeed. Most people grieve acutely over a period of about one year, have a significant relapse at the anniversary date of the loved one's death, and only then begin to look forward to a new and meaningful life. It is as though the mind needs to go through the four seasons of the year before it can come out of the darkness. One of the reasons for this is, that during the first year following the bereavement, a person will often think, "Last year at this time Susan was alive and we were on holiday together." This triggers the acute sense of loss all over again. Once the anniversary date is past, this kind of memory is no longer so painful because, of course, last year at this time Susan was already gone.

The mourner may then do well for a time but have a bad grief experience at the next anniversary date and so on for a few years, but each time it is of less and less intensity.

Grief at the death of someone we love is often somewhat lessened if there has been a prolonged illness prior to the death. During the sickness we are able to do some grief work, bit by bit, as we see our loved one deteriorate and approach death. This is called *anticipatory grief* and it is not a bad thing. It can greatly reduce the intensity of the grief we are going to feel when death finally takes place.

However, there is a very difficult aspect of grieving which has been termed *The Lazarus Syndrome*. This refers to a situation where a loved one is clearly dying. We enter into anticipatory grief, expecting her to die very soon, and then the patient makes a dramatic recovery. This raises two problems for the family. First of all, if we have interiorly said good-bye to Susan then it can be incredibly difficult to welcome her back into the land of the living and give her once more a place in our hearts. Secondly, when Susan relapses, we find it very hard to let ourselves grieve again for fear she may recover unexpectedly once more. *The Lazarus Syndrome* is an extremely difficult emotional crisis for family members. If it occurs more than twice, people can find themselves wishing that Susan would get on with it and die. They then feel deeply guilty about entertaining such "dreadful" thoughts. A good therapist knows how to deal with that guilt and helps a family member to understand that very few people can cope with the roller-coaster intense feelings which attend such a problem. The need for relief from the overwhelming emotion is so great that one might entertain a death-wish, something one would never have dreamed possible before.

The truth is that grieving is a necessary process. Left alone, and allowed to proceed naturally, it will result in self-healing. A grief therapist will compassionately allow the bereaved person to go through the process in his or her own way and at his or her own speed. Grief is not healed by aggressive intervention, but by patience and compassion. It is vital that the therapist affirm a person's unique way of grieving and reassure him or her that what they are experiencing is normal. The only time that grief can be considered to be abnormal is when it becomes blocked and is no longer progressing towards resolution. Blocked grief definitely requires therapy, otherwise it will persist for many, many years. Some people do not recover at all. This blockage can occur where a loved one died a sudden or violent death, or where the loved one was a young child. It can also occur if the survivor experiences crushing guilt (because she feels responsible for the death) or where she had not given or received forgiveness from the loved one. Guilt is a powerful obstacle to the grieving process.

As a rule, normal grieving passes through the seven *"R's."*

1. Realization

It is essential for the bereaved to fully realize that the death has actually occurred and to make some kind of sense out of it. This can be very difficult where death was sudden and unexpected, such as in a motor-vehicle accident. It is much more difficult where the death was a suicide or a murder. The stage of shocked disbelief can be very paralysing and the bereaved simply refuses to accept that the loved one is really dead. It takes a lot of love to gently help her accept the terrible truth.

As the person gradually allows reality to sink in, then the floodgates of loss can be opened up and she can give herself permission to feel the pain.

2. Remembering

A grieving person should be given permission to reminisce about her past life with the deceased. She should be allowed to bring back all kinds of memories of what they did together, trips they enjoyed, humorous times, and even sad times. There is no agenda here. The bereaved can talk about any memory at all and we should be very patient in allowing her to go over a memory as many times as she needs to. She should never be cut off just because she has already told someone the same thing many times before.

3. Realistic Recall

This is very important to healthy grieving. Very often the bereaved will focus only on the good qualities of the loved one as though it would be disrespectful or somehow sacrilegious to do otherwise. Most people believe that one should not speak ill of the dead. Yet, there is a big difference between the sin of slandering the dead and simply accepting the truth. All human beings are the usual mix of good and bad. The loved one was all of that as well. To "canonise" the deceased, as it were, is not only unrealistic but can lead to blockage of the grief process. The bereaved should be encouraged to remember good times, but should also acknowledge that the loved one was no saint and be able to talk about past hurts or hard times. This keeps the memory balanced and rooted in reality.

4. Releasing

If the grief is progressing in a healthy way, then sooner or later the survivor has to let the loved one go. There has to come a point at which she accepts the death, and releases the deceased into his or her eternal life. The fact is, of course, that the deceased is already in eternity, but the griever still fiercely holds on to the loved one in her heart. For healthy progress, she must cut the cord and allow the loved one to be really dead. It is very important to understand that this releasing does not mean the severing of a *relationship* with the deceased. On the contrary, therapy encourages the one left behind to develop a new and meaningful relationship with the loved one. This is a more spiritual connection, understanding that the loved one is not only still alive elsewhere, but is able to be closer to the survivor than ever before. The loved one is not constrained by the physical limitations of the body and so is able to be close to the bereaved in a new and beautiful way. As Catholics we believe we can and should pray *for* the souls of the dead, that they will be released from Purgatory (if they stand in need of purification), and we can pray *to* them asking for their intercession with Jesus on our behalf. This is the wonderful doctrine of the Communion of Saints and it is a source of great consolation to anyone who is grieving. The relationship with the deceased is not over. It is simply transformed.

5. Reassessment

With the death of someone very dear, all our assumptions about the world are drastically changed. The survivor up to that point had lived in a world where the newly deceased was intimately present. Perhaps the deceased had been the principal breadwinner. Perhaps he had always cut the grass and tidied up the yard. If the bereaved is a woman, perhaps she enjoyed a world in which her husband took care of the garden, looked after the family budget and organized vacations. Whatever the survivor was used to, she can no longer make those assumptions. The world has now changed drastically and in order to survive, she will have to make a whole new set of assumptions. She must learn to live in a world which has changed dramatically, a world wherein the loved one no longer resides.

6. Readjustment

Once the bereaved is able to accept that the old assumptions are no longer viable, she can begin the process of adjusting to a world without the loved one in it. This means finding new ways to secure income, to begin to prepare one's own meals and to perform the many other tasks previously done by the other. This may mean having to learn new skills. It could mean enlisting help from others in the family or co-opting friends. Naturally, this readjustment to a new and frightening world is more difficult the older one is at the time of the bereavement.

7. Resolution

The final stage of grieving is reached when the bereaved is able to look forward to a new life, to have a sense of future without fear, and to formulate goals for a productive and happy life. She is able to give herself permission to be happy without feeling that it betrays the memory of her loved one. She will still experience some pain on the anniversary dates of the death, but as time goes by, the anniversary becomes more of a nostalgia than a pain. It becomes a day or two of quiet reflection and gratitude.

The effects of grief upon a person are profoundly psychological, physical and social. Psychologically, the immediate reactions are similar to those of any major crisis in one's life and were first described by Dr. Kubler-Ross. These are denial, anger, bargaining, depression and acceptance. Denial is a period of shock which functions as a defence mechanism against the overwhelming reality of the death. There may be a period of anger at a cruel world which would callously take the life of a loved one or anger at whoever was deemed to be the cause of the death, or even anger at God. Bargaining means to indulge in behaviours which try to avoid experiencing the awful pain of grief. This can be so intense that it leads to blockage and so healthy grieving cannot proceed. Acceptance is simply the point at which the survivor enters into the first of the seven *"R's,"* namely realization. She accepts that the death has actually occurred and now gradual movement towards resolution can begin.

A very important feature of early grieving is a phase of yearning and searching. The bereaved manifests a strong urge to find, recover and reunite with the lost person. Many bereaved persons will confide that they keep "seeing" the loved one going into a store, or getting onto a bus, or walking down the street. They feel alarmed at this and think they must be going mad. This is a perfectly natural part of grieving. The yearning is so great that the mind plays tricks on one's perception and so the bereaved will connect to anyone who looks like the deceased and want it to be him. The bereaved merely needs to be reassured that she is not going insane, that this is to be expected and that it will become less intense with the passage of time.

This phase is also characterised by restlessness and irritability directed towards the self or to others. She may sit down, then immediately get up and pace around, perhaps going from room to room in the house searching for the loved one. She then sits down again only to get up once more. She may think she hears the loved one's voice from the kitchen and respond to it only to be overwhelmed when she realises it could not have been him. If the phone rings it must be him. If the door opens and someone comes in, it must be him.

Everything seems to remind the bereaved of the loved one. Items of clothing, photographs on the dresser, garden tools, or the deck he built last summer, all take on a dramatic significance. The survivor will at first tend to hold fast to these reminders, hoping thereby to somehow keep the loved one "alive." It will usually take a long time before she can slowly release these items one by one. She might allow her son to have dad's fishing rod or might finally bundle up his clothes and give them away, but there will always be something she retains in an effort to keep his memory alive.

Some persons find it comforting to create a special kind of shrine to their loved one. They set up a corner of the house to display special photographs, trophies and mementoes, perhaps with a candle burning as a sign of remembrance. She may adopt little rituals such as kissing a photograph of her loved one every night before going to bed and greeting the loved one in the same way in the morning. She might adopt some of the habits of the deceased such as watching his favourite T.V. show on Tuesdays, or cooking his favourite meal on Sundays. She may play family videos over and over again or constantly go to the family photograph album and remember old times. These are necessary rituals and should never be discouraged.

After a while other people who were less attached to the deceased might become impatient with one who continues to grieve and remember. This is cruel and to remark on it or to tell them to snap out of it will only add pain to the pain already being experienced. Everyone grieves in their own way and should be allowed to do so. Only when it is clear that the grieving is unhealthy should one seek professional help and advice. I have been in therapy with grieving persons sometimes for years, but the process was able to proceed mainly because I validated their unique way of grieving.

A very important point to make is that while we have described the stages of grief in terms of the seven *"R's,"* these are not chiselled in stone, nor do they necessarily have to take place in a rigid sequence. Such thinking often causes care-givers to deal with a grieving person according to the stage she is "supposed to be in" rather than dealing with the stage she is actually in at any given moment. Grieving people do not read the text books and adhere to nice theories. They grieve and follow their own instincts. The theory is only a way of coming to a better understanding of the individual and must be applied uniquely to each individual. Grieving people will tend to move in and out of phases seemingly at random and a good care-giver recognises the reaction of the moment and accepts it.

The physical manifestations of grief can be many. The following is a list of the more common responses:

- Anorexia and other gastro-intestinal disturbances.
- Loss of weight.
- Inability to sleep.
- Crying.
- Tendency to sigh.
- Lack of energy or strength.
- Physical exhaustion.
- Feelings of emptiness or heaviness.
- Feelings of "something stuck in the throat."
- Heart palpitations.
- Tremor and shaking.
- Nervousness and tension.
- Restlessness and searching for something to do.
- Loss of sexual desire or increased sexual desire.
- Slow thinking.
- Shortness of breath.

These physical features can be very debilitating and may require medical intervention to bring about some relief. For example, insomnia may require some form of sleeping medication since prolonged insomnia merely intensifies the grief and could progress to utter exhaustion and collapse. If the picture becomes one of a deeply entrenched depression then again an anti-depressant medication may have to be considered. The depression may have to be lifted for the grieving to proceed normally.

The social consequences of grief can be quite devastating. The bereaved often finds it impossible to initiate or maintain useful activity. Her actions tend to be pointless, without purpose and seemingly random. She cannot do the budget where she had previously been skilled in this area. She does not plan the shopping and so runs out of food for the daily meals. The laundry piles up. She begins her housework and does not complete it. She may just sit and stare while everything around her demands attention.

Social withdrawal is a major problem for many. She may sever all contacts with others, never lifting the telephone, staying at home and taking no part in conversations. This prevents her from creating new relationships to offset the one she has lost. It also perpetuates the stress she is already feeling. Again, the only compassionate approach is to accept her inertia and to gently encourage her to make some small non-threatening forays back into society. This can only begin by visiting the bereaved in her home then hopefully enticing her to a brief outing, perhaps for a drive, then to the grocery store, and so on. She must never be overwhelmed by large crowds of people during this withdrawal phase.

One of the most potentially dangerous forms of grieving is known as pining. Pining is an extreme combination of the psychological, the physical and the social. All grief involves some pining for the loved one, but it can become so over-powering that it leads to a rapid wasting away in spite of the best efforts of the family and of the doctor. It can progress to death and in such cases it is referred to as "dying of a broken heart." It usually occurs between six months to a year after the bereavement.

Children who are grieving require special understanding and care. A child may exhibit some or all of the following reactions and some reactions may occur right away, while others may be delayed.

For the following I am grateful for the work of Theresa Huntley and her book, ***Helping Children Grieve***.

1. Denial

This is not unusual. Death often comes as a shock and if the reality is too dreadful to face, a child will shut it down for a while. Often a child will resume playing as soon as she hears of a death. This does not mean that the child did not love the deceased. It is simply her way of coping. She may make such statements as "My daddy didn't really die. He is just away. He'll come back." "I want my mommy to come home."

2. Panic

Once a child accepts the reality of death, particularly the death of a parent, she may become fearful of her own survival or fearful for the survival of others whom she loves. She may become convinced that she will be bereft of all adults who care for her and so will starve to death or have no where to sleep or live. She may be heard to ask, "Mommy, are you going to die too?" "Who will take care of me?"

3. Anger

A child may find herself being angry at the death of someone whom she loved. She may see the death as an abandonment and rejection of her personally. She may be angry at the person who died, or she may be angry with the doctor or with God. The anger may be manifested by acting out, or by refusal to pay attention at school. Adults need to validate the child's feelings, letting her know it is normal to feel that way, then to listen to her concerns, and gently correct any misconceptions she may have. The angry child may make such statements as "Why did daddy leave me all alone?" "Why did God let him die?" "It's not fair."

4. Guilt

Children often feel responsible for the death of a loved one. They may blame themselves and believe that they must have been bad. This needs to be spotted by an adult as soon as possible before it becomes a deeply entrenched belief. They need to be told that they could not have caused the death and that the death was due to an accident, or a disease beyond anyone's control. It can be very difficult to shake that belief and the adult must be prepared to persevere with the child and keep on stating the truth. The signals from a child who believes she is responsible are such statements as, "If only I hadn't disobeyed him." "I shouldn't have said I hated him." "It's my fault. I was bad." "I was mean to my friend and so God took my daddy away."

5. Regression

A child who is experiencing shock may begin to exhibit infantile or childish behaviour. She may start to suck her thumb, she may soil herself, having been previously well toilet-trained, or she may indulge in baby-talk. This is simply her way of going back to a time when she was secure and lovingly provided for. She should never be scolded. Sooner or later, she will come out of it and get on with growing up. She needs to be reassured that her needs will be met and that she will be loved and looked after. Care should be taken to avoid adding any new stresses at this time. She has enough to cope with.

6. Anxiety and Physical Distress

A bereaved child may experience actual symptoms. These can be symptoms which the deceased exhibited during his last illness such as stomach pains or refusal to eat or headache. The child may also experience her own bodily distress because she is afraid that she is also going to die. She may say, "I can't sleep." "I'm not hungry." "My stomach hurts." This child needs to be reassured that she is safe and will always be loved.

7. Clinging

Some children are so fearful and threatened by a death that they become overly attached to an adult, usually the surviving parent. "I don't want to be with the baby-sitter." "Don't go out,

Mom." The adult needs to gently reassure the child that she will come back, but that she needs to go out at this time. Only reassurance will help, together with lots of demonstrations of love as in hugs, sitting closely together, reading a story and so on.

8. Preoccupation with the Deceased

Often a child will idealise the deceased. She becomes obsessed with the lost relative and is compelled to keep on remembering him or her as though not remembering was some kind of betrayal. "Mommy. Remember when dad and I went fishing?" "Dad would have done it this way." Each remembrance causes more pain for the child. She needs to be told that this is quite normal and that you too are remembering. By sharing your memories with the child, you help the child sort out her own memories.

Other manifestations of grief in a child include hyperactive behaviour, poor attention span, withdrawal from social contacts, assuming the mannerisms of the deceased and idealisation of the deceased.

One of the more profound consequences of grief in a child is that she feels she must fill the deceased's shoes in some way or another. As a result, a boy may feel compelled to become the "man of the house" to replace the father who was lost. Many well-meaning adults will say to a child at the funeral, "Well, you must take care of your mother now," or some similar call. The child hears these words and takes them to heart. He then gives up all playing and all childish things and tries to do what his father would have done. Likewise, a girl suddenly becomes a house keeper, a cook, and a laundry maid and forsakes her right to be a child. This loss of childhood can come back to haunt a person in later adult life. It can take the form of grieving for childhood, angry outbursts or bouts of depression. Adults of a grieving child must allow the child to be a child. She should never be robbed of her normal growth by being forced to become an adult before her time.

Just as in adult grieving, it is important for Catholic parents to encourage the child to rejoice that her loved one is still alive but in a better place and that she can still talk with that loved one at anytime. She can ask Jesus to take care of grandma and to believe that Jesus will do that. She should come to know that one day, she too will go to be with grandma in heaven and it will be a wonderful reunion.

The Incarnation of Jesus the Son of God changed the meaning of death for ever. Jesus died on the cross "that through death he might destroy him who had the power of death, that is, the devil" (Heb. 2:14). Death may be inevitable, but it need never be the end, "for since by man came death, by man came also the resurrection of the dead. For as in Adam we all die, even so in Christ shall all men be made alive" (1 Cor. 15:21-22).

St. Peter Damian, praying with a dying friend, put it so beautifully, "As your soul departs from your body, may the shining cohorts of angels hasten to greet you, the tribunal of apostles acquit you, the triumphant ranks of white-robed martyrs accompany you, the lily-bearing bands of glorious confessors surround you, the choir of virgins bring up your train with rejoicing, and in blest tranquillity may the patriarchs receive you into their loving embrace. May our Lord Jesus appear before you gentle and eager of countenance and assign you a place amid those who stand in his presence for evermore."

With thoughts such as these, grieving becomes bearable. We can latch onto Christian hope and while the present world may be empty for us without our loved one, it can be filled with anticipation of a far better world, one which lasts for ever and where there will be no more grieving for there will be no more death.

POSTSCRIPT

The major purpose of *Volume 1* has been to give Catholics a new and more exalted appreciation of what family life is intended to be in the mind of God. In particular, it is a call for Catholics to come to a new understanding of the Sacrament of Marriage, that it is a very lofty vocation indeed, much higher than most of us have realized in the past. It is true to say that, if anything, there is much more to be explored and revealed as the Church ventures deeper and deeper into the mystery of the marital union of a man and a woman. We will probably never ever reach the bottom of this mystery but surely, just as God continues to reveal himself to us in endless ways, he will also continue to shower the Church with ever new insights into the beauty and challenge of the married state.

Volume 2 will be concerned with the kinds of moral values and standards which a holy Catholic family should espouse. If we enjoy the privilege of belonging to a Catholic family, then we must also accept the responsibilities which accompany that privilege. This means learning, embracing and practicing good Catholic morality, which is founded upon the teachings of the Magisterium of the Church. When it comes to faith and morals, the Church can only teach the truth since it is forever under the inspiration and guidance of the Holy Spirit. As members of the Catholic Church, we stand on the Rock of Peter upon which Jesus built his Church and which therefore has God-given authority with which to impart his pure truth.

Volume 2 addresses some of the more important moral issues facing Catholic families in our time and is intended to provide not only good solid principles, but also to offer helpful practical advice on how to more easily live out these obligations.

Finally, the last chapter of all is really the very foundation upon which this whole work is built. The title of this book is ***The Catholic Family: Image and Likeness of God,*** and since God is a Trinity of three Persons, I make an attempt to explore the ways in which the Catholic family might also be seen to have "trinitarian" characteristics. This is by no means to suggest that the Divine Trinity and the human family are somehow comparable. That would be absurd. Nevertheless, since God informed us that he wished to make us in his own image and likeness, then we should be able to discern a "three-ness" about our individual natures and about our family relationships. If I have done this well, then the reader should develop a deeper appreciation of the awesome mystery and miracle of who we are and how we all, in some tiny way, reflect the infinitely greater mystery of who God is.